wisconsin lore

WISCONSIN LORE

BY
ROBERT E. GARD
AND
L. G. SORDEN

HEARTLANDPRESS
an imprint of NorthWord inc.

Twelfth Printing, October 1987

ISBN 0-942802-79-9

Direct all inquiries to:
Heartland Press
NorthWord Inc.
Box 128
Ashland, WI 54806

Library of Congress Card Number 62-12168

Printed in the United States of America

For FIDELIA VAN ANTWERP
Beloved First President of the Wisconsin Regional
Writers' Association

acknowledgments

To the Wisconsin Regional Writers' Association we owe the most in the work of assembling the material in this book. The members of the Association, under the great leadership of Fidelia Van Antwerp of Wisconsin Dells, came to our aid with bits of lore from every portion of the State. Miss Van Antwerp, indeed, at the time of her death in 1956 was beginning to collect new material, and had she lived longer she would have assembled a great collection of Wisconsin folklore. As it was, a collection was established in her name by the Association and is kept now in the archives of the Wisconsin State Historical Society at Madison.

We have made a sincere effort to acknowledge the sources of our material in the text of the book, and if there are omissions it is because names have been omitted from manuscripts, letters, and memoranda, and records have become obscured. We owe kind thanks to the Graduate School Research Committee of the University of Wisconsin; the State Historical Society; the Extension Service of the Wisconsin College of Agriculture; the Extension Division of the University of Wisconsin. We are indebted to the pioneer work of Charles Edward Brown, who was really the first Wisconsin citizen dynamically interested in Wisconsin lore. As director of the Folklore Section of the Federal Writers' Project in depression days, he, in association with his wife Dorothy Moulding Brown, was able to pull together rare materials upon which we have drawn for certain sections.

We owe gratitude to *The Milwaukee Journal, Milwaukee Sentinel,* and many other weeklies and dailies in Wisconsin. We wish especially to credit Professor Jonathan Curvin and his valuable pamphlet: *Early Wisconsin Through the Comic Looking-Glass*. In this admirable small work the author made the first attempt to estimate the humor of Wisconsin in terms of the frontier.

Our gleanings included looks into many county histories, and into innumerable small, curious items tucked away in file boxes in the State Historical Society Library. In terms of active work on material we owe deep obligation to Mrs. Margaret Ebert Kelk and her mother, Mrs. Isabel Ebert of Lake Tomahawk, who searched out much material and who were completely dedicated to the task; and to Margaret Gleason, head reference librarian of the State Historical Library.

Finally the following persons, all devoted to the Badger State and its traditions, gave us information or complete tales, songs, proverbs, or other lore:

Mrs. L. Aaseth, Stanley; Dr. Harriet Anundsen, Monroe; Mrs. Dan A. (Ruby) Anderson, Holcombe; Mrs. Neva Argue, New Glarus; May Augustyn, Fond du Lac.

Miss Melba Baehr, Eau Claire; Grace Baertech, Portage; Alice Baker, Eagle; Agnes M. Bale, Sparta; J. M. Bennett; Mrs. Ruth M. Blumber, Campbellsport; D. V. Brecka, Baraboo; Allen Brown, Rhinelander; Spencer Brown, Rhinelander; Mrs. L. G. Bryan, Madison; Mrs. L. Buchler, Reedsburg; N. E. Buehner, Fond du Lac; Frances Burt, Brodevik, Cal.; W. R. Bussewitz, Horicon.

Meloa F. Callins, Dalton; Frances Caldwell, Superior; Mrs. Dorothy Carey, Green Bay; Mrs. J. E. Carlson, Ogema; Mrs. Walter Case, McAllister; Mrs. George Coggins, Ladysmith; Delores Chilsen, Merrill; L. R. Clausen, Racine; Ida Cook, Spooner; Mrs. J. W. Cox, Mineral Point; Harold Crosby, Madison.

E. M. Dahlberg, Ladysmith; Grace Danlton, Galesville; R. M. Dessureau, Antigo; Virgil Drake, Menominee.

Mrs. Pauline Easterson, Eleva; Mrs. Charles Ecker, Holcombe; Walter K. Ecker, St. Louis; Betty Epstein, Millston; Ellis T. Evans, Delafield.

Mrs. Ben Feldt, Monroe.

Hans D. Gaebler; Sam B. Gary, Rhinelander; D. M. George, Westboro; Mrs. Rona Guenther, Antigo; Dorothy House Guilday, Rhinelander.

Rosa A. Habelt, Superior; Harland Hays, Gays Mills; Clarence Herbert, Richland Center; Mrs. M. Herrington, Ogdensburg; Olive M. Hope, Salem; Pearl House, Whittlesey; Comrade Howard, King; Mrs. Wm. A. Huntley, Baraboo; Floyd Hurlbutt, Rhinelander.

Annie M. Israel, Marshfield.

Mrs. Adeline Jackson, Owen; Helga Jackwitz, LaCrosse; Gertrude Jacobs, Park Falls; A. P. Jones; Mildred Jones, Baraboo; Mrs. Harriet Jordan.

James Kestol, Janesville; Thelma Kiger, Montello; Clara Kirkwood, Chicago, Ill.; Mrs. Frances Knapp, Lancaster; Edna Kraft, Merrill; Mrs. John Kruse, Middleton.

Mrs. Maurine Lescher, So. Milwaukee; Ruth C. Lembke, Milwaukee; Mrs. Don Linchan, Beaver Dam; Mrs. John Linzmeyer; John A. Lonsdorf, Birnamwood; Mrs. Archie Lorimer, Stoughton.

Arlyle Mansfield, Sheboygan; Mrs. George Mawhinney, Darien; Howard Mead, Madison; Mrs. Paul Meier, Rudolph; Alex Michie, Harshaw; Mrs. Belle Miller, Richland Center; Mrs. Sabrina Miller, West Salem; C. B. Miniatt, Bruce; Mrs. P. L. Mitler, Baraboo; Mrs. Herbert Mohns, Brodhead; Mrs. Clarice Moon, Delavan; Mrs. Lucinda Morken, Taylor; Mrs. Elizabeth Mott, Neenah; Mrs. William A. Mueller; Mrs. Leo Murray, Pepin; Maude McDaniel, Boscobel; Florence McNitt, Ft. Atkinson.

Celia Nieman, Mukwonago.

Mrs. Alvin Olsen, Poy Sippi.

Sadie Padley, Lodi; Mrs. B. H. Parie, Milton; Mrs. Marion Paust, Richland Center; K. F. Peabody, Star Prairie; Mary Pease, Portage; Norma Pelunek, Alma; Dora Pernot, Eau Claire; Mrs. Charles Peterson, Curtiss; Mrs. Lillie Peterson, LaCrosse; Nina Peterson, Comstock; Katie Pettis, Fairchild; Mrs. Jennie Phillips, Waupaca.

Jessie Quackenbush, LaCrosse.

Mrs. J. A. Rayburn, Durand; Ronald Reardon, Rhinelander; John Remo, Rhinelander; Del Richards, Ladysmith; William Righten, Fond du Lac;

Estella Ringhand, Brooklyn; Viola Robertson, Menominee Falls; Mrs. H. E. Rodman, Neillsville; Hazel Rohrbeck, Fall River; Alberta Russell, Endeavor.

Willie Crandall Saunders, Janesville; Dorothy C. Schraeder, Evansville; Edna Schroeder, Monroe; A. M. Schuttler, Wauwatosa; Mable Sedin, Poplar; Etta Sherman, Adams; Esther E. Smith, Augusta; Helen C. Smith, Evansville; Mrs. Julius Stangel, Kewaunee; Fritz Sterling, Rhinelander; Helen Stieve, Baraboo; Viola Stout, Edgerton; Paul Swanson, Antigo.

Lloyd Taylor, Rhinelander; Mrs. H. V. Tennant, Portage; Mrs. Maud Totten, Delavan; Mrs. Frank Trumpy, Monroe.

Fidelia Van Antwerp, Wisconsin Dells; Guy Van Antwerp, Eugene, Oregon; Ethel Van Patten, Evansville; Dorothy Vaughan, Manawa.

W. W. Ward, Soldiers Grove; Wanda Waters, Wauwatosa; Audrey Weaver, Colfax; Ruth Westover, Waukau; Mrs. Martin Williams, Green Bay; Dora Winn, Granton; Mrs. Bert Winterling, Jefferson; Mrs. Edgar Wholust, So. Milwaukee; Grace V. Woodard, Wisconsin Dells.

Bernice Yonkee, Deerbrook; and Alberta Young, Rhinelander.

contents

wisconsin lore

chapter 1

A WORD FOR BEGINNING

T HE first time we heard "The Little Brown Bulls" sung, it was by an old lady in Forest County who was sitting in a creaking Boston rocker. She was a very heavy old lady, and she sang as she rocked back and forth.

She said her Kentuck folks came up to Wisconsin in the Seventies to help knock down the big timber. She said, "Boys, my daddy was a ram-horn roller, and I am as hard to comb as he was. Don't come around here after dark or y' might git a sudden hole in ye." Then she glamed a deer rifle, and sitting in her Boston rocker she pretended she was going to plug a few windows into us. But she didn't. She preferred a drink of whisky any day to blood, and it was easy to get more songs and more talk out of her about those logging days when her pappy was the he-boss of the lumber camp.

When you come right down to it, Wisconsin hasn't had too much digging into her folklore skin. A lot of the old-timers who could have narrated a bucket full of good yarns are dead now, and everywhere you go the older folks who are left will give a sort of groan or sigh and say, "Son, you ought to've been around when Billy Coggs was alive. Heavens-a-day! Billy could spout for twenty-four hours about loggin', and hell-raisin', and Lord knows what! He knew 'em all,

Billy did, and nobody ever wrote down a thing he said! You're fifteen years too late, son. Maybe twenty."

But even though we were too late for some, a bushel of good lore remains. We were up in the Oneida County woods one day when the cold was knocking the nails out of the low rungs on the ladder. It was twenty below zero that morning, but we were out with a tape recorder and we went to see an old fellow who knew a lot of Scotch songs with a North Woods flavor.

We tried to make the machine run, but it was too cold. We set her on top of the cookstove, and when she warmed up and began to wheeze and turn a little bit, the old guy began to sing. He sang up all our tape and went on singing after the tape recorder gave up the ghost. We were there for two days and had to promise him a barrel of beer to get him to stop.

And so it goes most places in Wisconsin; there are plenty of people willing to talk, but until recently there were precious few who'd sit still to listen. The long-winded yarn spinner of the olden times gave way to the long-winded television programs and our young folks, at least, seemed to prefer the box with the hole in the middle to the real live McCoy.

A Professor of Rural Sociology at the University of Wisconsin was complaining to us one day about how rural and urban were really one and had merged, married, amalgamated—fused, so it was hard as Satan for a self-respecting sociologist to tell the difference. "Oh, for the old days," he cried, and sitting down, he began to bay the moon.

He was right in a way. The vast communications of the present have tended to destroy the quaint little pockets of lore and folksay that were viewed once with such scholarly complacence by the folklorists.

But on the other hand, something more splendid has taken the place of quaintness. The people must have their say again to keep from being bored to death by the ineptitudes of modern mass communication, and individuals are beginning again to enjoy communicating with one another. A joyous kind of folksay is evolving that has roots in the past and in the present, and the stories that have always been a part of the pleasures of daily community life are being created, or resurrected, and told once more.

We went over to Gays Mills, Wisconsin one day and talked to Harland Hays and some of his friends over there in the apple-raising country. We sat in the car at the top of the great hill above Gays Mills, and Harland Hays, who has done plenty of living in the Kickapoo—grown gray with living and full of pride for his beautiful home country—said, "Boys, if you knew all I know about the Kickapoo, you wouldn't write about it. You'd just enjoy it."

We went down into the village, and at the office of the *Crawford County Advocate* Pearl Swiggum told us that there were lots of folks back in the hills who knew great stories. We offered a ten-dollar prize in her paper, and a local yarn-spinner named Clarence Herbert brought in the story of the "Bone-Crusher," which won the prize.

That Bone-Crusher was a wonderful tale and a long one, so long we couldn't run it in the book, but it illustrates that people are hankering again for those characteristics of nobility and heroism that have always created the greatest aspirations in men and have made their greatest folktales and literature. The Bone-Crusher was an immense Indian who was so affectionate and so powerful that he crushed all the loved beings and objects he touched affectionately. When he so crushed and killed his mother he exiled himself from his tribe and lived as he could alone in the forest. His name arose from his ability to crush the bones of animals with his bare hands to get the marrow. At last he attached himself to a couple—white settlers in the Kickapoo—and while they seldom saw him, he watched over them, finally saving them both from the flood waters of the quick-rising Kickapoo River, but losing his own life as he rescued them.

Perhaps it's not so much that ours isn't an age of heroism, or regard for the hero, for certainly we must have folktale heroes in the making now, among us. But the habit of telling folktales has only been obscured by other habits and keener necessities.

We believe that in Wisconsin a sincere and deep love of places and people has been reborn. This State has basically that kind of warm, affectionate regard for past events and present scenes which generates a spirit of true neighborliness, and respect among many nationalities for one another, and folksay and folktales, if they have disappeared, are certainly not lost—only sleeping. Our hope is that this collection, which has been generously aided by more than two hundred Wisconsin citizens, will do something to focus interest again on the basic humor, tragedy, and folksay of the state.

We are, of course, far from being the first to bring some Wisconsin lore together, though our collection may be the largest one. Notable among the earlier works were those of Fred Holmes, well-known Wisconsin writer, who doubtless loved Wisconsin as deeply as any man of his time.

We were on the State Centennial Committee with Fred Holmes in 1948, and we saw how in a way he gave his life for the sense of duty and affection he carried for Wisconsin. He died on the speakers' platform in his home town of Waukau, where he was making the Centennial address, recalling precious events and lore to the minds of his friends and neighbors. He finished his speech and that was that. The curtain fell.

Maybe that isn't such a bad way to go out—back in one's home town after many years, speaking about the meaning of that place. There are many of us who would like that kind of identification; but so few of us really ever go back.

The lore in this book is essentially home-town or home-place lore. It is definitely attached to people who were or are in particular places at particular times.

And there is a lot of tradition attached to it; in fact, wherever we have gone, we've noted that there seems to be a heightened curiosity about Wisconsin traditions. We are often asked what the term "Badger State" really means, and how it got that way. We always reply that Louise Kellogg, so long associated with the Wisconsin State Historical Society, had decided the correct answer and that her explanation is the one we go by, too. Miss Kellogg maintained that during the mining boom which began just prior to 1830 in the southwestern portion of the state, the people who came from Illinois for mining came in the good season and left in the bad season just as the suckers in the streams did. Consequently the Illinois folk were called "suckers," while the people from Wisconsin, too busy digging lead either to leave or to build houses, moved into the abandoned mine shafts to live and thus became known as "badgers."

While we're considering traditions, we better say something about "Miss Forward," the golden figure on top of the state capitol at Madison which symbolizes the state's motto. Of course, "Forward" is part of the coat of arms of Wisconsin and has been since 1851. It seems that Nelson Dewey, first governor of the state, had asked John H. Lathrop, Chancellor of the University, to have a new seal prepared. The Governor, not liking the result, decided to have a "go" at it himself. So, during a trip to New York, he and Edward Ryan, later to be Chief Justice of the Wisconsin Supreme Court, sat on the steps of a Wall Street office and evolved the new seal. First they thought of "Excelsior," which made them think of "Forward," "Upward," "Onward." "Forward" was finally selected.

The State tree is the sugar maple. The maple tree was first selected in 1893 by a vote of school children. In 1948, the Centennial year, another vote was held and this time the school children voted for the sugar maple. The Legislature officially recognized this tree in 1949.

The State flower, the wood violet, was voted in by the school children on Arbor Day, 1909, and the State bird, the robin, led two to one in a vote held in 1926–27. The robin was made official in 1949.

And, of course, the State has a multitude of "firsts" which have in their own way become folklore. There are many tales about the liberation of the American woman through the invention of that devilish contraption, the typewriter, by a Milwaukee man, Christopher Latham Sholes. Wisconsin's "first" in dairying has led to the glorification of the American cow, an activity which far outshines the feeble efforts of Ziegfeld and his like with the American girl. And Fort Atkinson, Wisconsin was the home of the first and foremost champion chicken-picker of all time, Ernie Hausen, who could pick a chicken blindfolded, with his feet, in three seconds. Gilda Gray, of Cudahay, was first with the world-shaking shimmy dance.

Young John Appleby, of LaGrange, sat under a tree one day and carved from wood a little gadget which became the twine knotter for grain binders and which revolutionized harvesting.

We are not sure just why it's so much fun for Wisconsinites to brag about "firsts," but it seems to be one of the favorite local sports. Other "firsts" that the folks will brag about a little are: the first county agricultural agent employed with public funds; the first rural zoning ordinance; the first school forest; the first workman's compensation law; the first kindergarten; the first organizational meeting of the Republican Party (at Ripon); the first butterfat test, invented by Dr. Stephen M. Babcock; the first state to have a system of marked roads; the first community theater in America (at Madison, started by Professor Thomas H. Dickinson); the first use of airplanes to detect forest fires; the first radio station in America to conduct steady broadcasts (WHA in Madison); the first cow to produce one thousand pounds of butterfat in a year; the first Christian Science Church in America (Oconto); the first Norwegian Church in the United States (at Cambridge); the first newspaper boiler-plate was used at Baraboo; the first hydroelectric generating plant in America (Appleton); Pat O'Dea, the greatest punter in football history, was the first and only kicker to punt one hundred and ten yards in the air (against Minnesota in 1897). Pat also punted one hundred yards against Yale in 1899. He dropped-kicked a field goal of sixty-five yards against Northwestern in 1898. Anyway the little list given here of the "firsts" is only a start.

As for the name "Wisconsin," the State derives the name from the great river which runs diagonally through her. "Wisconsin" first appeared in the law approved by President Jackson, April 20, 1836, establishing the Territorial Government and providing that "the country included within the following boundaries shall ... constitute a separate territory ... by the name of Wisconsin."

And what of the name itself? Louise Kellogg says that Marquette in his Journal of 1673 gives the name Meskousing. Joliet's map, on the other hand, gives the name Misconsing. Father Hennepin in his map writes the word as Ouisconsing. Judge James Doty, early political great of Wisconsin, insisted in the 1830's that Wisconsin came from a Winnebago Indian word, Wees-koos-erah, which meant "river of the

flowering banks." An American woman who married a Menomonie
Indian says that the Menomonie always called this land Wisc-coh-seh,
meaning "a good place for a home."

Miss Kellogg says finally that the name with the most consistent
meaning for her is the Winnebago: Wees-koos-erah, and that it
means simply "the river." The Winnebago, after all, lived at the
portage between the Wisconsin and the Fox Rivers from the time
Wisconsin was discovered by the French; their name is most likely
to have been early known and to have long persisted. Wisconsin
thus meant "the river," or as Judge Doty said, "the river of the
flowering banks." Other names in the state have their own kind of
interest.

No other town in Wisconsin and perhaps no other community in
the nation received its name in a more peculiar manner than did
Eleva. Before Eleva obtained its present name, it went by the grand
cognomen of New Chicago.

New Chicago lost its impressive name by accident one early winter
years ago. A grain elevator had been erected that year alongside
the new railroad tracks, but a severe cold spell set in late in the fall,
before the painting of it could be finished. Just the first five letters
of the word "elevator" had been painted near the top of the structure
at the time the men left their scaffolds for the season. As no other
name was visible, newcomers assumed that the uncompleted one
on the elevator was the town's name. The name caught on, and
before long was substituted for the original one. Eleva demonstrates
the convenience and economy of using things at hand, a philosophy
that has had something to do with Wisconsin's emergence as a great
state.

We might, of course, say the same thing about the legendary reason
for the naming of the southwestern Wisconsin town of Boscobel.
Sure! A farmer calling his cows: "Co Boss! Co Bell!"

Not that Wisconsin names necessarily follow any reason or pattern. The names in the whole state, as a matter of fact, while often
names of beauty or high yarn interest, are pretty well mixed up.
The Milwaukee Journal some while ago illustrated this confusion
by reporting that Wisconsin has a Juneau County, but the city of

Juneau isn't in it. Instead, Juneau city is the Dodge County seat. Then is the village of Dodge in Dodge County? No sir. It's in Trempealeau County—and Dodgeville is the county seat of Iowa County.

Wisconsin has many such cities and villages that aren't in counties with the same names. Dodge County seems to be involved in more mixups than others.

The village of Burnett is in Dodge County, not in Burnett County. Iron Ridge is in Dodge rather than Iron County. Brownsville and Woodland also are in Dodge County, not Brown and Wood Counties.

Wisconsin's list of mismatches goes on and on. Monroe isn't in Monroe County, it's in Green County. Portage is in Columbia, not Portage County.

In fact, all the following places (some are mere hamlets) are in the "wrong" county. Marquette is in Green Lake, not Marquette County. Forest is in St. Croix, not Forest County. Lincoln is in Kewaunee, not Lincoln County. Oneida is in Outagamie, not Oneida County. Rusk is in Dunn, not Rusk County. Washburn is in Bayfield, not in Washburn County. Taylor is in Jackson, not Taylor County. Jackson is in Washington, not Jackson County.

Despite all the mixups, Wisconsin has twenty-eight counties that contain communities with matching names. Many are county seats, but not all. They are:

Milwaukee, Waukesha, Racine, Kenosha, Jefferson, Walworth, Dane, Adams, Ashland, Barron, Bayfield, Buffalo, Clark, Eau Claire, Florence, Fond du Lac, Green Lake, Kewaunee, LaCrosse, Manitowoc, Marathon, Marinette, Oconto, Pepin, Shawano, Sheboygan, Trempealeau and Waupaca.

As an appendix we include a list of place names of Wisconsin and the sources of their origin. We make no claim of accuracy or authority. All we can say is: here they are. If you know a better source or reason for a name, well, that's fine. Help yourself. At any rate you'll have to remember that many of the place names of Wisconsin are of Indian origin. Wisconsin was the meeting place of two of the greatest ethnological divisions of the red men east of the Rocky Mountains. These divisions were, of course, the Sioux and the Algonquin, and thus the Indian names of towns and places are Chippewa,

Winnebago, Menominee, Potawatomie, and Sauk. Whatever tribe the name arose from, it sometimes had high romantic and story interest. Perhaps our entire approach to this book of lore is somewhat colored by the spirit of the imaginative red men who were able to attach so much that was wonderful, curious, strange, or humorous to the everyday events and the familiar places of their lives.

The Winnebago Indians say that when their people and the Prairie Indians (Potawatomi) camped on the banks of the Rock River, there lived in that stream a huge and terrible water monster. This demon was a long-tailed animal with horns on its head, great jaws and claws, and a body like a big snake. It ranged over the whole length of the stream from its mouth to the foot of Lake Koshkonong. It preyed on both animals and men, seeming to favor one no more than the other. Hapless deer that went to the banks of the river to drink or walked into the water were seized and swallowed by the monster.

At the fording places of the river the demon especially hunted for victims. Indians crossing at these places were dragged down out of sight beneath the water and were never seen again. Canoes were overturned and their occupants swallowed. Only a few persons ever saw the Terror of Rock River, but its presence was known by the churning and boiling of the water.

In the springtime its movement in the river broke up the ice and heaped it against the river banks. Its dens were in the deep places; there it slept and devoured victims. Some Indians believe that there were several of these huge serpents in the river. Offerings of tobacco and precious articles were cast into the river to appease their wrath.

When the Indians ceased to camp in numbers along the "River of the Big Stones" after the white men came, the water demons also left the river. Some Indians thought they established dens in the Mississippi River, where they live today.

But if the monsters of the Rock River have departed, the yarns in this book, at least, are here to stay. We hope that you will enjoy them, and that you will accept them for what they are: stories told by people about people and places; stories that have been told not just once, but many, many times; stories that are history in a sense, but in a very special sense, arising more out of the imagination than out of chronology, more out of the individual memory than out of recorded fact. Anyway, here they are. Take them, enjoy them or not; treasure the book, or toss it over your shoulder. All we can say is: *The people spoke, and we put down what they said.*

chapter 2

THE RIDGEWAY GHOST AND OTHER CURSES,
HAUNTS, AND QUEER CRITTERS

W ISCONSIN contains, if the yarns are an indication, more ghosts
per square mile than any state in the nation. Apparently the fabrica-
tion or perception of haunts has been an important pastime of Wisconsin people, for there is seldom a community that does not have
its haunted house, or its favorite ghost story. Werewolves and other
unsavory critters range the Wisconsin farmlands and woods, and
are either native to the Badger State or else have been transposed
here from haunted spots in the Old World.

Many legendary ghosts of Wisconsin seemed endowed with a
puckish sense of humor, and of all the mischievous ones, the famous
ghost of Ridgeway, in Iowa County, was (and indeed is) the most
notorious. The Ridgeway Ghost ranged over the length of the old
Military Road from the early Pokerville settlement at Blue Mounds
to near Dodgeville, a distance of about twenty-five miles. Ridgeway
was approximately halfway between these two mining communities
and was the definite headquarters of the pesky phantom.

Over this early highway, known itself as the Ridge Road, were
driven the creaking, ox-drawn lead wagons proceeding to Milwaukee
from Mineral Point, Dodgeville, and other towns in the "lead region"
of southwestern Wisconsin. Along the Ridge Road between Dodgeville and Pokerville were no fewer than a dozen saloons, most of

them with somewhat soiled and dented reputations. They outnumbered the other businesses and had sprung up as indispensable adjuncts to the post offices, hotels, and groceries which were established along the route to the lead markets at Galena and Milwaukee. Ridgeway was a strategically located stopping-off place for the traveler and teamster and offered liquid sustenance and rest at the Sampson House or Messersmiths Hotel. The taverns were frequented by toughs and gamblers as well as by the miners from the area. There were many fights and robberies, and murders were common.

The miners had spread into the lead district, coming from Cornwall, Wales, Ireland, and from the American South, as many as ten thousand a year for a time, to lay claim to every available likely piece of lead-bearing land. Drinking and gambling were their milder amusements. Justice moved so slowly as to encourage spirited knifing frays, shooting contests, and miscellaneous brawls. Deaths were frequent, burial services informal. As one county historian wryly remarked: "Preachers didn't prove indigenous to this uncongenial soil."

It was in this environment, among people already steeped in Old Country superstitions, that the Ridgeway Ghost worked his own special havoc in the 1840's and 1850's. He ranged the Highway and the surrounding farmlands, playing his mischievous and harmful pranks upon travelers and inhabitants alike. He was that most exasperating of phantoms, the practical joker, and one who shamelessly exploited his obvious advantage, played according to no rules whatever, and generally turned out to be a downright nuisance.

Some think that the Ridgeway Ghost was originated by wags who were hopeful of ridding the district of an undesirable element which frequented the taverns. In any case practical jokers spread the growing popular belief in the Ghost, whose presence and pranks soon became more or less feared by nearly all the settlers.

In the course of many years inhabitants of the Ridge Road settlements and of the adjoining valleys had, or thought they had, experiences with the Ridgeway Ghost.

After the Chicago and Northwestern Railroad line was built into Mineral Point, in 1857, the hauling of lead and supplies over the Military Road was discontinued, and with it came the end of most of the saloons and the taverns. Strangely, the Ridgeway Ghost also largely vacated the region he had haunted for so many years, yet the scare and the superstition remained. It was said that the famous night visitor left because he could not stand the whistle and puffing of the railroad engines, and the rattling over the rails of the trains of freight and passenger cars. Indeed, the Ghost was reported to have been seen seated on the cowcatcher of an engine as it was leaving Ridgeway. Perhaps it was then that the wraith took his departure from the scene of his countless exploits. The yarns, however, never did stop. He has been seen by many persons, some of whom were sober.

THE POKER GAME

One night three men sat down to a game of cards in a saloon in old Pokerville. It is said that they had been doing some really serious tipping of the jug and were ready for anything.

There was a fourth vacant seat at the poker table. They played several hands, and considerable money on one hand of "stud" lay in the center. The miner with the full house won the pot and was about to reach for his spoils. Suddenly an unseen hand seized the deck and began to deal the cards. They appeared to fly from a ghostly hand to the table in front of the three men. They now noticed that the fourth seat was occupied by a stranger whom they had never before seen. His hat was pulled partly over his face.

The stranger began to play and the cards performed all sorts of peculiar tricks as he cast them down. When a player tried to pick up a card it would instantly leave his grasp and fly around the room. Soon cards of every suit were circling the table. The poker players couldn't stand the strain. They rushed for the door, stumbling over each other, and in their hurry carried the door right off its hinges as they went out. The money on the table disappeared, and so, of course, did the mysterious stranger.

Obviously, the Ridgeway Ghost had come to the tavern. Seeing a vacant seat, he took a hand in the game. The tavern keeper dropped behind the bar when he recognized the Ghost and remained behind the bar for some time. While there, it is said, he consumed several bottles of the stock-in-trade.

STRANGER ON A STOVE

There was a young fellow who lived at or near Ridgeway and went one evening to call on his girl at the settlement. The house where she lived was a two-story house with an outside stairway leading to the second floor. The young lady's home was on the second floor, and another family lived on the ground floor.

On this particular evening the calling suitor mounted this outside stair and paused on the landing before his sweetheart's door. From this landing he looked down, and saw, on the ground, seated on an old iron stove, a man whom he had never seen before. As he watched, the suitor decided there was something queer about the fellow, but soon he entered his sweetheart's home. He was very nervous and immediately told her about the strange man. In fact he was so nervous that he was not particularly pleased with the idea of going home alone in the dark. The young woman invited him to spend the night, but he felt that, since he was a gentleman, he must leave.

As he climbed down the stair and reached the bottom the strange man appeared beside him and walked with him step for step. Silently they walked side by side. The stranger made no move to interfere with the young man's progress, but the young man couldn't shake him, either. When they were within sight of the young man's home there was a sound like a little explosion and the stranger disappeared.

As he broke into the fastest running he had ever done in his life, the young man knew that he had been walking shoulder-to-shoulder with the Ridgeway Ghost. He never went back to see that girl again.

GHOST ON A PLANK

Two Pokerville citizens were walking one evening along the road carrying a plank or a rail on their shoulders. As they were passing a brush thicket the brush parted and an apparition in white leaped onto the plank between them. The men, badly scared, began to run. They held onto the plank and the Ghost, standing in the middle of it, lashed them painfully with a switch as they ran. Finally they fell down exhausted, and when they could bear to look the white thing had vanished.

OXEN HITCHED WRONG WAY TO

John Riley, a teamster, who was hauling a wagon load of pig-lead, stopped at a saloon in Jennytown for a couple of drinks of "bug juice." He knew that he was near the stamping ground of the Ridgeway Ghost and needed something stronger than water to transfuse his courage. When he returned to his wagon after dark he noticed that his oxen had been hitched to the rear. As John Riley looked down the road he saw the Ghost walking away with his lantern and whip. John put up for the night at Jennytown.

Such antics were typical of this pest. Most of his tricks seemed to have no meaning at all, and were simply designed to make settlers' lives unbearable. The Ghost milked cows dry as they stood in the pasture; he loosened carriage-wheel pins and caused several bad accidents; he stampeded horses by mounting one and plaguing the others until they rushed madly around the field. In fact, most of life's misfortunes could be traced directly to the Ghost of Ridgeway.

THAT WAS GOOD RUNNING

Welshmen and Cornishmen had the most adventures with him. One day at dusk a Welshman was trudging along the road just west of Ridgeway. This was in the 1840's. As he walked along the dusty road he noticed that he was being followed by someone. Taking a good look at this hazy person, the Welshman decided that it was the Ridgeway Ghost, and he quickened his pace. The apparition did likewise, always keeping the same distance behind. The Welshman, determined to lose this evil phantom, broke into a dog-trot. The Ghost did the same. The Welshman now became downright terrified and began to run, faster and faster. (And a frightened Welshman can travel mighty fast!) He ran so hard that he was soon out of breath. Finding a log by the side of the road, he sat down to rest on its far end. The Ghost, running close behind him, now came up and sat at the other end of the log. It was one of the few times when the Ghost uttered a word. He said, "That was some good running you were doin'."

"Yes," the Welshman said, fighting for breath, "and I'm goin' to be doin' some more in just a minute." And he did.

THREE "SOMETHINGS"

There was another Welshman named Johnny Owens who was walking toward Ridgeway one night, singing some Welsh songs to keep up his spirits. As he approached a big roadside tree he saw three dark "somethings" hanging from a limb. They were swaying in the moonlight.

When Johnny came nearer he saw that the three things were human bodies hanging by their necks. Johnny didn't hang around to do any investigating. He ran all the way to Ridgeway. The next morning, with several friends, all sober, he returned to the tree. No bodies were hanging there.

The Welshmen had a continuing battle with the Ghost. One teamster from the mines swore that he encountered the Ridgeway Terror in the guise of a drove of phantom pigs. On his approach the pigs dissolved into a cloud and were blown away by the wind. Many came to know the specter as an old woman who would trudge on for a distance ahead of their wagons, then suddenly vanish in a ball of fire. Very commonly the Ghost appeared as an itinerant peddler, who would vault agilely upon hub or whiffletree. There he would ride in apparent comfort, staring fixedly at the horrified driver.

GHOST PUMPS WATER

A Welsh farmer living near Ridgeway went to his pump one evening to get two pails of water. When he reached his house with the full buckets he looked back at the pump and in astonishment saw that the pump handle was still going up and down and water was still pouring out of the spout. He had heard stories about the Ghost, and now he knew that the rascal was haunting the pump. He ran into the cabin and blocked up the kitchen door.

FINGER MARKS IN WHIP

A Welsh settler who was riding over the hills on horseback thought he saw something move in a deserted cabin he was passing.

Dismounting from his horse, he went to the cabin and looked in. There he saw the Ghost, who was visiting the cabin on some nefarious business of his own. The rider struck at the Ghost with his whip and the Ghost disappeared. The man noticed next day that in his own fright his fingers had sunk into the stock of the whip with which he had struck at the Ghost. The impressions made by his fingers were plainly seen. This man's name was Lewis.

IRISHMAN WOULDN'T LIVE THERE

The Irishmen had their troubles too with the Ghost. One time an old Irishman built quite a large house on a lot he owned. He was going to live there in the best style. After the house was completed and before he moved into it he went one evening to inspect. He entered by the front door and wandered through the rooms on the ground floor. Suddenly he saw before him in the dining room a hazy white light which he made out to be a human figure. He rapidly decided that this must be the Ridgeway Ghost, also come to look over new quarters. The Irishman tore up a few boards leaving by the front door. He would never live in that new house. He built himself a small house in the rear and lived there while the large, new house stood empty.

Sometime later this same Irishman was walking one night up the railroad track toward Barneveld. As he was approaching the town he saw a white light coming toward him along the track. This mysterious light was dancing up and down, now bright, now dim. The Irishman didn't wait to see anything more. He jumped off the track at right angles and legged it fast across the fields.

THE RAILROAD CREW

One yarn tells about this Ridgeway Ghost really being the spirit of a Virginia man killed in a duel in Mineral Point over a pretty woman in 1825. The ghost of the Virginia man haunted his antagonist, a Missourian, until he was dead. Then the haunt stayed right on along the Ridge Road doing his dirty work. Certainly he was still haunting the Ridge Road country in 1869 when the railroad was being built through Ridgeway. The members of the construction crew at this time were quartered in an old frame building.

This building had a trap door in the ceiling leading into an attic above. When the men were all in bed one of the crew, unable to sleep because of the snoring of his fellow workers, retreated to this attic. Here he conceived the idea of playing a great joke. He knew that the Irishmen were all frightened of the Ridgeway Ghost anyway, and figured that he would use this to his advantage.

So sometime during the night mysterious noises from the attic awoke some of the Irishmen sleeping below. One man who was of strong courage decided to investigate the cause. A table was placed in the center of the floor and a chair lifted on top of that. The courageous one mounted the chair and lifted the trap door to the attic. As he did so a pair of ghostly arms reached down, lifted him up and dashed him down, chair, table, and man crashing down together.

The thump aroused all of the sleepers who were not already awake and in the dim light the whole crew rushed for the door. In the stampede several of the crew were slightly injured. Convinced that the place was really haunted, none of the crew would return to the building that night. Some slept in trees and elsewhere. Some never did return to the construction crew. They had fled the Ridge Road country for good.

A WHITE THING

The Ghost nervousness infected others than the railroad gang. A young farmer went out to hunt small game for his home larder. He was returning in the early, misty evening when he suddenly saw a mysterious white object directly in his path. The thing appeared to be very threatening, and the farmer knew that he was about to have an encounter with the famous Ridgeway Ghost. Quickly he raised his shotgun and fired. The white object remained just where it was. He managed to load and fire again, but with no effect. Then, tossing away gun and gamebag, he took to his heels.

Next day he managed to persuade himself to return for gun and game. The white object was right where he'd seen it before: a large fencepost from which the green bark had been removed. The post had plenty of lead in it, but the farmer never bragged too much about this encounter.

CHASING THE GHOST

One summer when the Ghost fever was high along the Ridge Road, a settler who wished to give his neighbors a real fright jumped into a partly filled flour barrel and covered his features and his clothing with flour. Then he visited the homes of several neighbors about dusk and, peering in doors and windows, accomplished what he came for. Several of the inhabitants took off across the country. In fact, he scared everybody except one salty old farmer, a hero of the Blackhawk War, who grabbed his shotgun and took after the "ghost."

It was now the "ghost's" turn to be frightened, and he fled through a woodlot, down into a ravine, and into another woods with the old farmer hot after him, trying to get in a good shot. The "ghost" was nearly dead with fright and exhaustion when he finally succeeded in hiding in thick brush until the ghost-killer had given up and gone home.

The ghost-hunter often boasted how he had run the Ridgeway Ghost out of the country.

GHOST ON WINGS

In those Wisconsin frontier days when all entertainment had to be homemade it was a temptation to take advantage of every opportunity to do something spectacular or dramatic. Scaring one's neighbors was a part of the neighborhood fun.

One day a Welshman was returning from a day's work on a farm where he had been helping to shred corn. On his way home he had to pass through the bars of a pasture fence. A friend, who wished to give him a real fright, had dressed himself up as a ghost and was waiting for the Welshman behind the stone pasture fence. This man had a white rooster which he held on top of his head.

As the Welshman, tired from his day of labor, climbed painfully through the bars this "friend" suddenly rose up from behind the fence. As he did so he released the frightened white rooster which flapped its wings and flew directly into the Welshman's face. The Welshman dropped the pitchfork he was carrying and with a loud yell burned up the sod across the pasture. He never learned of the hoax his friend had played on him, and often told of the day he had met the Ridgeway Ghost and how the varmit took the wings of a great white bird and pursued him across the fields.

GROWING PIGS

Old Mr. Lewis was returning home one evening from a farm where he had been doing some butchering. As he trudged homeward along the Ridge Road he noted the presence of a sow and some young pigs in the road just ahead of him. They were moving up the road very slowly. Every time he looked at them the pigs and the sow grew in size. As he drew near they were already as large as cows. They were growing larger and larger. He struck at them savagely with his butcher knife. At this they disappeared from sight, vanishing in the air. He now knew that these were ghost swine, and that they were the brood of the Ridgeway Ghost. The old man reached home, but his experience was too much for him, and he sickened and died soon thereafter as a result of his fright.

THE HAUNTED GROVE

Just west of Ridgeway on Highway 18, formerly known as the Ridge Road, is the area which old timers called "the haunted grove." This is now peaceful open farming country; but as late as fifty years ago anyone who had to travel through this area did so only in broad daylight. If they were forced to travel through "the haunted grove" at night they whipped up their horses and sped through with their eyes straight ahead and their ears closed to all sounds.

It seems that in the earlier days someone, nobody knows who, encountered a ghost in this timbered area. The haunt had appeared driving a great team of black horses hitched to a black rig. This phantom carriage rushed straight at the traveler and passed over him, leaving him senseless in the trail. Later stories recounted a strange, flitting, white critter which dashed among and beside horseback riders as they were passing through the grove. Some of the riders also said they heard a wailing sound at night in the woods near the roadside.

Natives in the Ridgeway region still talk about this "haunted grove." In fact it's unlikely that the Ghost will ever quit the imaginations of the Ridgeway people. In 1910, at least, Pat Burns one night put the matter of the Ghost to a waggish test. Driving north from the Ridge with "a man named Smith," Pat clucked to his team and said suddenly aloud, "Come on, get up here on the seat. You don't have to ride on those eveners."

"Who you talking to, Pat?" Smith asked, turning white.

"Why that man sitting down there on those doubletrees," Pat said. "Don't you see him riding backwards and looking at us?"

Smith looked but saw nothing. Nothing at all. Meanwhile Pat had edged along the seat, as though making room for another companion. He settled himself and remarked, comfortably, "There, friend, that's better. You'll be easier up here on the seat with us."

Smith, according to Pat, departed rapidly, and didn't budge from the local tavern for several weeks.

THE HOUSE ON THE RIVER

Leaving the country of the Ridgeway Ghost we go north for a different kind of a tale—a story of a haunted property known as the Fehlhaber house, or perhaps as the Barsanti house, or, going back further, as the Kuechle house, or the Scott house. The place is now, incidentally, part of a convent for an order of Catholic Sisters.

This mansion, on a high knoll near the city of Merrill, stood for nearly forty years and scarcely ever, in all that time, knew the sound of human footsteps in its spacious halls and chambers.

Great amounts of money were spent by different persons on the construction and the reconstruction of the old house, but none of the various parties ever enjoyed, at least for very long, what they had built.

All about this beautiful estate on which so much time, effort, and money was spent there seemed to hang an evil omen, a sinister curse which worked its misfortune on all those persons who tried to live on the hill, or even work on it. If ever a house was haunted, this old mansion at Merrill was certainly more beset by evil spirits than most of the haunted houses one reads about in fairy tales. Here there were no ghosts, spooks, or any of the apparitions so well known to traditional haunted houses. Nor were there any rattling windows or clanking chains, yet something worse seemed to be present, a grim spirit of disaster and calamity which remained for years and claimed everyone who presumed to make his home on the hill.

And how did the curse start? Well, when the big timber push was on in Northern Wisconsin a party of men, timbermen, came down the Wisconsin River. Their boat passed the rapids, rounded the Big Eddy, and suddenly one of the men exclaimed, "Look! That splendid stand of timber on the hill to our left!"

There was a peaceful Indian village that lay on the river's bank opposite the hill. The French traders called the village Squitee-causippi, and when the white men disembarked the Indians crowded to the water's edge. Then down came the chief with his friendly greeting: "Welcome, white brothers!" To his people the chief explained, "These white men will be fair to us. They are our brothers."

In the chief's wigwam the strangers were served by his only daughter, whose pleasing ways and beauty had made her a favorite with the entire village. Now she glanced shyly at the white men.

"Pity that young 'un hasn't a respectable name," said the youngest stranger. "Think I'll call her Jenny," and Jenny she became.

More white men came. Lumbering operations began, and the fame of Jenny's beauty and sweet temper spread until the settlement was called by her name. It was inevitable, perhaps, that the youngest stranger should make secret love to her, and in her shame the girl dealt herself a mortal wound and died without revealing the name of her betrayer.

In terrible grief and anger the Chief ordered that she be buried on that hill across the river.

"I shall pronounce a curse upon that ground," he said.

The Chief stood before the grave. He raised his arms and said, "Oh, our Father, grant me this place for my child. Let this ground be sacred to her memory, and let it never do any white man any good."

The years passed, and in time came the railroad and a new name for the village—Merrill, in honor of S. S. Merrill, general manager of the St. Paul road. Before long the Indians had all disappeared, and the people almost forgot the name of Jenny. All that was left was the dim memory of the curse upon the hill.

This hill was the last piece of land in the vicinity to be purchased from the Government. T. B. Scott owned the largest mill in Merrill at that time, and he purchased the hill, but he didn't log it off. Instead he decided to build a mansion there fit for a lumber king, and in 1888 the work was almost finished when Mr. Scott died. His widow planned to carry on the work, but she, too, died suddenly. Then the property passed to their youngest son, Walter.

No one knows whether Walter Scott planned to finish up the house, for during a hot argument with the architect in a Chicago hotel, young Scott was stabbed to death with a paper knife. The architect, Mr. Sheldon, proved self-defense.

The Scott estate then sold the house and property to a man named Kuechle. Kuechle was a millionaire who wished to finish the Scott house for a summer home. This was at the time of the World's Fair in Chicago, 1893, and Kuechle purchased many prize-winning accessories for the building. There were prize doors and plate glass throughout, beautiful mirrors and an elaborate mantel. Workmen were sent to complete the house.

In the meantime, Kuechle had invested everything he had in a gold mine in the west. The mine had everything but gold, and in his despair Kuechle obtained a five-thousand-dollar mortgage on the Merrill place from Barsanti, a Chicago saloonkeeper. Just when Barsanti was about to foreclose an uncle of Kuechle's died and left him another million.

Immediately, Kuechle determined to win back the money he had lost and took an enormous contract for the Northern Pacific Railroad. He had no experience in engineering, would take no advice, and so lost his second fortune. Some clever scoundrel then persuaded Kuechle to trade the Merrill house for a business block in Chicago. However, there turned out to be no property in Chicago of the description furnished. Kuechle was able to save the Merrill property, but had to mortgage it again to Barsanti, who in time did foreclose. Kuechle went insane.

Barsanti decided to travel to Merrill to inspect his new property. He never got there. He was stabbed and killed in the Union Station in Chicago by a member of the Black Hand organization. The Barsanti estate sold the Merrill property to George Gibson from Illinois, who planned to establish there a home for old lawyers. Gibson established an office in Merrill and received donations from all over the country. The grounds were laid out and work of completing the house began.

One night Gibson failed to return home for dinner. No one had seen him since he left his office. There was no apparent motive for his disappearance; he was devoted to his family and liked by all who knew him.

Searching parties were sent out. The Wisconsin River was dragged, the booms were watched, but Mr. Gibson never appeared dead or alive. Nobody to this day knows what became of him. Only one thing was certain: after his disappearance, the house went back to the Barsanti estate, since all the payments had not been made.

Now for years the property remained idle; no one lived there and the house had never been completed. There was usually a caretaker on the property, and one of these caretakers was an Englishman known as "Popcorn Dan" because he kept a popcorn stand. Dan went to visit relatives in England. He made a fatal mistake. He booked passage home on the *Titanic*.

By this time the place had attained a reputation as being cursed and haunted. For a long while it was up for sale for thirty-five hundred dollars. And finally a Mrs. Fehlhaber bought it.

One day, after she had lived there a short while, she was driving along the road in her horse and cutter. She suddenly felt ill. She drove into the nearest farmyard, but before a doctor could arrive she was dead.

Sometime later the city of Merrill purchased the property with the vague idea of using it for a hospital, but when an order of Catholic Sisters offered to construct a hospital in Merrill, the city gave the Sisters the old house.

Now, at last, the house is finished and is used as a convent. Beside it is a beautiful hospital building. Nothing unusual has occurred. So far.

Told by Delores Chilsen

THE INGRAHAM CURSE

Another strange curse with a Wisconsin flavor was the yarn of the bitter luck that plagued the English Ingraham family.

The people of Milwaukee especially, in the early 1860's, told and retold the tragic tale of the excursion steamer *Lady Elgin,* which sank in Lake Michigan on the night of September 8, 1860, carrying more than three hundred citizens of Milwaukee to their deaths.

Most of these victims were of Irish descent, and the tragedy is said to have broken the Irish rule in the city.

Now it happened that there was in Chicago on September 8 a wealthy British gentleman, Sir Herbert Ingraham, with his wife.

In a sense, Sir Herbert was visiting Chicago as part of an extensive trip which his wife, at least, hoped would break the family curse. Ingraham was founder and publisher of the *Illustrated London News,* an important man, apt to scoff at such things as curses and coincidences. Yet a series of unusual events made him aware of these things, and his wife urged the trip to help establish a more normal point of view.

Sir Herbert's father, on a visit to Egypt in the 1850's, played a chief role in the excavation of a tomb in which a roll of papyrus was discovered in the case of a mummy. When translated, this papyrus said simply that anyone touching the mummy or desecrating the tomb would be cursed and his family cursed, and that his children and his children's children must suffer the fate of untimely death. The curse was widely publicized at the time.

Not long afterward Sir Herbert's father was trampled to death by an elephant while hunting in Somaliland, and his younger brother died under very mysterious circumstances.

It was after the brother's death that the Ingrahams' American trip was arranged, and in Chicago the publisher conceived the idea of traveling up the Lake shore to Milwaukee. The boat he picked on which to make the journey was the *Lady Elgin.* The wife protested, but Sir Herbert stood firm. He would take the *Lady Elgin* and no other.

So the man and wife embarked on the evening of September 8, along with a gay crowd of excursionists from Milwaukee, on an excursion arranged to help pay for new muskets for the Milwaukee Union Guard regiment.

It was a lowering night with a very high sea running. Who was to blame for the tragic accident no one has ever decided, but when the *Lady Elgin* was beating up the lake opposite Winnetka, Illinois, she was rammed in the side by a lumber schooner, the *Augusta*. She sank immediately, in three hundred feet of water. Among those who perished were the Ingrahams.

The *Lady Elgin* tragedy was the subject of a very popular ballad widely sung in the last century.

> Up from the poor man's cottage,
> Forth from the mansion's door,
> Reaching across the waters,
> Echoing 'long the shore;
> Caught in the morning breezes,
> Borne on the evening gale,
> Cometh a voice of mourning
> A sad and solemn wail.
>
> Lost on the Lady Elgin,
> Sleeping to wake no more,
> Numbered with that three hundred,
> Who failed to reach the shore.
>
> Oh, 'tis the cry of children
> Weeping for parents gone;
> Children who slept at evening,
> Orphans who woke at dawn.
> Sisters for brothers weeping,
> Husbands for missing wives,
> Such were the ties dissevered,
> In those three hundred lives!
>
> Lost on the Lady Elgin,
> Sleeping to wake no more,
> Numbered with that three hundred,
> Who failed to reach the shore.

THE THREE BONES AND MISCELLANEOUS TALES

As an example of how certain immigrants to Wisconsin brought a tendency to ghostly experiences with them, Mrs. L. Brechler of Livingston tells this story.

Back in York State, several years previous to coming to Wisconsin, her grandfather found himself the owner of a tavern or roadhouse.

It was in a rather run-down condition when he got it, but the owner gave him such a bargain he could scarcely refuse to buy it. The grandfather thought he certainly could make some money at the price asked. However, before the final papers were signed, the owner reached down behind the desk and brought out a small box. On lifting the lid, grandfather beheld three small dried bones. They looked like human finger bones.

Grandfather found that before he could take possession, he had to swear that he would make every guest handle those old dry bones before they would be allowed to stay the night. After some deliberation, he promised he would do as the owner said.

As time went on, grandfather got used to asking his guests to handle the bones. The former owner had left a letter explaining that years ago there had been a foul murder committed in the tavern and that the body was buried in the cellar. Three small bones from the body had been kept to catch the criminal. The letter explained that some day the murderer would return to the scene of his crime and these three small bones would figure in his capture.

One dark, stormy night a shifty-eyed gent came up to sign the register, wanting a room for the night. When the box with the bones was brought out, the man turned pale and refused to touch them.

When told he would have to find shelter elsewhere unless he handled the bones, and on hearing the gusts of wind and rain on the window panes, the visitor finally consented. The moment he touched the bones three drops of blood fell from them and stained his hand.

Immediately the grandfather exclaimed, "You are the man!"

After being confronted with this phenomenon, the gent readily admitted that he was the guilty one. Next morning he was escorted to jail. Later he was tried and sentenced to life imprisonment.

When this same grandfather of Mrs. Brechler's decided a little later to come to Wisconsin, he thought it best to come on ahead of his family and find a suitable place to live before they would arrive.

He arrived at a certain town one evening about dusk, and decided he would have to look for a place to spend the night.

He found there were a considerable number of travelers in town that night, too, all looking for a place to stay. The only available hotel left was a rather old weatherbeaten place that looked far from prosperous; but he thought he could stand it for at least one night. Being very tired, he retired early. He was asleep almost before he "hit the tick," so he said.

Suddenly grandfather was fully awake, lying tense in the darkness, except for a beam of light from the moon that filtered through a dusty windowpane and fell on an old bookcase full of books. He had noticed the bookcase there when he went to bed.

He saw something move. It was the figure of a woman dressed in gray. She had on some kind of a loose garment that covered her head like a shawl. She had her back turned and was on her knees noiselessly taking the books out and piling them on the floor. Grandfather didn't say a word, just breathed evenly as if he were asleep.

Finally, after all the books were on the floor, she began arranging them back in the bookcase again and then suddenly disappeared.

When grandfather awoke the next morning, he decided to get breakfast and then ask some of the townspeople if they knew anything about this apparition he had seen. One old man explained that this ghost had been coming to that certain room for years, and it was imperative that no one speak to her while she was there.

As grandfather could find no other room, he had to take the same one the next night.

As on the previous night, he slept soundly for a while, but all of a sudden he was fully awake. Sure enough, there was the woman at the bookcase!

After watching for some time, grandfather decided to speak to her, so he said, "What the h—— are you doin'?"

Immediately she arose and glided towards him. He saw her face clearly then. It was just a grinning skeleton, with two black holes for eyes.

She placed two bony thumbs on his forehead and pressed his head right down through the straw tick. When he became conscious enough to realize where he was, he was choking and gasping for breath. His ears, eyes, and mouth were full of chaff, and he had a terrific headache.

He carried the marks of those thumbs for years afterward.

THE ROCKING CHAIR STILL ROCKS

A surprising number of murdered people who died violently have remained active as Wisconsin ghosts.

One evening about seventy years ago, near the old site of a grove of great oaks, the first murder happened in Oshkosh. A man, accompanied by his little boy, was carrying a rocking chair home. He became tired, and when he had gotten down a ways on the high boardwalk which had been built bordering the grove, he stopped to rest and sat rocking in his chair.

Two drunken men came by and became angry at seeing him at such leisure. There was a quarrel; the drunks killed the man and ran away. The little boy had, in the meantime, hid under the sidewalk, but finally ran across the street for help. When the neighbors came the man was dead in his chair.

For a long time thereafter wayfarers could hear his groans and the creak of his rocker under the oaks at night, and even today on a stormy night, one may hear the sounds, the echoes of the first slaying in Oshkosh.

MILWAUKEE HAUNT

Dr. E. J. W. Notz of Milwaukee told Charles E. Brown about a haunted house, one of many in Milwaukee.

In the year 1908 Dr. Gerhard Bading and wife were residing in an old-fashioned large frame house which they had rented on the west side in Milwaukee. This house, located on Upper Wells Street between 25th and 26th Streets, had a staircase which led from the front of the house to a hallway on its second story. At the rear of this hallway a similar stairway connected the second story with the downstairs kitchen. Both the staircases and hallways were carpeted, as was formerly the custom. Dr. Notz, then a young man, had been requested to sleep in the house to look after the furnace, etc., while the tenants were away on a trip.

The first night after the Badings left, after attending to everything that required attention, the young man retired for the night in a bedroom on the second floor of the house. He slept very well, but shortly after midnight he was awakened by a tremendous crash. It was so loud that it awakened him from his deep sleep, and he found himself sitting bolt upright in bed. While he was trying to recover his senses and to determine what might have happened, be heard in the hallway a noise, as if some person were walking over the carpet in his or her stocking feet. Then he could hear the footsteps treading down the rear staircase.

Certain now that there must be someone besides himself in the house, the young man quickly arose, turned on lights, and made a thorough search of the entire house from basement to attic. But there was nothing amiss anywhere, and the owner of the mysterious stocking-clad feet was nowhere to be found.

Now satisfied that there was no intruder on the premises, the young man again retired, only to have his repose again disturbed by a sudden crash and, a few minutes later, the same hurried tread of stocking-clad feet through the hallway and down the staircase. Again he arose and made a second thorough search of the house, but again without result. No trace of the mysterious night prowler or of the cause of the tremendous crash was to be found. Once more, before morning, the same terrible noise was heard, with the same ghostly footsteps in the hall and on the staircase. When the same things happened several times on the second night of the young man's stay in the house, he was very much disturbed. There was something very uncanny about it all. He mentioned the matter to two aunts of his who resided in town, but they had no helpful suggestions to offer.

When Dr. and Mrs. Bading returned he told them of his experiences, and they informed him that they had also often heard the same night noises in the house, but they had become accustomed to them and were not particularly disturbed.

In the meantime his aunts had made some inquiries and learned that the residence which Dr. Bading had rented had the neighborhood reputation of being a "haunted house." Its owner was the proprietor of a summer resort hotel in the Waukesha Lakes region.

He had in his employ as a domestic a girl or young woman. Early one autumn they had sent this girl to town to prepare the house for their coming. While thus engaged this girl had, in a fit of despondency, committed suicide on the premises. Thereafter her spirit was believed to haunt the house. After several families who had rented it had had peculiar experiences with this haunt within its walls, the house acquired the evil reputation in the neighborhood of being haunted. Dr. Bading, soon after his return, removed to a new home on the east side of the city.

There were also in the city of Milwaukee a number of other vacant residences which had the reputation of being haunted. One of these was located at the northwest corner of 12th and State Streets, and one at about 11th and National Avenues. A third was on Grand Avenue (now W. Wisconsin Avenue), at the western limits of the city.

No one cared to live in any of these dwellings. Some stood untenanted for years; boys threw stones through their windows and they soon fell into a state of general dilapidation. There were similar deserted farmhouses in the country around. All were shunned by superstitious persons. In nearly every case a murder or a suicide had at some time or other taken place within their walls.

COUSIN GOTTLIEB'S BROTHER

From Fremont comes the tale of Cousin Gottlieb's brother. This was told by Mrs. Franklin Neuschafer.

Cousin Gottlieb's brother was very ill. Indeed, he was on his deathbed. He lived about thirty miles from Gottlieb's farm. There was no way of communication then, for it was the age before telephones were in every home. And transportation was by carriage or wagon, by horse, or on foot.

One evening after the children were all in bed and Gottlieb was quietly sitting downstairs with his wife, a thumping sound began to sound upstairs, going from room to room, so it seemed.

The children awakened and became very frightened. They ran for the stairs, and one of them tumbled all the way down.

By the time all this excitement was over the thumping had stopped.

Gottlieb took a lamp off the table and also picked up a stick and went upstairs, searching all the rooms. There was no one.

He came down and stood in deep thought, then turned to his wife and said, "My brother is dead."

In the matter of twenty-four hours a message came to them telling them Brother August had passed away.

At the funeral Gottlieb asked the time of death. He had died at the exact time of the thumping disturbance in the upstairs rooms.

DREAMED HIS OWN FUNERAL

In the same tradition, when strange phenomena lead to real events, there is the famous story of Robert Laurie. Laurie was born in Scotland in 1825 and came to this country in 1852, settling in Buffalo, New York. In 1854 he came to live in Door County, Wisconsin. He was the seventh son of a seventh son, and the Scotch of his day believed such a man to have unusual perceptive powers. His great-granddaughter, Dorothy Carey of Green Bay, tells this story:

One of Laurie's daughters, Isabelle Laurie Drumb, was my grandmother. I remember her as a person who was not superstitious in any of its usual manifestations. However she believed strongly in the truth of the material herein stated. She didn't try to explain the reasons for these incidents, she just stated them as facts, telling the story many times to my mother, who passed the story on.

When my Scotch ancestors emigrated to Wisconsin in 1854, they brought with them their families, their possessions, and their superstitions.

Among them was my great-grandfather, Robert Laurie. He had been born in Scotland, the seventh son of a seventh son, an event not to go unnoticed among the Scotch of his day. For did not the seventh son of a seventh son have supernatural powers to foresee future events?

As a child these supernatural powers had not been apparent, but from the time Robert became a young man, more and more heed was paid to his words. Had he not correctly foretold the coming of a baby boy to the Fergusons, who had despaired of having a boy after the birth of seven girls?

Then, too, they remembered the time he had foretold his brother's death. His brother Alex, together with a neighbor, had left Sturgeon Bay in a boat. They were going to Green Bay for supplies.

After they had been gone for some time a storm had sprung up, and the waters of the Bay washed high upon the shore. Robert Laurie had watched the waters and paced along the shore, an anxious look upon his face.

Catherine Laurie, seeing her husband's restlessness, watched him with fear and apprehension. What did it mean? Finally she could stand the suspense no longer.

"What is the matter, Robert?" she asked.

"Alex and his neighbor have drowned," he informed her. "We will never see him again."

It was early afternoon, and there was still time for Alex and his friend to return safely. Yet Catherine went about her task with a heavy heart. Should she tell Alex's wife or wait until later? Maybe— pray God—Robert was mistaken this once. But as the hours wore on and the boat did not return, fear lay heavy in their hearts. Alex Laurie was never to come home.

Then there had been the time a neighbor's boat had been caught in a storm and capsized.

"Do not despair," Robert had comforted the distraught wife. "Your husband is safe. A cabin door has torn loose from the boat and he is clinging to it. He will be saved."

Later the cabin door was washed ashore, the man still clinging to it, semiconscious but alive! It was enough to bring the goose-pimples to your flesh!

One night when Robert Laurie was in his sixties he had a dream. The dream was so real to him, he felt it was an omen. The next morning he told his wife about it.

"There is going to be a big funeral in Door County soon," he said. "People are going to come for miles to attend. Many will spend days reaching here, but they will come—by foot, by boat, and by carriage. There will be many carriages there, their horses sleek and shining out of respect for the dead." He went on, giving minute details about the funeral, the minister who would give the eulogy, the names of the various mourners, etc. It was very real to him.

But there was one important detail he didn't know—whose funeral it was.

One month later this funeral was held. People came for miles to attend, by boat and by carriage. Their horses shone and their buggies had been freshly cleaned.

The minister who spoke and the mourners who came were the same as Robert Laurie had foretold. Everything about the funeral was exactly as he had predicted. And whose funeral was it, do you ask? Robert Laurie's.

A VISION

Of a similar nature is the yarn related by Mrs. J. G. Slater of Cleveland, Wisconsin:

This authentic tale happened when I was about twelve years old and lived on a farm near Cleveland.

One night my father entertained a group of friends and business associates. It was a pleasant evening with serious talk first and laughter and jokes over a glass of cider later. When it was time for the guests to depart, my father went outside to tell the hired man to harness up the horses and bring the conveyance to the door.

When he returned we were all surprised to see him being led in by the hired man. He looked queer and had great beads of perspiration on his brow. When he wiped them off, others returned.

Mother rushed forward, deeply concerned. One of the men exclaimed, "Did you see a ghost, Hencel?" They wanted to laugh but could sense that their friend was under a great emotional strain.

Presently my father lost his agitation and detailed the following experience:

On his way to the stable he had been halted suddenly by observing in the gray shadows of night the figures of men in somber garments, passing through a side gate, followed by a coffin borne by pallbearers. Strangest and most shattering was his realization that the faces of all the pallbearers were those of the men sitting, at that moment, in his house, with one exception, for he could not see the face of his best friend—a miller and dealer in grains—among the figures in the ghostly apparition. He himself was one of the pallbearers also.

After the vision faded away, he could only stand horror-stricken in his tracks. He feared his legs would not support him if he attempted to walk, for there is something in the supernatural that strikes terror even into the bravest heart.

Fortunately the hired man came out of the stable with a friendly lantern and, noticing something was amiss, helped my father back into the house.

His friends were openly skeptical of his story and hinted slyly that he must have drunk more cider before he went outside. However, their carriages were at the door, putting an end to further talk on the subject. After cheerful good nights they went home.

At ten o'clock the following morning one of the previous night's guests arrived on a bicycle, deep concern stamped on his features. He came to report that the miller had died of a heart attack while sitting at his kitchen table, where his wife discovered him when she went down to start breakfast.

His had been the only face my father had not seen in the shocking vision at the farm gate.

The surmise was that in the phantom funeral the miller was the dead man, for at his funeral a few days later everything else was just as my father had seen it in his out-of-the-ordinary vision.

THE STRANGE NIGHT

There's no doubt about it, very strange things have happened in Wisconsin. Erva Loomis Merow of Kenosha relates that near the Mound at Platteville, Wisconsin, there stands a very old stone house. About ninety years ago a young German farmer called Carl Nodolf bought that house and many acres of land around it. He was sure his bride-to-be would love the view of the Mound and the rolling hills of good farmland. So he went back to Germany to marry her and bring her back. He arrived there only to discover his bride-to-be had died of diphtheria weeks before. The farm in Wisconsin did not seem like a beautiful dream now, but rather like a very sad nightmare. Slowly Carl lifted himself out of his grief to discover that, of his bride-to-be's family, only two people had survived, her mother and a young sister. Carl looked at the sister, just sixteen years old, and once again his farm became a beautiful dream. He asked the mother and sister, called Louise, to go back to Wisconsin with him.

The stone house by the Mound must have been a quiet haven to a young girl who had been through so much. Soon Carl and Louise were married. Three years later their first child was born. They called her Minnie Louise. Two years later a son, Louie, was born to them. Minnie and Louie Nodolf were to become the center of a legend—a legend which still lives among the people near the Mound.

One night Louise and Carl put their two children to bed upstairs, as usual. This night the wind had become stronger after dark, so Carl locked every shutter tight. They went back downstairs to sit before the fire, reading and sewing. Usually Louise liked to mend, but tonight the wind howled like a fall blizzard, instead of a June thunderstorm. They stayed up longer than usual because the wind became so intense. Great streaks of lightning and cracks of thunder filled the air. Finally Carl decided it was just another summer storm and they prepared for bed. The wolves, which were a common sound of every night, howled with the wind. Louise remembered wondering why they seemed so close to the house that night. Carl closed the shutters at the windows and barred the doors securely. Louise, carrying a lamp, led the way upstairs. She covered the children and soon they were all asleep. Toward morning a very loud crack of thunder woke Louise and Carl. Louise said she heard Minnie crying for her and ran to her bed. Neither Minnie nor Louie were in their beds. She lighted a lamp and looked around the room, thinking they must have been frightened by the storm and gotten out of bed. They were not in their room. "Carl," called Louise, "they must have gone downstairs in the dark!" She ran down, Carl following, both calling for the children. They were not downstairs.

"Minnie! Louie!" screamed Louise. Then, between the battering of the wind and cracking thunder, they heard the children crying! They listened, unbelieving. Carl ran to the door, sliding the heavy bar back. He swung it open and there outside, on the step, stood Minnie and Louie!

"Children!" cried Louise, and they carried them in by the fire.

"Wrap them up," began Louise, "I'll get their dry—" She couldn't go on, for Carl was feeling their nightgowns. He touched Minnie's hair. "You don't have to get dry clothes, Louise. They're not one bit wet!"

"But that's not possible! It's pouring rain," whispered Louise.

"How did they get out there, Louise? That's not possible either," said Carl.

Louise stooped down to Minnie, who was four years old. "Minnie," asked Louise, "Minnie, how did you get outside?"

"I-I-I-I don-don-don-don't kno-kno-know," stuttered Minnie.

"Carl!" screamed Louise. "She's stuttering!" So she was. And so was Louie, just learning to talk. Both were stuttering for the first time! From that moment on they stuttered. Of the eight children born to Louise and Carl, Minnie and Louie were the only ones to stutter, and they do, still, to this day.

Every window in the house had been closed. The doors were barred with high sliding bars. It was impossible for the children, four and two years old, to open them, get out, and then slide the bar back into place. Everything was locked from within!

Just how the story reached the neighbors and got into Platteville isn't known. The family thinks perhaps Carl asked if anyone had seen a tribe of gypsies near the Mound. Perhaps Carl thought that gypsies had stolen the children out of an upstairs window, which didn't explain how everything was still locked from within. Legend has it the neighbors hadn't seen gypsies near the Mound, but they had been worried about the Nodolf family. The storm had seemed to be right over their farm. Unusual streaks of lightning, balls of fire, and torrents of rain had beat down on the small stone house. Had gypsies taken the children and become frightened and returned them? How? Without opening doors or windows?

Did Minnie and Louie somehow get out of the house, locked from within? Why, then, weren't they wet? The children couldn't explain how they got outside. Not that night, nor in the many years to come. Yet they were so frightened they stuttered from that night on!

Did Carl or Louise, walking in their sleep, take the children out of their beds, down the stairs, and put them outside to be devoured by hungry wolves? Wouldn't the children have awakened and cried out?

Was it perhaps a freak storm?

People near Platteville refer to all this as "the Nodolf incident— on that strange night." Perhaps there isn't an explanation. It did happen, but there isn't an explanation. It was just—a strange night!

UNEXPLAINED FIRES

More in the nature of queer happenings:

Up in the Indian Head country in northwestern Wisconsin there is a yarn which tells how, when the district was first opened up, a house was built and occupied. One evening the family returned late to find that a window curtain had completely burned, the ash falling to the floor but causing no greater fire. About a year later in much the same way they returned to smell smoke and to find the cushion on a chair smoldering. About a year later still they returned to find the house burned to the ground. They rebuilt it, and the following year it burned again, almost trapping the family, who were asleep upstairs. They abandoned the place.

After a lapse of many years a stranger bought the land and hired a carpenter to build a summer cottage on it. After the building was well under way the carpenter returned one morning to find that his nail apron, which he had thrown on the floor the night before, was completely burned. The rough floor lumber, having been green, did not catch fire. The new owner only then learned the history of the place. He paid off the carpenter and was seen no more.

THE EVANSVILLE HOUSE

Ethel Van Patten of Evansville tells another strange happening. She says that her parents were good, dependable Yankees who would have admitted anything rather than that they were superstitious. This is Mrs. Van Patten's story:

In the year 1894, my parents bought and moved into what was known as the Evansville House. It was an old remodeled structure at that time. I was a little girl of eight. The place must have been sixty or more years old then. In the days of stagecoaches it had been a stage stop, and the old barn, with its hand-hewn log rafters and sills, still acted as a livery stable.

First maybe I had better describe the layout of the old hotel. The office was on the west with a door opening onto a long, wide veranda. In the front, which faced the south, was another huge door which led into a long hall, from which opened several and various rooms. Like most old places it had its legends of mystery, tragedy, and romance. One of them was about a lovely young girl who, while working as a chambermaid, had been strangled by a lover who already had a wife and family and who, not being able to have her himself, had decided that she should never belong to anyone else. After killing her he had dashed out to catch an outgoing freight, had fallen, and had himself been killed.

Even as young as I was I can remember enough about the happenings to make this story very real to me. Through the years however, I tried repeatedly to persuade my mother to tell of their experience that winter, but she was always reticent about it and put me off, saying, "Oh, that. That was only one of your father's and my nightmares," or "Why quiz me? Your father knows more about it than I do." But one day she said to me, "Well, I might as well set you as straight as I can about it. I don't believe in mysteries and I never will. There was a solution to our phantom, but we didn't have the courage to stay and search it out. There was a solution as sure as there is life, but we never found it."

Among the steady boarders at the Evansville House was an old sea captain, Pat McGlinn. He wore brogans and danced the hornpipe to the music of an old wheezy mouthorgan. It was sure fun to learn the steps from him and then hear his tall stories of the "Terribal disasthers upon the sae." His brogue was rich and resonant and his vocabulary a constant disturbing element in my little mother's life, for I was an apt pupil and so were all of my pals in the neighborhood. I loved Pat, so one day when I heard him and father having heated words in which Pat was pounding the desk and swearing by all of the saints good and otherwise, I listened in.

About that time I guess Pat had father more or less convinced that it was not he who was clumping all over the place at all hours of the night, for they parted with a congenial attitude which put me more at ease, but it made me more conscious of the happenings about the place.

It seems that every morning about three o'clock someone wearing heavy shoes came clumping down the stairs, which were right beside my folks' room. I can remember what I, too, thought was Pat come clump, clump, clumping down the stairs. It would not have impressed me at all but for the realization that my folks were so disturbed about it, and I did not want them mad at Pat. Later, after mother made it clear to me, the whole thing came back. It seems that my father ran a race, as it were, with the phantom all winter. At first he would take time to slip on his trousers, then he began opening his door quietly, but no matter how careful he would be, the footfalls would stop if only halfway down the stairs.

One snowy night my folks just lay and listened. The footfalls went out into the office; the outer door, which was locked, opened and closed. My father dashed out then; the door was still locked and there was not a single footprint in the newly fallen snow. Then father dashed up to Pat's room to convince himself that it was not he and found him snoring peacefully in his bed.

If I hadn't heard the footfalls myself I would have thought that my folks had dreamed the whole thing, but I heard them just as plainly as they did.

Throughout the years I have heard and read about happenings to people who were just as staid and unsuperstitious as my people were, but had to admit something beyond their comprehension happening to them, and I've wondered if, in some strange incomprehensible way, Pat's spirit did leave his body and roam restlessly beyond his control, paying penance for some crime committed at sea, or if the young lover was still fleeing from his terrible crime. Be that as it may, we shall never know.

That spring my father sold the place. We never heard whether with our leaving the phantom stopped its restless roaming or not. Maybe it retired back from whence it came, whether it be into the sea or otherwise.

LANKY NIGHT WALKER

When most of the men of the Northern settlements went to the lumber camps every fall and were away till late spring, the women and children were left alone during the winter. One winter a person of fabulous height, enveloped in a long black cape, walked through a street of West Algoma every night at midnight, continuing on past the end of the sidewalk, and on into the blackness. He walked with a slow measured tread, and apparently with the aid of a cane. He walked for exactly one and one-half hours, and never varied the time of his coming or departure.

One of the older boys of the village chanced upon "him" one night. The boy was terrified, of course; beyond the fact that the face was absolutely colorless, and had no expression whatsoever, the boy was unable to describe him.

His appearance must have been bizarre in the extreme, because no one in the entire settlement slept at night until he had come and gone, and not a soul in all West Algoma offered to interfere with him or investigate him in any way. When the men returned in the spring, his perambulations ceased, and he never returned.

ELEPHANT ROCK LEGEND

Once Elephant Rock near Wisconsin Dells was called the Devil's Hitching Post. Children were told that when a death occurred in the community, a man on a coal black horse tied his mount there, and wandered over the hills and valleys, bringing the death angel. In very early days, tradition says, a man once saw the horse tied there and approached to investigate. The horse seemed friendly, and the stranger advanced to inspect and admire him. Suddenly a man appeared above on the cliff, and the horse turned and kicked, striking the curious man and killing him instantly.

THE SERPENT "BOZHO"

Along with the ghosts and haunted houses are the strange critters. In about the year 1917, says Charles E. Brown, a University of Wisconsin student found on the beach of the north shore of Picnic

Point, on Lake Mendota, an object resembling a fish scale. It was of large size, thick and very tough. Never having seen anything just like it before, he took it to his professor. This man, being from New England and acquainted with the species, identified it as a scale from the body of a "sea serpent." This was, so far as one can learn, the first well-verified indication that there was such a creature at large in the fairest of Madison's Four Lakes.

Nothing was seen of this strange water denizen until one day in the early autumn of that year. A fisherman angling for perch off the end of Picnic Point received the fright of his life when he suddenly saw a large snakelike head, with large jaws and blazing eyes, emerge from the deep water not more than a hundred feet away. The man was paralyzed by the fearful sight for a few minutes. Upon recovering his senses, he quickly fled from the shore, leaving his pole and fish-basket behind. He told friends of his experiences, but no one believed his story. He was well laughed at.

Not so very long after this a University boy and coed companion were one day suntanning their backs at the end of a fraternity house pier. They were lying on their stomachs with their feet toward the lake. They had been in this position but a short time when the girl felt something tickling the sole of one of her feet. When this happened she looked at the young man, thinking it might be he. But he was lying quietly with his eyes closed. So the young lady lay down again and closed her eyes, too. A few minutes later something began to tickle the sole of her foot again. This was not to be tolerated. Turning over quickly she saw the head and neck of a huge snake, or dragon, extended above the surface of the water. It had a friendly, humorous look in its big eyes. With its long tongue this animal had been caressing the soles of her feet. She quickly aroused her companion, and the two bathers were soon running as fast as they could go to the shelter of the nearby fraternity house.

Another couple, who were canoeing one evening in University Bay, next saw this marine monster disporting there. Being somewhat familiar with pictures and accounts of Eastern States sea serpents, they readily recognized this creature and hastily paddled to the shore. After this incident other students and citizens of Madison reported that they had seen the serpent at different times and places in the lake. Fishermen stated that they had noted its presence several years before this time. Skeptical persons thought the reputed serpent only a large pickerel, or perhaps a gar fish, with a collection of artificial baits clinging to its head.

This mysterious creature obtained the name of "Bozho," no doubt an abbreviation of the name of the old Indian hero-god, Winnebozho. Several waterspouts which occurred in Lake Mendota were explained as probably caused by this sea serpent. He was taking a shower bath.

Bozho was, on the whole, a rather good-natured animal, playing such pranks as overturning a few canoes with his body or tail, giving chase to sailboats and other lake craft, uprooting a few lake piers and frightening bathers by appearing near beaches. People made more use of the lake when he finally disappeared. It was thought that he left it by way of the Yahara River.

A MENOMINEE LEGEND

In the western part of Marinette County, Wisconsin, stands Thunder Mountain, a relic or root of a mountain range that was older than the Alleghenies or the Rockies. The remnants of this range extend diagonally across the state through the granite quarries at Wausau and end in the Baraboo Bluffs at Devil's Lake.

Before the white settlers came to Wisconsin, this region was inhabited by several tribes of Indians, including the Winnebagoes and the Menominee. Thunder Mountain was in the territory of the latter tribe. About this mountain cluster some very interesting legends, one of which I will give as a sample of their nature.

It is well known that Indians made deities of some animals and birds, such as the bear and the eagle. There also was an imaginary bird thousands of times larger than an eagle, which they called the Thunderbird. The Thunderbird ruled the sky and rode upon the storm, beating out the raindrops with its wings. It made its nest on the top of Thunder Mountain. Some of its eggs rolled down the sides of the mountain and were petrified into stone, which may be found there today in the form of round boulders larger than bushel baskets.

Near the mountain's top is a little lake, and in this lake dwells a serpent that is longer than the length of the tallest trees. It has a copper tail with which it defended itself against the huge creatures that existed in the long ago.

One day an Indian who was hunting on the mountain heard a great commotion in the lake. Peering through the foliage he witnessed a fierce struggle that was going on between the Serpent and the Thunderbird. Seeing him, the Thunderbird called to the Indian to shoot the Serpent, and as a reward it would give good luck to him and to his family. "Shoot the Thunderbird," cried the Serpent, "and I will give good luck to you and to all of your tribe." Not knowing which to trust, the Indian closed his eyes and let fly an arrow to choose its own victim. The arrow hit the Thunderbird, which enabled the Serpent to make a prisoner of the bird beneath the water. Anyone who doubts this story may find evidence of its truthfulness today, when the storm cloud hovers over the mountain. The rumble of the thunder is the noise of the struggle still going on, and the lightning in the cloud is the flashing of the Thunderbird's eyes. Why should more evidence be asked?

The Menominee are now on a reservation along the Wolf River, about fifty miles southwest of Thunder Mountain. At a roadside is Spirit Rock, a stone that is gradually disintegrating. It is a legend with the Menominee that when the stone is gone their tribe will disappear with it.

Told by Colonel A. D. Dorsett

THE WILL-O'-THE-WISP ON THE BIG EAU PLEINE

Will-o'-the-wisps have always been companions of ghost legends, and Mrs. Adele Cline of Eau Pleine remembers how the will-'o-the-wisp was a visitor on their homestead winter and summer, but not very often:

When my father pioneered in the 1880's among the pine and timber along the Big Eau Pleine River, he was the first to see the will-o'-the-wisp. When he was walking home one evening from his parents' place, which was located about a mile away, this light appeared suddenly beside him. By the time he was near his house it disappeared.

It had the appearance of a man walking with a lantern, which was the common way of traveling in those days, and when it was seen by others not too much thought was given to it.

We who lived there knew it was something different, something unexplained. Our neighbor boy Paulie, knew it; my grandfather did; also my aunt and uncle.

My father built the big timber barn and put a board fence around the yard. Until the board fence was put up the light came up to the house.

Not too far from the buildings is the Big Eau Pleine River, and right close by is the lake. Before you get to the lake and river there is about an acre or so of stone, sort of a hill of stone. Some stones lie in long slabs and high ridges and there are also a few scattered boulders. We always classed the area as "the acre of stone," as all around it the land is almost stone-free and under cultivation.

The light always came from the direction of the lake over this hill of stone. It would first be seen when it was turning dark, and never after midnight. Except once, when my mother witnessed two of the lights, chasing one another, leaping up at great height, until two o'clock in the morning.

Sometimes the light would travel faster, as though it was really in a hurry, but regardless how fast it came over the hill it never came over the board fence and gate. It would hover there a moment and disappear. Then suddenly it would be seen about half a mile away in a northern direction, along the river or south of the lake.

Pioneers were brave and God-fearing people, but that mystery gave one such an eerie feeling that one's bravery vanished.

One summer my aunt, who was twelve years old, and my uncle, nine years old, were visiting us and were late in getting the cows home. It was just turning dark when in front of them was that light, flickering, making a hissing sound. Our brave, faithful dog, Shep, left for home like a streak of lightning. The cattle sensed something unusual and everything sure got home in a hurry that evening. For several days after that the dog was afraid to come out from under the house porch. My grandfather, coming home from working late one night, saw the light and thought sure it was going to be the end of the world. All at once there was such a roaring noise, as though big rocks and boulders were falling thousands of feet below, with an echo. My grandfather had been an East Prussian soldier in the Kaiser's Army. He was familiar with the sound of a cannon roar, but he said it was impossible to describe those awful roaring noises underneath the hill that night.

This was also experienced many years later by our neighbor boy, who lived about a mile away, as he was taking this path on his way home. He was not afraid of anything, but he knew fear then. From that time on, he carried a gun.

My grandfather experienced this in the winter and our neighbor boy Paulie in the summer, when he was helping my parents during the haying season.

We moved to an adjoining farm where my father had purchased a cheese factory, so this homestead farm was rented all these years.

Once in a while a renter remarked someone going across the field with a lantern and wondered who it could be, going in such a direction.

Most people think the will-o'-the-wisp is some remote idea of the imagination, but if they could live near this place by the Big Eau Pleine River they would see it. It was last seen in 1948 by the bulldozer operator who worked there late one August night, because next day he came to my father and said, "Why, Mr. Radke, you needn't have walked over the field with a lantern. You could have seen the field riding with me on the bulldozer." My father in a very much surprised and thoughtful manner looked up at him and smiled, but said nothing.

WILL-O'-THE-WISP

Alfred Ulrick, Sr. tells us about a will-o'-the-wisp:

I want to relate the experience I had of seeing a will-o'-the-wisp at a distance of about sixty feet away. Webster's dictionary defines it as gas from low marshy soils. It forms into a bluish fiery ball and floats along on the surface of swampy areas or wanders out onto adjoining areas. It appears to move along in hops, skips, or jumps. The distances vary, and when molested, it seems to have the power to lead one astray.

It had appeared for several years and became a common sight to everybody in our area. Cattle grazed in the fields unalarmed when it was present. No one tried to interfere with it.

We noticed that it never appeared in an open field, but would hop alongside the cross-fences. Our neighbor built a new line fence to replace the old one, which was in poor condition, but that did not make it change its course. That farm was its domain. Never did we notice it hop over the fence onto our land. The weather didn't have any effect on it either. It would appear on light or dark moons and on rainy nights as well. It seemed to be more brilliant in the rain.

I owe a lot of my courage and bravery to my deceased grandfather, who had lived his young manhood years long ago with a similar phenomenon. He told me to have no fear of its presence, to go about my work unconcerned, but not to be a smarty or a wisecracker. Back in the month of July, 1909, my father and I left home in our milk wagon, drawn by my favorite horse, Dick. He was a good pacer and a good traveler, and I took him out to get five bags of oats to tide us over till we had our grain thrashed, as our supply was getting low. My father was a strong man, five feet eleven inches in height and weighing around 175 pounds. He never became frightened of anything. He did not seem to know the meaning of fear, regardless of what the situation was.

That night on our way home we took a town road near which the will-o'-the-wisp frequently appeared. Shadows fell and night was taking over the land. Dick paced confidently along the road, which looked like a white ribbon laid out in the darkness. The cool evening breeze made it a pleasure to be out. Both my father and I sat silently on the seat of the wagon and looked across the field to see if the will-o'-the-wisp would appear. There were not many nights when it was not seen.

Sure enough, there it was, hopping about towards us. My father was one of the curious type. He had seen it many times before but never close by, so he tightened the reins on Dick and slowed him down to a walk. I didn't like this, I was beginning to feel butterflies winging their way around in my stomach, but I didn't say anything to my father. I knew him too well for that.

We drove on a short distance, and then Dad brought Dick to a complete stop. It was just like him to want to see what the "ghost" would do. Suddenly, like magic, it came hopping towards the road about forty feet to the rear of us. That was the limit I could take. I think my body was covered with more goose-pimples than a chicken has feathers; seconds seemed like hours; and I know I stopped breathing. I think my father felt alarmed also, because he didn't look back but gave Dick the starting signal and drove on home without stopping again. We didn't find out whether the "wisp" followed us very far or not and we didn't want to.

I was a lad of twelve years at the time. I'm in my sixtieth year now, and whenever my thoughts wander back to this incident, goose-pimples begin to creep along my spine, and I'll remember it the rest of my earthly life. If my father were alive today he would verify this story as being true in every detail.

PERSONAL EXPERIENCE WITH A WILL-O'-THE-WISP

K. F. Peabody of Star Prairie told us this:

The following is a true experience that can have no value except that it is a thing seen once in a hundred years. My father, who was a missionary here, drove many hundreds of miles by team, and I am sure that if he had ever seen this phenomenon he would have told me so. But it was left for me to see it myself over fifty years ago.

In the early years of the century, before automobiles began to stray into the country from city streets, a few cyclists traveled about with powerful headlights. One night when I was driving home in my horse and rig, it was very dark, and a fine rain was falling, but there was no lightning, no thunder, and no wind. Suddenly a light began to glow around the rig, and thinking a cyclist was coming up from behind, I turned clear out of the rather muddy road. No one passed me, and I looked back to see an empty road. Thinking that the light must come from the sky, I held the umbrella aside and looked up. To my shocked surprise I saw a flame on the metal tip. In momentary fright I furled the thing and laid it in my lap. Instantly the flame appeared on the tip of the whip which stood in the socket on the dash. Taking stock of myself, I decided that I was neither dead nor in imminent danger thereof. I also remembered reading about St. Elmo's fire which sometimes struck sailors with terror. St. Elmo's fire is a flamelike appearance sometimes seen in stormy weather on prominent parts of a ship. St. Elmo is the patron saint of sailors. I held my right hand high with one finger extended and removed the whip. Yes, I had captured the spook and had a good look at it. It was very white, very bright, and very like the flame of a large candle, except that it was cold. I put back the whip but kept the umbrella down as I wanted to watch. I drove with it for about half a mile to the top of a long hill. As we went down it began to fade, and before we reached the bottom, it was done.

Perhaps many have seen this phenomenon on land. At any rate, I would like to know.

THE WITCHES OF PICNIC POINT

Charles E. Brown, while talking with Mrs. Anna White Wings, was told how several Indian families were long ago living on Picnic Point in peace and comfort. Then witches came. They carried away some of the small children. They fed them and fattened them and ate them. The Indians were very sad over the loss of their children, and they prayed to Earthmaker to help them.

Earthmaker caught the witches and restored the children to their homes. He transformed the witches into hackberry trees and placed them near the end of Picnic Point. There they must stand forevermore because of their wrongdoing. When the Wind Spirit comes, they wave their limbs, moan, and ask to be released. When the winter comes one can see twists of witches' hair at the end of their branches. They must stand where they are forever.

THE NIGHT RIDER

Many farm people in Fond du Lac County have heard tales of the "Night Rider," one of the most elusive of the strange ghosts which haunt the Wisconsin land and air. Norma E. Buehner of Fond du Lac relates a version of a Night Rider tale she heard from her uncle, a farmer.

Mrs. Buehner recounts how her car stalled one evening and how she took refuge with her Uncle John and Aunt Em, who lived nearby:

Late in the evening, Aunt Em remarked, "My, it's been a long time since any of us talked about the Night Rider."

Knocking the ashes from his pipe into the coal heater, Uncle John agreed. "Yes, Em, a long time. But none of us ever will forget about it, I guess."

Idly I inquired, "Night Rider? What's that?"

"Come, now," Aunt Em said, "I'll give you the nice feather bed you liked to sleep in when you visited us as a little girl."

I was appalled at the thought of retiring at such an early hour. Besides, I still hadn't received an answer to my inquiry about the Night Rider. Aunt Em's fluttering concern served to heighten my curiosity. Uncle John never had been able to refuse me anything. Again I turned to him. "Please tell me about this Night Rider."

Aunt Em, with a warning eye, turned to him also. "No, John, she hasn't known all these years. Why tell her now?"

Uncle John looked uncertainly from one to the other of us. I had become quite excited. Aunt Em saw the story bursting to be told from my uncle. With a resigned sigh she assented.

"Well, all right. But I don't want any part of it. I'm going to bed. John, give her the big lamp and be sure it's filled. She might want to leave a light burning all night. Be sure to bank the fire before you come to bed." Giving us a disturbed look, she shook her head and retired to her room.

Uncle suggested a hot toddy. Remembering the warming, spicy tang of his winter bedtime drink, I quickly agreed.

We went to the kitchen. The room was warm and I felt a growing sense of well-being as I viewed the filled woodbox, the bread mixture rising for the next day's baking, the covered tub of homemade sausages waiting to be smoked. Uncle John put the teakettle on the kitchen range, placed two heavy cups and a thick bowl from the pantry shelves before us on the table. Then he gathered the rum, sugar, eggs, and spices. He was slow and I was impatient.

"When do we begin the story, Uncle?" I asked.

Painstakingly measuring the sugar, rum, and spices into the bowl, he answered, "You really want to know, I guess. I'd like to tell you. Then again, I don't. It's hard to believe, for anyone who never had it happen to them. Don't want you to think I'm lying. Never did tell a lie, you know."

"No, Uncle, I won't think you're lying." And I reflected upon his indisputable truth and honesty.

He carefully broke and separated the eggs, then beat the whites into a miniature mountain of frothy whiteness. He added the precious mixture, then gently ladled the foaming goodness into each cup. I went to the cupboard drawer for teaspoons and placed them in the cups. He filled them with water from the steaming teakettle and we sat down to stir our drinks, facing each other across the table. He spoke.

"If I was the only one who had ever heard the Night Rider, I wouldn't expect you to believe me. I would doubt my own senses. But all the old neighbors have heard the same thing for at least seven, eight miles around. I can't tell you exactly what they heard, but I can tell you what I heard. It happened many times, many years ago. I'll tell you about the first time it happened to me. Couldn't help thinking about it tonight. It was on a night just like this, after a storm of snow and ice. The moon was so bright that the night was almost as light as day.

"Aunt Em and I were very young. We hadn't been married a year. As you know, Grandfather lived on the old farm then. It's only a mile from this place if you take the short cut through the woods. Grandpa took our cream to the creamery every morning, so usually every evening Em and I would take our cream to him. We enjoyed those walks." He paused to sip the toddy, then continued.

"Grandpa had told me about the Night Rider. Everyone around here had. I had never heard it myself, so I laughed at the mention of it, laughed at the mystery of it, the terror everyone had for it. I was young and smart. I wasn't afraid of anyone or anything.

"Like I said, it was on a night like this, only there was a little wind. I was taking the cream to Grandpa's. Em didn't go along that night because of the snow and ice. I had a cream can in cne hand, a lantern in the other. Didn't need the lantern, but it was one I had borrowed and I was taking it back.

"The trees in the woods were mighty pretty that night. The pine branches hung low with snow and sleet. The oak branches reflected the moon like big crooked icicles sticking out from the trunks. I always liked to hear the wind in the pines and I stopped a few times to listen to it then. It wasn't as cold as it is tonight so I didn't hurry; walked slowly.

"You know where the foot bridge crosses the stream that runs through Grandpa's marsh. I stopped there, too. It was so light out that I could see the tracks in the snow where the muskrats had gone down to the water.

"After having gone through the woods I thought I kept hearing the soughing of the wind in the pines, so I listened again for a while. I heard something, all right, but it wasn't the wind. I was sure of that because it kept getting louder and closer. I looked all around and then up at the sky, because it sounded so much like thunder. I knew it couldn't be thunder that time of year. Besides, the sky was clear. What had been a blowing sound changed to what seemed like many ponderous things rolling over something big and hollow, like gigantic wagon wheels on a big, wooden bridge. Suddenly I remembered all I had heard about the Night Rider. This must be it. I meant not to let it scare me the way it had scared everyone else. Then I heard woeful wailing like unnumbered souls in agonizing torment; faint at first, but rapidly becoming louder and closer along with the other noise, now roaring and crashing. The tumult was above and all around me. My eardrums hurt with the growing intensity of it. I started to run. It was like trying to run against a strong wind, and yet the branches of the river willows were barely swaying. The noise pressed upon my shoulders like heavy weights. This unknown force pushed against my chest and legs and arms and my arms became very weak. I dropped the cream can and lantern in my eagerness to escape more rapidly from the threatening peril. Whatever the noise was, I had no further desire to see what caused it. It pressed closer and closer and became so heavy against my throat and chest I thought I would surely strangle. I became completely enveloped in a horrible, overwhelming noise. It kept pushing me down until by the time I reached the hill to the house I was crawling on hands and knees. Grandpa had heard the weird commotion in the sky. He had been expecting me, and came to meet me. With an encouraging word and a firm hand he lifted me to my feet and half-dragged me to the house where Grandma helped us in. No one said a word. We all felt thankful to be alive and safe. I stayed the night and slept like a man completely drugged.

"The next day I went home the way I had come the night before. I saw my footprints in the snow, the tracks of the muskrats at the river's edge and I saw where I had dropped the lantern and the can of cream. They were gone, but I could see where I had dropped them. They were gone, and mine were the only tracks to and from the spot where they had fallen. I know that once they had dropped from my hands I had not touched them again."

Uncle John had finished his story. Our hot toddies, barely tasted, had grown cold.

Aunt Em had been right. I burned the lamp the rest of the night.

THE GREENWOOD GHOST

Dr. Harriet Anundsen, Monroe, gave us this one about Bill and the Greenwood ghost:

It was really dark when I headed for home with a fresh can of carbide on my running board and a couple of beers under my belt. I was breezing along at almost fifteen miles an hour. I like to ride fast. I was pitying the folks who must ride behind plodding horses and admiring the way my headlights bored through the darkness as I approached Greenwood cemetery. The road goes straight toward the cemetery, and just at the gate it turns sharply to the left. I was just a few rods from the gate when I saw a white, iridescent figure flitting about among the tombstones and monuments. I stopped my car and the figure stood still. I started again and it moved too. Then, as I made the left turn, it disappeared just like that!

I'll admit the Buick did something better than fifteen the rest of the way home, and when I got there I drove right up to the back door instead of to the machine shed. If the doorstep had been lower and the doorway wider I'd have driven right into the kitchen. I didn't tell Betina what I'd seen. I knew what her explanation would have been, and I also knew that I hadn't had that many beers.

I didn't mention it to anybody. I didn't want to be a laughing stock, but I kept my ears open and the next Saturday night I heard Emmet Wild ask the crowd at Joe's place whether they'd seen anything queer in the cemetery. They all looked blank. They were probably asleep by the time they got that far from town. Horses don't have to be driven home on a Saturday night. That is, they looked blank excepting Jack Thomas and, I suppose, myself. He sort of gravitated toward Emmet and retired from the bar to compare notes.

All three of us had seen the same thing on the same night. Come to think of it, we were the only ones in our neighborhood who drove cars.

Jack thought he had seen a woman, but Emmet said it was too tall for a woman, and besides, what would a woman be doing in the cemetery at that hour?

Anyway, we decided to go home together and see what we could figure out. It was clear when we left town with a moon as big as a washtub, so we didn't light our headlights. We didn't waste carbide in those days. Well, we drove up to the cemetery and back and forth along the road, and didn't see a thing. But the next night I took Betina in to a special meeting at the Methodist Church, and on the way home, just where I'd seen it before, the figure appeared. Betina screeched and grabbed my arm. Almost put us in the ditch. "Bill," she yelled, "there's a ghost in the cemetery!"

After that everybody knew about the Greenwood ghost, but only a few people saw it. When the young bucks took their girls buggy riding, they would head for the cemetery, and the girls would screech and grab the boys around the neck. They didn't, as it turned out, really see anything, but they had a good time.

It was the science teacher at the high school who solved the mystery. He had somebody drive out there in a car one dark night. Then when they saw the figure they stopped the car and he got out and walked straight for the ghost. Took nerve, I'd say. It was a new monument he had put on his lot—a marble pillar polished till you could see your face in it. The headlights picked it up as they approached the cemetery, but lost it when the car turned.

How did it move? It didn't. It was we who were doing the moving.

THE GIRL IN WHITE

Jessie Quackenbush of La Crosse says this really happened:

This is a true experience of John Groat's while he was working in the community somewhere in the neighborhood of Menominee. One

evening, I think he said in July, he and another young man, a friend
of John's in the neighborhood, decided to walk into town, a distance
of perhaps a mile and a half. On their way back they intended to
stop at a farmhouse where two young ladies lived—sisters whose
company they had been enjoying. The farmhouse was situated near
a small, shallow stream of water which crossed the highway and had
an old-fashioned wooden bridge built over it for better traveling.
The stream was only about five rods from the farmhouse. No cars
or even buggies were used then for conveyances. Everyone either
walked or rode horseback; and not owning horses, the two young
men walked. On this particular night it took them longer than they
had intended.

As they stood leaning on the bridge and trying to decide if it was
too late to call at the farmhouse, Ed said to John, "Look, there's
a girl coming down the road dressed all in white." She came right
towards the bridge, then swerved, and crossed right down to the
little stream.

John said to his friend, "That's too bad! She has seen us and feels
afraid to cross the bridge!"

They both watched her, and Ed said it might be Carrie or Anna
from the farmhouse, but where was she going and why was she
going to wade through the stream at night? They watched breath-
lessly. She walked right into the stream and appeared to go right
in over her head.

The boys made a mad rush down to the place where she had disappeared. There must be a deep hole there, they both thought.
They walked right in the shallow water around and around and
back and forth where she had apparently disappeared, but no hole
could be found. "Well, let's go to the farmhouse and report this,
even if it is late," said John. "It must have been one of the girls, and
what has happened to her?"

They went on to the farmhouse where the old couple were sitting
on the front porch. John said, "It's quite late, but we thought we'd
stop anyway." They asked if the girls were home. Their mother
answered that they had had company and were now in the kitchen
finishing the supper dishes.

The girls came out on the porch then, and the boys told them what they had seen and showed them their wet and muddy shoes. The girls said there was no deep hole in the stream. It was so shallow they had waded through it many times.

What was it they had seen? They couldn't find an answer. "This story I would never repeat," said John, "if I alone had seen it, but Ed witnessed the sight also."

The people at the farmhouse were mystified also. They had no explanation for the strange phenomenon.

chapter 3

LUMBERJACK LORE

The lumberjack had a language all his own. It was a rough language, and some of it was lost because it was unprintable. It was a man's language. He lived in a man's world. Women had no part of it in the early logging camps. There were no women cooks. It was only after the spring break-up that there was any social life or any drinking.

An Irish lumberjack was brought into a hospital in the early logging days with a few broken ribs. The nurse, full of sympathy, asked him how it happened. He replied, "Well, Sister, I'll tell you how the whole thing happened. You see I was up in the woods a-loading. One cold morning when I was sending up a big burly schoolmarm on fourth tier, I see she was going to cannon, so I glams into it to cut her back when the bitch broke and she comes and caves in a couple of my slats."

To the uninitiated, lumberjack lingo sounds like so much double-talk. Actually it's quite simple. The worker was loading a big forked log onto a sleigh full of logs. When he saw that it was going to upend, he tried to hold it back, then the chain broke. The log fell on him and broke a couple of his ribs.

LIFE OF THE LUMBERJACK 1880–1910

"Daylight in the swamp" was the call which started the lumberjack on his active day. He crawled from the muzzle-loading (end-loading) bunk, filled with balsam boughs or straw for a mattress, and which had a straw-filled sack for a pillow. The deacon seat, hewed from a log or plank and placed at the end of the lower bunk, was his only dressing table. Heavy two-piece wool underwear, heavy Chippewa or Malone stag pants (pants cut off just below boot-tops), two or more pairs of warm wool socks inside packs, one or two wool shirts, a heavy Mackinaw, wool cap and mitts kept him warm in many-degrees-below-zero weather. The stag pants legs were worn over the packs, not inside them, to keep out the snow. The packs were made of rubber bottoms with sewed-on leather uppers eight to sixteen inches high. They were made by a local shoemaker. Some of the earlier lumberjacks wore all-leather, well-oiled boots.

There was no indoor plumbing. Two poles behind a clump of hemlock or balsam, or in a rough enclosure to keep out snow but not cold, served in lieu of steam-heated facilities. You then walked or ran back to the camp in the dark, washed up, often in cold water, but felt full of vim and vigor and believed you could lick your weight in wildcats.

At 6 A.M. the gabriel (dinner horn) was sounded or a steel was struck with a stamping hammer (a heavy hammer with the company's brand on the face), and you crossed the dingle (alley between men's camp and kitchen) or raced to the cook-shack if the buildings were separated. You took the same place at the same oilcloth-covered table for all meals. You had to hurry or be the last one to leave the table. Some men could eat and run in five minutes. Everyone was through in fifteen minutes. Chewing your food was a mistake. You had to learn to bolt it. The cookee (cook's helper) had the table set with tin plates and cups, knives, forks, and spoons, and no one left the table hungry. There were logging berries (prunes), oatmeal or cornmeal mush, stovelids (sourdough pancakes), sometimes french toast, sowbelly (salt pork) murphys (fried potatoes), dish water (coffee) or swamp water (tea), bread and doughnuts. Always doughnuts. Lard, margarine, or butter and jam provided the spread. Cookies and left-over pie or cake were generally on the table.

The jacks were in the cuttings before daylight and usually waited for light to begin work. Sawyers felled the trees, swampers trimmed the branches from the logs, and skidders with teams of oxen or horses snaked the logs from the woods to the landing. Jammers loaded the logs on sleighs (not sleds) which ran on ice roads with ruts for the sleigh runners. Although the loads of logs were immense they were generally pulled by one team. A huge horse-drawn water tank sprinkled the roads, and during the night the water froze solid. The sprinkler was used at night in order not to interfere with the sleigh haul and because the water froze faster. A rutter cut a groove in the ice for the sleighs hauling the logs to the rollway (decks of logs) on the bank of a stream, there to await the spring breakup.

There was no coffee break for the lumberjack. At eleven-thirty the gabriel was blown again and the men came into camp if it was close (less than one mile), but generally the shanty boss (chore boy) or cookee hauled the dinner to the woods in boxes on a jumper (sled drawn by one horse). Dinner was the big meal. There was red horse (corned beef) or roast pork, murphys or rutabagas, bean-hole beans, dried apricots, peaches, currants, raisins, or prunes, or fresh-baked raisin or pregnant women (dried apple) pie, cookies, doughnuts, coffee cake or raisin cake and mountains of bread and jam, and again java (swamp water).

For supper they "kind of let up a little." There was soup, hot biscuits or johnny cake (corn bread), cold meat or hash or beef stew, potatoes, pie or cake and cookies, and left-over dinner food.

There was no talking at the table unless it helped to speed up the eating process. Talking took too much time. The cook was the absolute boss in the dining room—there was no higher authority.

Bread, pancakes, and doughnuts were made from sourdough. Bread was set and part of it was kept for the next batch. On the river drive it was banick, made from flour, baking powder, and water, and it was not very appetizing.

In the evening the men usually sat around. Some patched mittens or other clothing, some read worn-out novels many times passed around, some played poker, some lay on their bunks, but most of the men just sat and smoked. There was talking and storytelling and occasionally a little singing, mouth-organ- or fiddle-playing. Generally however this type of entertainment was reserved for Saturday night and Sunday. If the cook or boss had some news it was given at this after-supper time.

One by one the jacks would go to bed. Snoring would start immediately and lights were out by eight o'clock. Snoring stopped only when the familiar cry, "daylight in the swamp" was heard after a too-short night.

Sunday was washday. In below zero weather this was a most unpleasant job. In front of the camp a large cauldron was filled with water and a fire built under it. There were tubs with washboards to wash and scrub the clothes. But first there was boiling-up to get rid of the crumbs (lice) brought in by a boomer. A boomer was a lumberjack who did not stay long on a job, just long enough to get a liquor stake and the wrinkles out of his belly.

There was surprising little sickness in camp. If sick or injured and he had a hospital ticket, the man was taken to the hospital by a tote team. Health insurance is not new; it goes back to the days of our lumberjacks. Salesmen went from camp to camp selling tickets at a cost of five to eight dollars each. This ticket entitled the lumberjack to hospital and medical care for a whole year. Aches and pains were cared for by a liniment rub.

One ailment was blanket fever. If a man stayed in bed in the morning he usually had blanket fever. About nine o'clock he would be in the cook-shack wanting breakfast. The cook could generally tell by the amount he ate whether the lumberjack was really sick or whether his ailment was blanket fever.

In early logging days lumberjacks went into camp in the fall and generally did not come out until spring. Some of them would roam from camp to camp looking for better wages, carrying all their belongings in a turkey (pack sack). Later, however, the professional lumberjack force was supplemented by farmers who took their teams with them to the woods in the winter. A man earned from $18 to $30 a month. A team was worth as much as a man.

A third-generation son of a lumberjack by the name of Lewis recalls: "My wife's grandfather used to live by Iola, Wisconsin. He always used to work in the woods in the wintertime to earn money to clear more land. His wife and kids would take care of the farm.

He would come home at Christmastime. It was probably why all her aunts and uncles were born at the same time of the year."

In the early logging days of northern Wisconsin there were no railroads or highways in the pinery (pine forest). The only way to get the logs out was to float them down the many streams. Only the pine logs would float; therefore, loggers cut only pine. The hemlock and hardwood was left standing. Almost every city in northern Wisconsin is built on one of these log-driving streams.

The entire winter's cut of one or many logging camps was hauled to the stream and piled along the bank awaiting the spring breakup. Melting snow and freshets raised the water in the stream to make log driving possible. Dams were sometimes built to back up the water; wing dams were built from the shore to guide the logs past an obstruction.

A crew of the best lumberjacks were chosen from those of the winter crew. These men made ready to start the drive the moment the head (amount) of water was sufficient. At a word from the boss, the logs were broken out of the decks with peaveys and cant-hooks, rolled into the water, and the drive was on.

The main job was to keep the logs moving and to prevent their causing a jam by piling up on an obstruction. The best of the drivers stayed at the head of the mass of logs. The more inexperienced followed to "sack the rear"—that is, to push logs that had floated into still water out into the current.

The river drive was probably the most dangerous of any occupation in the history of the state. Many, many river drivers, or "river rats" or "river pigs" were drowned. Many more had legs or bodies broken. A driver who met death was buried on the bank, and often no stone marked his grave. He was simply forgotten. Injury or death was considered a part of the job. Regardless of danger, the logs had to move.

The log-jam was the nightmare of the rivermen. There were many rocks and other obstructions that the logs could pile up on, causing big trouble. Breaking the jam and finding and loosening the key log took skill, experience, and a disregard of danger—for once the logs started moving, men working on the jam could be crushed by the moving mass. On a bad jam, dynamite was used. Speed was essential because every minute's delay caused additional logs to pile up. The jam was eventually broken and the logs were again on their way. But there was many a driver who knew the Wisconsin version of the ballad, "The Log Jam on Gerry's Rocks" and knew that, sentimental as it was, it was based on truth.

Come all you true born shanty-boys wherever you may be
Come sit here on the deacon's seat, and listen unto me.
It's about a gay young shanty-boy, so gentle, strong, and brave,
Was at the jam on Gerry's rocks, he met a watery grave.

Was on a Sunday morning, as you shall plainly hear,
The logs were piled a mountain high, we could not get them clear.
"Turn out brave boys!" Monroe did cry, his voice devoid of fear.
"We'll break the jam on Gerry's rocks and for Eagleston we'll
    steer."
They had not pushed off many logs, before Monroe did say:
"I'd have you all be on your guard, this jam will soon give way."
He had no more than spoke these words before the jam did go,
And swept away those six brave youths, and foreman young
    Monroe.

When the rest of all the shanty-boys the sad news came to hear,
They gathered up the river boys and downward they did steer.
And there they found to their surprise and sorrow, grief, and woe,
All cut and mangled on the shore, the form of young Monroe.

They picked him from the water, pushed back his raven black
    hair
There was one fair form among them all whose cries did rend
    the air
There was one fair form among them all, a girl from Saginaw
    town,
Whose mournful cries did rend the air, for her lover who was
    drowned.

Throughout the drive, the drivers were often wet the entire time. Sometimes they rode the logs, sometimes they walked along the bank on a path called the gig trail. Trout fishermen still use these old trails. The men slept where they could, often under the stars on the ground, or on a bed of balsam boughs. Some lumberjacks were superstitious and would not change wet clothes, but let them dry on their bodies for fear they would get pneumonia. Following the drive was a bateau or a wanagen, carrying food and supplies. The bateau was a flat-bottomed boat tapered at each end. The wanagen was the cook's raft, and was generally used on large rivers.

A long drive could last several weeks, part of which was without contact with the outside world. Generally, however, there were a few points where the tote roads ran to the river and where fresh supplies could be brought in. Food was carried in a "river pig's nose bag" (tin lunchbox) strapped to the back of the river driver.

When there was only one logging company there was no problem of ownership. On the larger streams, however, many owners drove each spring and boom companies were organized to drive all the logs at one time. To identify ownership a log mark was made with a stamping hammer, with raised letters which marked the logs on the end and side for identifying in the water. The log marks were to the logger what the brands were to the cattlemen of the west.

Eventually the drive arrived at the sorting gaps at the mills where the logs were sorted according to ownership and placed in booms (log corrals) awaiting the saws.

After the spring breakup and after the logs were delivered to the mill, the lumberjack usually went on a spree. And a great spree it was. The shanty-boy had a special affinity for women. However, he had also a set of standards of his own, and it was his boast that he never offended a respectable woman. Fights were common. They were a form of entertainment. Grudges were seldom held. Towns were rough as a result of the lumberjacks' desires and demands. An often repeated statement was "Hurley, Hayward, and Hell," in the order named.

There will never be another sleigh haul and there will never be another log drive in Wisconsin, but the memory of this group of lumbermen will never be forgotten. It is all a part of the story of the building of the Great Midwest.

THE LUMBERJACK AS A FAMILY MAN

Mrs. Pauline Easterson, whose father worked in timber camps and sawmills, says that her father had worked in the forests of Norway and Sweden before coming to America:

His name was Paul Anderson. Mine is Pauline, which is the feminine of Paul. Among the Norwegians you often hear such names as Christine, Josephine, Melsine, or Jensine. They are names in honor of the father. I've always been proud of mine as I could always be proud of my father.

My childhood days were spent in Eau Claire, Wisconsin, which was called the "Sawdust City." There were at least a dozen sawmills in Eau Claire at that time. It wasn't until I finished Rural Normal and went to teach in Taylor County that I saw a lumber camp. I, therefore, sort of have the cart before the horse.

We lived on the west side of Eau Claire, within a half mile of four sawmills. When the whistles of these mills blew, as they did morning, noon, and evening, we youngsters all ran for home. We had no excuse for not knowing it was mealtime. We also recognized which mill the whistle belonged to. Each whistle sounded differently.

Father worked mostly for the Daniel Shaw Lumber Co. He was either in the loading shed or in the yard where the lumber was piled.

Sometimes we had to bring him his dinner. I always volunteered for that job. The mill fascinated me, especially the loading shed. This was close to the Chippewa River.

We were forbidden to go inside the mill where the big logs came up the ramp from the water. I'll have to admit that my best friend Clara and I weren't the most obedient daughters. We would sneak in there and stand transfixed, watching the logs as they came up from the water. They were then sawed by the huge saws. We were soon spotted by one of the men and chased out of there.

My father and others took the lumber, sorted it, and loaded it onto the wagons that were backed up to the loading shed.

He worked ten hours a day for $1.75 a day. No wonder he was too tired to walk home for dinner. I can see him yet as he took that pail. It was a tin pail with a tray and cover combined that fitted in the upper part of the pail. This held the tea or coffee. The lower part held the food.

The yard was so large that the company had built tracks through it. The lumber was piled in high piles and in rows, like houses in a city block. The tracks ran between these rows of lumber. The lumber was loaded on the carts that ran on these tracks. They were pushed by hand by the men.

We youngsters would wait until the cart was empty. Usually the men with that cart would be on top of the lumber pile by this time. We then shoved the cart away, taking turns to ride or push. The men would scream at us, but we had lots of fun before we abandoned it, way off in the other end of the yard.

The latter part of October father would begin his preparations for going to camp for the winter. Mother would always plead with him to get a job in town. His answer was, 'You will be all right and I'd much rather work in the woods.' We were all right, but how we missed him.

He never left home without the woodshed stacked with wood, split and piled in neat piles. The cellar contained potatoes, rutabagas, and a barrel of apples. We had beef and pork, frozen or salted. He arranged for credit at the grocers. We had warm clothes, shoes, and rubbers. The only cash mother got was the rent from the upstairs apartment, which was $6.00 a month.

Father and his friend, Christ, always hired out as a team. The foremen were there early in the fall bidding for their services. They were experts at felling trees. I've met several old woodsmen that they worked for. One said, 'So you are little Paul's daughter. There never was a better team of sawers than little Paul and Christ!' They were both short but oh, so stocky and strong. They were also kind and good Christians.

I remember only one Christmas that father felt he could afford to come home. It was a gala occasion.

When he came home in the spring, he had all his winter's wages. He would pay the grocer and we really had a treat. It was usually oranges and candy. There have never been such sweet juicy oranges since. I am sure of that. Father could afford some improvements on the house. Mother got some much-needed piece of furniture.

When I went to Taylor County to teach, I saw a primeval forest for the first time. As I walked a mile and a half through the woods to school, I could understand why father loved the woods.

One Sunday the teacher in the adjoining district, and I, with two friends, drove to the nearby logging camp. I had heard so much about it that I was very interested. This camp had eighty men. We saw the building with the bunks, the blacksmith shop, and the building "wanigan," where they sold clothes and things for the men who didn't have enough to last through all winter. We ate in the "diner" on tin plates and drank from tin cups. The food was good. The men were not supposed to talk while they ate. The knives and forks against the tin plates made noise enough. We ate at the cook's table.

On the way home we discovered someone had filled our coat pockets with raisins and prunes. These were considered great delicacies.

THE LITTLE BROWN BULLS

One of the great ballads of Wisconsin is "The Little Brown Bulls" which tells the story of a log-skidding contest between a team of "white spotted steers" and a team of "little brown bulls." It has often been referred to as a lumberjack classic and a true Wisconsin song. Folks up in Northern Wisconsin will mention the ballad. A few old-timers will even sing it for you.

Not a thing on the river McClusky did fear,
When he drew the stick o'er his big spotted steers,
They were young, quick, and sound, girting eight foot and three.
Says McClusky, the Scotchman, "They're the laddies for me!"

Bull Gordon, the Yankee, on skidding was full,
As he cried "whoa hush" to his little brown bulls!
Short-legged and soggy, girt six foot and nine.
Says McClusky, the Scotchman, "Too light fer our pine!"

It's three to the thousand our contract did call.
Our hauling was good and the timber was tall,
McClusky he swore he'd make the day full,
An' skid two to one of the little brown bulls.

"Oh no!" says Bull Gordon, "that you cannot do.
Though it's well we do know you've the pets of the crew!
And mark you, my boy, you would have your hands full
If you skid one more log than the little brown bulls!"

The day was appointed and soon it drew nigh
For twenty-five dollars their fortunes to try.
Both eager and anxious that morning were found
And scalers and judges appeared on the grounds!

With a hoop and a yell came McClusky in view,
With the big spotted steers, the pets o' the crew!
Both chewing their cuds—"Oh boys, keep your jaws full!
You can easily beat them, the little brown bulls!"

Then out came Bull Gordon with a pipe in his jaw;
The little brown bulls with their cuds in their mouths.
And little we think when we see them come down,
That a hundred and forty could they jerk around!

Then up spoke McClusky, come stripped to the skin!
"We'll dig them a hole and tumble them in!
We'll learn the damn Yankee to face the bold Scot!
We'll mix them a dose and feed it red hot!"

Says Gordon to Kennebec, with blood in his eye,
"Today we must conquer McClusky or die!"
Then up spoke bold Kennebec, "Boys, never fear!
For you ne'er shall be beat by the big spotted steers!"

Oh, 'twas up to the logs and fasten 'em on!
Hurry up, boys, for it's no longer dawn!
The daylight is running, and if you'll take a hunch,
You'll hook to the logs and forget about lunch!

McClusky, the Scotchman, showed nothing like fear,
As he cried, "Whoa hush!" to the white spotted steers!
For it's on, boys, and gone, boys! Take hold of the snow!
We're hooked to the log, and now let 'em go!

Bull Gordon he worked with a pipe in his mouth,
And the wind blew the smoke from the North to the South.
Says he to his helper, "John, I'm scared as can be
That those white spotted steers 're too much fer me!"

The sun had gone down when the foreman did say,
"Turn out, boys, turn out! You've enough for the day!
We have scaled them and counted, each man to his team,
And it's well we do knew now which one kicks the beam!"

After supper was over McClusky appeared
With the belt ready made for the big spotted steers.
To form it he'd torn up his best Mackinaw,
He was bound he'd conduct it accordin' to law!

Then up spoke the scaler, "Hold on, you awhile!
The big spotted steers are behind just one mile!
For you have a hundred and ten and no more,
And Gordon has beat you by ten and a score!"

The shanty did ring and McClusky did swear.
He tore out by handfuls his long yellow hair.
Says he to Bull Gordon, "My colors I'll pull,
So here, take the belt for the little brown bulls!"

Here's health to Bull Gordon and Kennebec John,
The biggest day's work on the river they done.
So fill up your glasses and fill 'em up full,
We'll drink to the health of the little brown bulls!

Professor Raney of Appleton says that the lumber camps of Wisconsin helped to create an entire cycle of native American folklore.

Paul Bunyan, the hero, was a mythical lumber operator who, according to Gene Shepard * had his camp about forty miles west of Rhinelander, Wisconsin. Paul had great ingenuity and was of gigantic stature; as in other states, he was the possessor of Babe, the Blue Ox, who measured forty-seven axe handles and a tobacco plug between the eyes; and much else in the camp was of equally heroic proportions. After his work in Wisconsin was done, Paul Bunyan logged in the Dakotas (witness their present treeless condition) and in the Pacific Northwest.

PAUL BUNYAN'S WISCONSIN NATURAL HISTORY

Inhabiting the big pine woods, the swamps, lakes, and streams in the vicinity of Paul Bunyan's old-time logging camps † were a considerable number of very wild animals. These differed considerably from the common bear, deer, wildcats, and wolves of the timber lands. Most of them are now extinct or but rarely seen. Some were quite harmless, but most of them were of a very vicious or poisonous nature. Most were active only during the winter months; during the summer they hid in thickets or windfalls, hibernated in caves or hollow trees, or migrated to the North Pole. Tall tales of encounters with some of these mythical wild animals were often told in the lumber camp bunkhouses at night to create mirth or to impress and frighten the greenhorns. The information here collected concerning these Bunyan beasts, birds, reptiles, and fish was obtained from various reliable, as well as unreliable and doubtful, sources. The descriptions of these are arranged in alphabetical order for convenience of ready identification.

ANIMALS

Axehandle Hound: Like a dachshund in general appearance, with a hatchet-shaped head, a short handle-shaped body, and short, stumpy legs. It prowled about the lumber camps at night looking for axe or peavy handles, this being the only kind of food it was known to touch. Whole cords of axe handles were eaten by these troublesome wild hounds.

* See chapter on Tricksters.
† Apparently on the Onion River.

Argopelter: This hoary beast lived in the hollow trunks of trees. From this point of vantage it dropped or threw chunks or splinters of wood on its victims. It but seldom missed its aim, and a considerable number of lumberjacks were annually maimed by its gunnery. No complete description of it has ever been obtained, and its life history is unknown.

Camp Chipmunk: Originally small animals, they ate the tons of prune stones discarded from Paul Bunyan's camp cook-shanty and grew so big and fierce that they killed all of the bears and catamounts in the neighborhood. Later Paul and his men shot them for tigers.

Flittericks: The variety of flying squirrels which frequented the vicinity of the lumber camps were very dangerous because of the great rapidity of their flight. It was impossible to dodge them. One struck an ox between the eyes with such force as to kill the animal.

Gumberoo: It lived in burned-over forests and was therefore easily avoided. It was very ferocious. It was "larger than a bear and had a round, leathery body that nothing could pierce. Bullets bounded off its tough hide. Often they struck the hunter on the rebound and killed him. The only thing that could kill a gumberoo was fire. Often at night the lumberjacks were awakened by loud explosions. These were caused by gumberoos blowing up in flames." A foolhardy photographer once took a picture of one, but this also finally blew up.

Gyascutus: Also called the Stone-eating Gyascutus. This sordid beast has been described as "about the size of a white-tailed deer. Has ears like a rabbit and teeth like a mountain lion. It has telescopic legs which enable it to graze easily on hills. It has a long tail which it wraps around rocks when its legs fail to telescope together. It feeds on rocks and lichens, the rocks enabling it to digest the tough and leathery lichens. It is never seen except after a case of snakebite."

Hangdown: Its Latin name is unknown. This utterly foolish animal lives in big woods "where it hangs down from the limbs of trees, either with its fore or hind paws, either head down or head on, either way making no difference to its digestion. It climbs along the bottom of a limb after the manner of a sloth. Its skin brings a high price. It is more easily hunted at night when a tub must be placed over it. It is then killed with an axe."

Hidebehind: A very dangerous animal which undoubtedly accounted for many missing lumberjacks. It was always hiding behind something, generally a tree trunk. Whichever way a man turned it was always behind him. From this position it sprang upon its human prey, dragged or carried the body to its lair and there feasted on it in solid comfort. Because of its elusive habits no satisfactory description of it has ever been obtained.

Hodag: The Black Hodag (Bovinus spiritualis) was discovered by E. S. "Gene" Shepard, a former well-known timber cruiser of Rhinelander, Wisconsin. Its haunts were in the dense swamps of that region. According to its discoverer, this fearful beast fed on mud turtles, water snakes, and muskrats, but it did not disdain human flesh.

Luferlang: A curious animal with a dark blue stripe running down the length of its back. Its brushy tail was in the middle of the back. Its legs were triple-jointed, and it could run equally fast in any direction. It attacked its prey without provocation, and its bite was certain death. "It bites but once a year, so if one met one that had already bitten someone, one was perfectly safe."

Roperite: A very active animal as large as a pony. It had a rope-like beak with which it roped the swiftest rabbits. Sometimes it got a tenderfoot logger. It generally traveled in small herds. Probably now extinct.

Rumptifusel: A very ferocious animal of large size and great strength. When at rest it wrapped its thin body about the trunk of a tree, a clever stratagem for securing its prey. A lumberjack mistook it for a fur robe, approached it, and was thereafter missing.

Sidehill Dodger: It lived on the sides of hills only. It had two short legs on the uphill side. It burrowed in hillsides, having a number of such burrows and always dodging in and out of these. It was harmless but its very strange antics frightened many a lumberjack into fits.

Silver Cat: This fierce denizen of the pineries was a huge cat with tasseled ears. Its fiery red eyes were in vertical instead of horizontal eye slits. It had a very long tail with a ball-shaped knob at its end.

The lower side of this knob was bare and hard, on its upper side were sharp spikes. The big cat would sit on a limb waiting for a victim. When one passed beneath it would knock him down with the hard side and then pick him up with the spikes. Paul Bunyan's crews suffered continual losses from the depredations of these big cats.

Teakettler: A small animal enigma. Its hind legs have the hoofs of a moose and its fore legs the claws of a bear, making it very hard to track. When it tires of using one set of legs it travels on the other set. It prowls along the tote roads devouring any coats or other articles of lumberjacks' clothing which it finds hung on trees or logs. It is fierce in appearance but is shy and harmless.

Tripodero: It had tripod legs. "Its beak is like the muzzle of a gun with a sight on the end. Going through the brush it raises and lowers itself to look for game. Upon seeing a bird or small animal it tilts itself to the rear, sights along its beak and lets fly a pellet of clay. A quantity of squids of this material it carries in its cheeks. It never misses a shot." This is more particularly an animal of the vicinity of the civil engineering and railroad construction than of the logging camps.

BIRDS

Goofus Bird: One of the peculiar birds nesting near Paul Bunyan's old-time camp on the Big Onion River. It was the opposite of most other birds—it always flew backwards instead of forwards. This curious habit an old lumberjack explained: "It doesn't give a darn where it's going, it only wants to know where it's been." It also built its nest upside down.

Gillygaloo: This hillside plover nested on the slopes of Bunyan's famous Pyramid Forty. Living in such a locality, it laid square eggs so that they could not roll down the steep incline. The lumberjacks hard-boiled these eggs and used them as dice.

Pinnacle Grouse: This bird had only one wing. This enabled it to fly in only one direction about the top of a conical hill. The color of its plumage changed with the seasons and with the condition of the observer.

Phillyloo Bird: It had a long beak like a stork and long legs. It had no feathers to spare. It flew upside down the better to keep warm and to avoid rheumatism in its long limbs. It laid Grade D eggs.

Moskittos: The naturalist in Paul Bunyan's camp classified these as birds. When Paul was logging in the Chippewa River region the mosquitos were particularly troublesome. They were so big that they could straddle the stream and pick the passing lumberjacks off the log drive. Sometimes a logging crew would find one in this position, quickly tie his legs to convenient trees and use him for a bridge across the river. Paul imported from Texas a drove of fighting bumble-bees to combat the mosquitos. They fought for a while, then made peace and intermarried. The result of this crossing made the situation worse than ever before for the loggers. The offspring had stingers at both ends.

SNAKES

Hoop Snake: A very poisonous reptile. It could put its tail in its mouth and roll with lightning-like rapidity after its prey. The only way to avoid it was to jump quickly through its hoop as it approached. This so confused the large serpent that it rolled by and could not get back. Its sting was in its tail. A hoop snake once stung a peavy handle. This swelled to such great size that Paul Bunyan cut one thousand cords of wood out of it.

Snow Snake: These reptiles came over from Siberia by way of the frozen Bering Strait during the very cold year of the two winters. Being pure white in color, they were always more plentiful during the wintertime. They were very poisonous and savage. Tanglefoot oil was the only remedy for their bite.

FISH

Cougar Fish: This savage fish, armed with sharp claws, lived in the Big Onion River. It was the cause of the disappearance and death of many river drivers, whom it clawed off the logs and beneath the water. Paul Bunyan offered a big reward for their capture and extermination, but the fish heard of it and stayed away. None were taken.

Giddy Fish: They were small and very elastic, like India rubber. They were caught through holes in the ice during the winter. The method pursued was to hit one on the head with a paddle. This fish would bounce up and down. Taking the cue from him, the other fish would bounce also. Presently all would bounce themselves out of the water onto the ice. There they were easily gathered up.

Goofang: This curious fish always swam backward instead of forward. This was to keep the water out of its eyes. It was described as "about the size of a sunfish, only larger."

Log Gar: These big fish had a snout so well-armed with large saw teeth that they could saw right through a log to get at a juicy lumberjack. Once in the water they made mincemeat of him.

Upland Trout: These very adroit fish built their nests in trees and were very difficult to take. They flew well but never entered the water. They were fine pan fish. Tenderfeet were sent out into the woods to catch them.

Whirligig Fish: Related to the Giddy Fish. They always swam in circles. They were taken in the winter months through holes in the ice, like their relatives. The loggers smeared the edges of the holes with ham or bacon rind. Smelling this, the fish would swim around the rims of the holes, faster and faster, until they whirled themselves out on the ice. Thousands were thus taken.

Bugs

Chiefly bedbugs and greybacks. The men soon got used to them and tolerated them. Wood ticks were in the brush, but were out of date and inactive in the wintertime.

Told by C. E. Brown

PAUL BUNYAN'S SHOES

In the logging museum at Rhinelander hangs a pair of shoes so huge that they could have been worn by no one but Paul Bunyan. The story goes that Paul once caught a baby muskellunge, carried it home, and put it in a rain barrel outside his cabin. Every day he took the little fish out of the rain barrel and placed it on the ground. In time the muskie learned to walk and, before many months, to abhor water.

One day when Paul was walking along the Rib River the fish followed him and tried to cross the fast stream on a fallen log.

Halfway across it lost its balance and fell in. Although Paul quickly pulled off his shoes and plunged into the river, his pal had drowned by the time he reached it. Overcome with grief, Paul returned to camp, forgetting his shoes, the pair that are now displayed in the museum.

ROUND RIVER DRIVE

'Twas '64 or '65
We drove the great Round River Drive;
'Twas '65 or '64—
Yes, it was durin' of the war,
Or it was after or before.

Those were the days in Wisconsin,
The good old days when any man
Could cut and skid and log and haul,
And there was pine enough for all.

Then all the logger had to do
Was find some timber that was new
Beside a stream he knew it ran
To Wausau or to Markesan.
That at the place a mill there was
To take the timber for the saws.
(In those old days the pioneer
He need not read his title clear
To mansions there or timber here.)

Paul Bunyan bossed that famous crew;
A bunch of shoutin' bruisers too—
Black Dan McDonald, Tom McCann,
Dutch Jake, Red Murphy, Dirty Dan,
And other Dans from black to red,
With Curly Charley Yellow-head,
And Patsy Ward from off the clam—
The kind of gang to break a Jam,
To clean a bar or rassle rum,
Or give a twenty to a bum.

Paul Bunyan and his fightin' crew,
In '64 or '5 or '2
They started out to find the pines
Without much thought of section lines,
So West by North they made their way
One hundred miles until one day
They found good timber logging land,
With roarin' water close at hand.

We put one hundred million feet
On skids that winter. Hard to beat,
You say it was? It was some crew.
We took it off one forty, too.
A hundred million feet we skid—
That forty was a pyramid;
It runs up skyward to a peak—
To see the top would take a week.
The top of it, it seems to me,
Was far as twenty men could see,
But down below the stuff were slides
For there was trees on all four sides.

At last, a hundred million in,
'Twas time for drivin' to begin.
We broke out rollways in a rush
And started through the rain and slush
To drive the hundred million down
Until we reached some sawmill town.
We didn't know the river's name,
Nor where to someone's mill it came,
But figured that, without a doubt,
To some good town 'twould fetch us out
If we observed the usual plan
And drove the way the current ran.

Well, after we had driven for
At least two weeks and maybe more,

We came upon a pyramid
That looked just like our forty did.

Some two weeks more and then we passed
A camp that looked just like the last.
Two weeks again another, too,
That looked like our camp came in view.

And then we realized at last
That ev'ry camp that we had passed
Was ours. Yes, it was then we found
That the river we was on was round.

And though we'd driven for many a mile
We'd drove a circle all the while!
And that's the truth as I'm alive,
About the great Round River Drive.

What's that? Did every one
Come on that camp of '61,
Or '63 or '65
The year we drove Round River Drive?
Yes, Tim Lawler, Tom Doyle and Me
John Moen, and some two or three
Of good and truthful lumbermen
Came on that famous camp again
In West of Rhinelander fifty miles
Where all the face of nature smiles
We found the place in '84—
But it had changed some since the war,
The fire had run some summer through
And spoiled the logs and timber too.
The sun had dried the river clean;
But still its bed was plainly seen.
And so we knew it was the place,
For of the past we found a trace—

A peevie loggers know so well,
A peevie marked with circle L,
Which you all know was Bunyan's mark.
The hour was late, 'twas gittin' dark;
We had to move. But there's no doubt
It was the camp I've told about.
We eastward went, a corner found,
And took another look around.
Round River so we learned that day
On section thirty-seven lay.

GENE SHEPARD

But the lumberjacks didn't need Paul Bunyan all the time. They created their own tales and humor.

SUMMER WHISKEY

One of the lumberjacks, preparing for a winter in the woods, began checking over his needs. Finding that he had overlooked one very important article, he visited his favorite drinking place and ordered a quart bottle and a half-gallon jug of good whiskey.

While on the train on his way to camp, he opened the quart bottle and passed it around to all his fellow jacks, but never once did he mention that he had a reserve of a half gallon jug in his "turkey." When he reached camp late that evening, he stealthily buried his jug alongside a large pine stump. There it was to remain until midwinter, when it would be brought out for his treat to the men who were remaining at work during the holidays. Christmas Eve came and, upon returning to camp from his day's work, he went out to the stump where lay buried his jug of Christmas cheer. He carefully dug away the frozen ground covering the jug, but, as he picked it up, it fell apart. Hurried examination proved that the contents of the jug had frozen and cracked the jug. His holiday cheer had vanished into the earth. Well, here was one angry Swede. Instead of remaining in camp at work during the holidays, he took the first train for town. Landing there with blood in his eye, he immediately set out for the saloon where he had purchased his jug of whiskey. Arriving there, he began berating the bartender for having sold him whiskey that would freeze. The barkeep, visualizing a good beating, hurriedly started to do a little fast talking. "Hey, hey, there Ole, don't get so tough—I made a mistake, that's all!"

"Mistake," screamed Ole, "*mistake!*"

"Yah, mistake," the barkeep sputtered. "You see, Ole, I sold you summer whiskey accidentally, that's all. I didn't know that you were not going to drink it until winter!"

Told by Fred C. Burke

THE DRUNK AT THE PUMP

A deep sense of humor was characteristic of the early lumberjack attitude toward life. It was apparent in many a half-wistful tale founded on temporary misfortune of some member of this vigorous fraternity. Illustrative is the whimsical yarn concerning the jack who had brought his payday from a hard winter's work into town and immediately proceeded to forget the lonesomeness of the forest lands by staging an extended spree. After two or three days of roistering, he awoke during the wee hours one morning with a terrific thirst. Finding himself back in his hotel room, and realizing that it was too late to get into a saloon for a "freshener," his thoughts somewhat reluctantly turned toward water to quench the internal fire.

Stumbling down the stairway and out into the dark yard in front of the hotel, he groped for the pump. After several minutes of earnest labor with the pump handle had brought no results, and not knowing that this particular pump needed to be primed, he stood back and sadly addressed the pump, saying, "I don't blame you a bit, Mister Pump—when I have money I never come near you —it's only when the saloon is closed, or I am broke, that I even think of you!"

Told by Fred C. Burke

INITIATION

When a novice crew came to a lumber camp there were often a few who would tell of the places they had been and the sights they had seen. When they got too cocky, their sentence from the older jacks was a blanket ride. Four to eight strong jacks with a double bed blanket would get outside camp, put him in, and begin an upheaval. Up and down, and up and down they'd toss him, and if he was game and lost his sissyness, he'd become a good lumberjack. If not, he'd better leave camp. Two young upstarts came to camp, where the custom was to get out to work before daylight and home after dark. They said their "Maw would not like that as she'd be afraid they'd cut their feet with the ax." They got onto the sissy custom and left before the blanket ride.

Told by S. B. Gary, Rhinelander, Wis.

BIG BOSS FIXES

At one time, Dad hired a rather large number of men of Hungarian and Polish descent who had worked in eastern coal mines, lived with their own nationality and did not speak or understand any English. One of them, who had never seen an ax, had a tree almost chopped down with a grub hoe before the boss discovered what he was doing. They seemed to have a lot of confidence in Dad—whatever he did was right, and there was nothing he could not do. So, when one of them—a strapping six-footer—accidentally cut off his big toe with an unlucky blow from his ax, he refused hospitalization, although he had a ticket. He kept shaking his head, and saying, "Big boss fix. Big boss fix." So Dad assembled boiling water, carbolic acid for a disinfectant, white silk buttonhole thread and buckskin needle, and without any anesthetic for the victim sewed the toe back on. He tied the foot to a shingle for splint or cast, and in a surprisingly short time the man was back to work.

By Mrs. D. A. (Ruby) Anderson
Holcombe, Wisconsin

LUMBERJACK CELEBRATION

A group of lumberjacks who were close friends came into town after a very long, hard, and boring time in the woods. They were going to celebrate and really enjoy themselves. The best way, or perhaps the only way, to achieve a real celebration was to get drunk —completely, totally, happily drunk. And it would be especially enjoyable to accomplish this feat by visiting all of the saloons in town.

So they started out in high spirits in the first saloon by downing a few strong drinks. But one of them, Charlie, quite suddenly gave a shudder and a sigh and rolled off his seat onto the floor. He had died of a heart attack. The others conferred for a moment after they examined his still body. They decided that "Ole Charlie" had just had too hard a time in the woods and it was indeed too bad that death had taken him—especially so early in the evening. They were sure he would not have chosen it that way if he could have had his choice. He would have wanted to enjoy this celebration with his pals. Furthermore, he would want them to enjoy it too. They reasoned that it was not right to allow Charlie's unfortunate end to spoil their plans for a big celebration that evening.

So they propped up his body on the bar stool and supported it between them as though he was still with them. They ordered drinks. For each round they also ordered one for Charlie and threw it in his face.

They went on to the other saloons as they had planned to do, dragging poor Charlie's remains with them. Wherever they stopped they always included Charlie, bought him drinks and tossed them in his face.

As the night ended and dawn came, the lumberjacks were very, very drunk, and their friend Charlie, had consumed as much liquor on the outside of his person as they had consumed inside.

Told by Otto Krasselt to Margaret Kelk

THE HOTEL WAS FULL

A lumberjack came into Rhinelander late one night and went to a cheap hotel down in Hungry Hollow. The hotel was full. He made quite a fuss, and finally the clerk told him he had a room with two beds with a curtain between. Although the room was occupied by a woman, since it was so late and he wanted to catch the five o'clock train, he might occupy the spare bed. This arrangement was finally agreed upon.

In a short time the lumberjack appeared in the office with boots and mackinaw in hand and hair standing on end, and said to the clerk, "Why, that woman is dead." "Yes, I know it," said the clerk, "but how did you find it out?"

MAN FIGHTS DOG

Once a belligerent lumberjack hit town in a mood for takin' on man or beast. In a barroom he heard of the feats of a pit bulldog owned by Jack Bolger. This dog, it seems, had cleaned up everything in the canine world and even vanquished a wolf.

"So this dog is a holy terror, is he? Well, so am I . . . and five dollars says I can lick him," boasted the jack. The bet was covered.

So the "fightingest jack" invaded the lair of the vicious dog, got down on his hands and knees and growled, expecting to slug the animal the first rush.

But when Minocqua's Dr. Torpy got there in a call, one side of the lumberjack's face had been ripped clear of the cheekbone, an ugly wound.

"So I sewed him up the best I could, and never a wince from him," says Dr. Torpy. "I told him to come back and I'd remove the stitches. He did, months later—this time he had a full beard covering the scar. When I asked him who had taken out the stitches, he looked amazed and answered, 'So that's why I haven't been able to shave.'"

—*Milwaukee Journal*, January 23, 1949

DRINKING AND FIGHTING IN CAMP

It was hard to control drinking in logging camps, although it was prohibited in most. There was a continuous "turnover" of at least 10 per cent of the crew, and it was not unusual for a few men to call at the camp office each Saturday for their time. Also, it was not unusual for several men to drift in Sundays, usually towards or after dark, going direct to the men's shanty to locate a place to sleep. The cookee or choreboy usually acted as chambermaid and placed the new men in an empty muzzle-loading bunk if any was vacant; if not, he had to crawl in with another man. This usually involved a three-cornered argument, between the cookee, the old employee who had been sleeping alone, and the newcomer, who in the majority of cases had a hangover and was more or less belligerent.

Hale-Mylrae Company Camp #1 was built out of logs, two separate buildings under the same roof, cook-shanty and men-shanty, with an open alleyway between.

The men's shanty had no windows in the walls, but a glass window in the roof about over the stove, which rested in a large sandbox in the center. This window was hinged on the upper side, the lower side attached to a small notched pole for raising and lowering it, depending on how smoky or foul the men's shanty got, with sixty-five jacks smoking on the benches at the foot of their bunks, or else the old iron box stove smoked, because it usually had several cracks in it. Damp clothes, washed underwear, wool socks of sixty-five men hung over the pole racks or on wire above the stove in all directions added to the atmosphere. Peerless or Standard smoking tobacco added their own aromas.

The bunks were in two tiers all around the walls except where the one door led to the alleyway and cook-shanty. There were home-made wooden wash benches sloping to one side wall and corner, where the wash water drained out in a pipe run through the log walls.

This one Sunday night stands out in my memory more than any other similar circumstance. I was awakened late in the evening by an unusually noisy commotion going on in the men's shanty. I got up, slipped into my Malone stag pants and a mackinaw. On investigation, it seemed several private fights were going on. The stove had been tipped over and the floor was smoldering. So I woke up Hale, who slept in a small shanty near the office. Hale wore heavy flannel nightshirts coming down to his ankles; his six feet four inches and 254 pounds were exaggerated in this attire. He put on a pair of stag rubbers, picked up a club, gave me the lantern to hold up high, and told me to stand on a bench inside the men's shanty.

It was difficult to see on account of the smoke, so we were not recognized until Hale told the men to get into their bunks, and that the party was over! After some argument and threats all hunted their bunks except August Lapinski, a young six-footer, who had worked for us a long time.

August weighed 225 pounds, and he was the only one who was not ready to go to bed. So the fight started between Hale and August. It was rough and no holds barred. The stovepipe came down on the upset stove, benches were tipped over crossways, and anything loose was soon in tough shape.

Hale finally got a bear hug on August, carried him to the four-foot-wide hardwood door made of inch maple lumber, homemade on strap iron hinges hung to swing the door in. Most doors swing out.

Hale slammed August against the door so hard it bent the iron hinges and the door was badly broken. Hale picked August up and threw him out through the broken door into the alleyway, then threw him back in the sleeping shanty. August couldn't get up, so Hale picked up the iron stove poker and asked if there were any more so and so's that wanted to carry on, now was their chance. No one asked, so we righted the stove and stovepipe, put a little water on the part of the floor that was smoldering, and went back to bed.

Next morning, Monday, every man in the crew, including August, was on time for 6:00 A.M. breakfast, and I could not see anyone had hard feelings, even August.

He and his brother Jake worked for us several years after that, with only their intermittent benders in Rhinelander or Hurley.

Told by Jack Mylrae

THE WHITE HEIFER THAT TRAVELED

The last of the pine log drives off the Pine and Popple Rivers were completed prior to 1905.

The Oconto Company rented their logging camp, spur, and log landing to the H-M Co. in 1909, as they had cut and shipped the timber they had owned tributary to these camps.

The H-M Co., Hale and Mylrae, consisted of two young men in their late twenties, one of whom had two teams, a white cow, and a small logging outfit. His partner had a small amount of capital, and both had had some woods experience.

Just prior to the renting of the Oconto camps, they had cruised and purchased from Max Sells, in Florence, Wisconsin, five or six million feet of hemlock, hardwood, and some scattering large pine on Section 6-38-15E for $12,500 ($1.00 down and the balance the rest of their lives).

The rail was still on the spur, but the switch and frog had been taken up and had not been replaced by the C. & N. W. Railway by the time the H-M outfit had arrived in a thirty-six-foot boxcar, including the white cow. She was two or three years old and weighed five hundred to six hundred pounds.

This car had not been expected until the spur was connected up, but the morning freight, which came down every morning, consisted of a large R-1 locomotive, a refrigerator car, this thirty-six-foot boxcar, and the caboose.

They were met by H-M and the few men who were putting new roofs on the rented camps. Like most freight crews in those days, they came right to the point, in no uncertain language, as to why this car had been shipped before the switch was in, and what the dam hell was H-M going to do about it?

The real problem was how to get the cow out. She was tied near the door, preventing the equipment from being unloaded.

It was solved, however, by "H," who agreed to catch the cow if "M" and some of the other boys would get behind her and shove her out. This took some time, as Bossy didn't like the looks of the situation.

However, away she went, half shove and half leap. "H" caught the six-hundred-pound heifer around the neck and foreleg, setting her down on the ground on her fanny, without a bruise or scratch.

About a year later, towards March, when the deep snows were slowly melting and the little creeks and Popple River were opening up in spots, our cow took off on her own one Saturday morning, following the sleigh road until it crossed Popple River. There she left it and started through the deep wet snow. This was a winding stream, with small hills in the open, on which much if not all of the snow had melted off. She was not missed at camp until Saturday night.

In the dark she could not be found, but some of the crew had seen her tracks as they came in from the woods Saturday afternoon, indicating she had gone down, following the stream.

Sunday A.M. she had not returned, so "M" and Charley Johnson, equipped with snowshoes and each with huge roast beef sandwiches, started at the bridge and followed her wandering tracks

until 3 P.M. Sunday afternoon. She was standing among some pine
stumps on a little bluff where the snow was nearly melted off.

On arriving they found wolf tracks and signs that she had fought
wolves all night. "M" and Charley said she sure was glad to see
them, but not as glad as when she was offered one of the big lumberjack sandwiches. Did she eat it? You bet your life. "M" said, after
their return to camp with her following like a pet dog, that he
thought she was going to kiss Charley when he went up to her with
the sandwich.

It was 9 P.M. and dark that night when the two men and the cow
reached camp.

In a straight line, it was five miles down the Popple River, probably nearer eight miles of actual travel, that she had wandered.

"M" and Charley didn't have to be rocked to sleep that night.
(Editor's Note: For the uninformed, the heifer was looking for a
boyfriend.)

Told by Jack Mylrae

LUMBERJACK'S HOSPITAL PLAN

The lumberjacks possessed a peculiar type of hospitalization unknown to most of us today. A lumberjack of Northern Wisconsin
could buy a 'hospital ticket' for the sum of $3.50 which was good
for one year. It was exclusively for the lumberjacks. Hospitals in
Tomahawk, Ashland, and Marinette, besides St. Mary's in Rhinelander, Wisconsin, used the plan in the years about 1890 to 1912.

Dr. I. E. Schiek, Sr., of Rhinelander explained the plan of operation. When lumber was King in Wisconsin, the lumberjacks were
a vital and necessary part of society. Every spring when the lumberjacks came to town to spend their winter wages, a man represent-
ing the Sisters would sell the men their hospital tickets. Sometimes
the man would go from lumber camp to lumber camp selling the
tickets before the jacks could get to town and spend all their money.
The men were always happy to have the opportunity to buy them,
because they knew most of them would return to the woods broke.
Naturally this agent for the Sisters received a commission based on
the number of tickets which he sold.

The $3.50 hospital ticket entitled the lumberjack to hospitalization any time during or for a one-year period. If there were extra medical bills which the patient could not pay, the men in his camp "passed the hat." Each man contributed whatever amount he felt like giving. It didn't make any difference whether a lumberjack worked in camp one day or five years. The other jacks automatically helped each other whenever it was necessary—a spirit common in pioneer days.

Incidentally, in line with a year's hospitalization costing only $3.50, the doctors on the staff at St. Mary's received the salary of $10.00 per month.

"Sometimes," remarked Dr. Schiek, "the men would need a rest before going back to the woods. They would often be flat broke. These lumberjacks would invent all types of aches and pains to try to get into the hospital for good food and lodging. Of course the colorful lumberjacks never fooled the Sisters at all. They knew many of the men spent all their money in Hungry Hollow, the favorite hangout of all the lumberjacks around Rhinelander."

Between the hospital tickets and passing the hat, then, a lumberjack possessed an excellent form of hospitalization and medical aid.

Told by Dorothy House Guilday

REPORT ON CONDITION OF LOCOMOTIVE #7

Thunder Lake Lumber Company,
Rhinelander, Wisconsin
The boiler is "busted" in a place or two,
The heads hold on by a rusty flue,
The crown sheet is burned and the wheels all flat,
A side sheet blister like a derby hat.
The whistle is missing and so is the bell,
The tank's all rusty and leaks like Hell,
And boiler patches she has a few—
For I think she was built in "Seventy-two."
The cylinders are oval where they ought to be round;
One end of the equalizer drags the ground.
I tried to run her and got her hot,
Every seam leaked and at every spot.

I opened the throttle with a good track ahead,
She gave two exhausts—groaned and went dead.
The cab is like steel but it's made of tin,
But she's a d—— good engine for the shape she's in.

"George Smith," Engineer

JOHN DIETZ—MARTYR OR OUTLAW?

In 1902 John Dietz was working as watchman for the Chippewa Lumber and Boom Company. Two years later he was its bitter enemy; and for eight more years he fought the company ruthlessly, only to lose out in the end. The sad thing about the whole unfortunate affair was that it was apparently due to a misunderstanding.

In 1904 the Dietzes purchased from Mrs. Hugh Cameron, a widow, a piece of land on the Thornapple River in Sawyer County. The Cameron Dam was across the river at this point and the east end of the dam rested on the Dietz land. The dam was built in 1874 by Daniel Shaw, who secured perpetual right to build and maintain the dam. When the transfer of land was made to the Dietzes the reservation of the right to maintain the dam, which right belonged to the Chippewa Lumber Company, was inadvertently omitted. Legally Mrs. Cameron could only transfer title to the land subject to the right of the lumber company. This the Dietzes did not know.

Consequently, when the company's men came to close the gates to get a head of water, Dietz ordered them away. He posted a notice at the east end of the dam forbidding trespass and told the Superintendent of the company that no more logs would go through the dam until he received toll pay of $8,000 for the eighty million feet of lumber he estimated had gone over since he acquired the dam. When the company lumberjacks appeared and said they were going to go ahead and sluice the six million feet of logs already behind the dam, Dietz stopped them with a rifle and told them to get out and stay out.

The company got out an injunction. Dietz ignored it, saying he didn't take any stock in courts. A warrant was issued for his arrest, and two armed deputies, joined on the way by two lumberjacks and a farmer, set out for Cameron Dam. Dietz and a neighbor met them with guns and began firing. The bullets flew from both sides. One hit the farmer's hat, another cut a deputy's suspenders, two bullets struck one of the lumberjacks. The deputies and their companions drove helter-skelter away from the scene; all except the farmer, who had fallen out of the wagon. Dietz and his companion ordered him to start running back toward Hayward and shot branches from over his head as he ran. No further attempt was made to serve the warrant. A Federal injunction was treated with similar contempt. Two United States Marshals attempted to serve it, but Dietz drove them from his land.

For five years John and Hattie Dietz and their children held the fort. The shooting ability of the whole family was held in wholesome respect, and attempts to arrest them were only half-hearted.

What finally led to Dietz's downfall had nothing to do with the dam. It was ten miles to Winter, the nearest village, and roads were impassable in spring and fall; so the Winter school board agreed to pay for a tutor in the Dietz home. In 1910 Dietz and his son, Clarence, drove to Winter and demanded an allowance for rent, fuel, and janitor service for the maintenance of a school in his home. He happened to meet the president of the Town Board and stated his claim to him, but was told that the agreement was to pay only the tutor's salary. The Chairman of the Town Board came up about that time and with him was Bert Horel, clerk of the School Board. There was a hot argument and then a fight. Dietz knocked Horel down. Horel got up and knocked Dietz down. Dietz came up with a Luger pistol and shot Horel, after which he and Clarence went home.

Horel then filed a complaint, and the sheriff sent word to Dietz to come in and give himself up. Dietz replied, "Come and get me." The sheriff deputized two of the best rifle shots in the county to watch the Dietz farm and issued a warrant covering the whole family. Thus it happened that when the two older boys and Myra, their sister, set out for town they were ambushed and commanded to halt and throw up their hands. When the command was ignored, the deputies fired, wounding Myra and Clarence, the oldest boy. Leslie Dietz escaped into the woods.

The deputies had made a big mistake in firing at the children. Myra was taken to the hospital in Hayward and became the headline heroine of all the big city newspapers, which in every instance made the affair sound very brutal. Nevertheless, Sheriff Madden decided to finish the Dietz case. He rounded up a small army of deputies and laid siege to the Dietz farm.

In the meantime the Governor had been receiving appeals to prevent bloodshed at Cameron Dam and in response had sent two envoys to assure Dietz of a fair trial if he would surrender. Dietz refused. Sawyer county authorities tried again, with no success, and then went into action. Dietz raised a small American flag aloft on a pole at his cabin and prepared, with set shotguns and all his family armed, to do battle. The shooting began about nine o'clock and increased in intensity as the day wore on. Dietz was shot in the left hand. Oscar Harp, one of the deputies, was killed. Inside the Dietz cabin dishes were shot off the table and shelves; a framed picture of the family was riddled with bullets. Bullets crashed into the organ, splintering its sides and shooting out the stops and keys. Quilts on the bed were covered with spent bullets fallen from against the thick walls. The attacking men gradually closed in. John Dietz was bleeding badly, and by midafternoon it was evident that he must have medical attention. Little Helen Dietz was sent out to the sheriff with a white flag and the siege was over.

John Dietz conducted his own trial at Hayward and did it very ably, but was found guilty and sentenced to life imprisonment at Waupun. Ten years later he was pardoned. The Dietz children appeared on the stage and also were the heroes of a moving picture which claimed to be a true relation of the events at the Battle of Cameron Dam.

There are so many angles to the story of John Dietz and the Cameron Dam, and so many versions of it, that perhaps it is well to add to the tale the comment of an unbiased individual. E. M. Dahlberg, of Ladysmith, tells of visiting with John Dietz through the bars of the county jail at Hayward, where he was awaiting trial on a charge of shooting a resident of the village of Winter. Mr. Dahlberg was a student at the time and had come to Hayward to play football with the Indian Training School at that place. He says:

"I do not propose to justify John Dietz, but the people with whom

I was associated at that time were disposed to stand on his side of the issue. I recall that by student subscription we sent flowers to Myra Dietz, who was in the hospital recovering from a gunshot wound received in the closing action at Cameron Dam. Our sympathy was naturally enough on the side of this pioneer family who were besieged and shot in their own house for attempting to prevent a lumber company from flooding their land to float their logs. The legal aspects, however, were apparently not so simple. There are many good people from that vicinity who hold that Dietz was wholly wrong and pursued a lawless course in the whole affair."

As told from an account by E. M. Dahlberg

THE GHOST OF FRENCHY LA PIERRE

"Back in '78," my old friend Mr. Larzelere said, "we floated millions of feet of good pine down the Wolf to Shawano and Oshkosh. They called Oshkosh 'the sawdust city' then. Right here, Bob, the logs jammed sky high. I happened to be at the Cabins then. It was a tricky job to get the mess untangled. The water was backing up and raisin' a ruckus. Now there was a hardy river rat working on the drive. He came here from Maine state. His name was Jean La Pierre. We all called him Frenchy. Now I saw Frenchy crawling up to the top of this log jam with my own eyes. They planned to set some sticks of dynamite in the jam, but before the blast went off the logs broke loose of their own accord. They made a terrific noise. They turned over end on end like matchsticks before settling down below in the river. Now just after the roar and a moment before the top logs gave way, we heard a voice. It was the bellowing voice of Frenchy. I looked and heared him roar from the top of those logs, 'Timbaire! Theyaire she goes!' That was the last we ever saw of Frenchy. No one who watched can forget how he threw up his arms and in an instant tried to steady himself with a canthook. His body was not found. It upset us all—Jennie Hill, Horace Rice, Seymour Mills, John Corn, and several others stood with me watching this tragedy, Bob."

"Yes, Mr. Larzelere, I have often heard that many rivermen lost their lives on the drives during the spring months."

Mr. Larzelere continued: "But this is the funny part of this story, Bob. Three years later in the same spot in the month of April, 1881, I was standing almost in this same path with Dick Healy, Sr. of Antigo, Squire A. Taylor of the Lily, Fred Dodge of Hollister, and I think Arthur Janes and Amessey Smith were in the bunch. The spring drive of logs was in full swing. There was trouble again in this same bend in the Wolf River. The foreman of the drive was Hank Edwards. News had gotten around that this jam would soon be dynamited. We were watching. Suddenly there was a cracking of plunging logs, and the spray of water and confusion forced us back somewhat. Just as the whole pile was about to collapse we saw it—it all happened so fast we were speechless. High up on top of that crumbling log jam, just as I had seen him three years before, stood Frenchy Pierre. We all recognized him. He was holding a long peavy as if he tried to balance himself. Then all of a sudden his great voice burst out in one great shout, 'Timbaire! Theyaire she goes!' and that was all. Was this a vision? We had heard of things like that. None of us had been drinking. None of us believed in ghosts. Each was glad someone else was on hand and saw it to corroborate his story. Well, Bob, we were pretty much shaken up and talked about this many times after that. But the payoff was this: Three days later down the river near Otter Slide the body of Frenchy La Pierre was found. There was a fresh deep gash in his forehead near an older scar close to the right temple. The body was otherwise in a good state of preservation.

"Now Bob, figure that one out, will yeh? If Frenchy had just been killed, where had he been the past three years? Why hadn't someone seen him around since '78? Some said he had lost his mind and was living as a squawman on the reservation; that he had been pulled out of the river and saved three years before. No one really ever found out. Some even said the body found near Otter Slide was that of one Gideon Cromber, but old Indians on the north end of the reservation always told the children to watch for the ghost of Frenchy La Pierre 'over the river after the geese fly north and the logs go down.'"

Fishermen plying the Wolf in early May when morning mists arise before the sun gets high sometimes in a confidential yet sheepish manner have been heard to say to wives or men companions: "You know something? Up around that bend by the Log Cabins this morning I saw the funniest thing. The mist . . . it looked like a man walking on the water. Drinking? Not me. I never do! It looked like he had his hands in the air and he was carrying a pole or something. It gave me the creeps, but of course I forgot it because I don't believe in ghosts."

And so the ghost of Frenchy La Pierre lives on and on . . .

Told by Robert M. Dessureau

A-RAFTING ON THE RIVER

The Wisconsin raftsman, sometimes called "pinery boy," was a rough and ready customer, hard-working, free-spending, ready at any minute for a fight or a good time. He lived a dangerous life, especially when the rafts passed those sections of the rivers where there was swift water, or obstacles. Today, many of those danger spots, still bearing the names given them by the raftsmen, are points of interest along the Wisconsin River. Among these names are Sliding Rock, whose sloping sides made it impossible to gain any foothold; Notched Rock; the Devil's Elbow, a right-angle turn making passage terribly difficult; and the Narrows, where the River is said to be turned on its side, since its width at this point is only fifty-two feet, and its depth is one hundred and fifty feet.

An old Wisconsin ballad describes the life of the raftsman:

Oh, a Raftsman's life is a wearisome one,
It causes many fair maids to weep and mourn,
It causes them to weep and to mourn,
For the loss of a true love that never can return.

Oh, Father, Father build me a boat.
That down the Wisconsin, I may float.
And every raft that I pass by, there
I will inquire for my sweet pinery boy.

Is she going to find him? Wait and see.

> Oh, raftsman, raftsman, tell me true.
> Is my sweet Willy among your crew?
> Oh, tell me quick and give me joy.
> For none other will I have than my sweet pinery boy.

Then the raft captain answered to her that they had seen the poor pinery boy, but it was at Lone Rock when his raft had hit the rock and smashed up into smithereens and splinters.

> She wrung her hands and tore her hair.
> Just like a maiden in great despair.
> And rowed her canoe against Lone Rock.
> You'd have thought this poor maiden's heart was broke.

> Oh, dig my grave both long and deep.
> Put a marble slab at my head and feet.
> And on my breast a turtle dove,
> So all the world will know I died for love.

And then she proceeded to die for love.

WHISKEY JACK

We are sure that Whiskey Jack was the most famous of all Wisconsin raftsmen. Marian Paust of Richland Center, who has admired Jack for years, describes him and some of his exploits:

Gently the river sweeps on and shakes off its lethargy. It recalls Whiskey Jack. Now there was a man! Mighty as Paul Bunyan! He taught the raftsmen their trade. His feats were fantastic. He was their ideal and their brain child—a seven-foot-tall Samson! He was never bested in a fight by any man, red or white. No man could down an equal amount of liquor. The river towns laid in a huge supply of "forty rod" and "tanglefoot" whenever they heard he was coming down the river with his crew. He joined all the celebrations along the river and never left until the last jug was "killed," but he made up lost time by rigging a sail on his raft and taking shortcuts across sandbars and islands. If his raft became wedged against a sandbar, he either picked it up and carried it to deep water or towed it.

On a certain day when Whiskey Jack tied his raft at Richland City, he had no money to buy drinks, but he took a bundle of lathe to the tavern to exchange it for "forty rod." "Put it outside the back door," the barman said. When Whiskey Jack left by this door, he picked up the lathe again and gave it to another of his crew who was approaching the tavern front door. This process was repeated over and over again. When all had gone, the barman looked out the back door and found only one bundle of lathe!

One of his crew hooked a great catfish one day which was so huge that he couldn't land it. The fish towed the raft so rapidly that the men fell on their stomachs and hung on desperately. The fish reversed directions suddenly and swam under the raft, pulling the front cribs and line after him, followed by the rest of the raft. The crewmen, who didn't jump into the river, were drowned and the raft was never seen again.

On a trip to St. Louis, after their pay was collected, Whiskey Jack and his men bought suits in a secondhand store. They put them on, visited the taverns as usual, and had only enough money to travel back by steamboat as far as Prairie du Chien. From there they gigged or walked back the rest of the way. Near Fort Andrew it rained steadily, and Whiskey Jack's suit began to shrink. By the time he reached Portage, the pants had shrunk to his knees, his coat sleeves to his elbows, and his vest halfway up to his chest. When he arrived at Stevens Point, his coat and vest had disappeared completely and his trousers had become shorts. The rain continued to fall. At Wausau, he was completely naked, and the sheriff threw him in jail.

Another time when Jack gigged back to Stevens Point (after imbibing "snake juice" at several taverns) he discovered a large blue racer snake following him along the trail. A blue racer is very poisonous, so he made tracks. At Sauk City he swam across the river, but the snake followed. At Merrimac and Wisconsin Dells he jumped from bank to bank, but the snake did the same. At Stevens Point his friends beat the snake to death with canthooks and pike poles. They measured and found that the snake was twenty-seven feet long!

Cooking was a primitive process on lumber rafts. A crude shelter had to be erected on windy days. The cook had only a frying pan, a kettle, and a coffee pot to cook in. Big John Marshall was Whiskey Jack's cook. The crew disliked eating the same food day after day. Jack asked him if he had ever used a cookbook. "I got one once but couldn't use it," John answered.

"Why not—too fancy?" asked Jack.

"Sure," John drawled. "Every recipe started out, 'Take a clean dish . . . ' and that cured me."

John served hash a great deal. "What's the recipe?" a crewman asked.

"It just accumulates," came the reply.

The years have changed all this. The river no longer calls to the adventurous. The lusty little river ports are dead, and the brave souls who built them lie long beneath soft green sod. Only the river is haunted by old, old dreams. At dusk, a whippoorwill calls from the lonely bluff. The night owl answers and a night heron joins the chorus. The valley stills. A leaping fish splashes, and the chorus is repeated again and again until dawn's smoldering fire breaks into the clear yellow flame of another day. Time leaves only the river to remember forever. . . .

WHISKEY JACK SIGNS HIS NAME

Whiskey Jack was not a scholar; he didn't care to read, and he could not write. When he signed the payroll or any other document at the sawmill or lumberyard office he signed with a big "X" instead of his name. He did this for a long time. But one day he signed with an "X X" instead of just an "X." The bookkeeper wondered at this and asked him why he signed with two "X's" instead of just one. And Whiskey Jack explained to him that he and a milliner lady in one of the river towns had just got "spliced," and he thought that now, being a married man, he ought to change his name. Hence the "X X."

Told by C. E. Brown

One of the ballads remembered by folks in the Kickapoo River Valley is called "The Fatal Oak." The ballad, said to have been written by Abbie J. Payne in 1870, tells the tragic tale of a raft which tied up for the night on the banks of the Kickapoo, under the protective branches of a great oak. We obtained the ballad from W. M. Ward of Soldiers Grove.

Sad is the story I relate of three young men who met their fate;
While folded in the arms of sleep they sank beneath the waters
    deep.
In blooming health they left the shore,
Ne'er thought they'd see their friends no more:
There were four brave boys upon a raft,
With DeJean, the captain of the craft.
Down they sailed on the Kickapoo,
Laughing and joking as raftmen do.
Never thought their fate would come so soon,
When death would rob them of their bloom.
When night came on they went to shore,
Stopped where they oft had stopped before,
'Neath the same oak that had been their stay,
They went to sleep at the close of day.
The Captain viewed this tree once more,
Spoke as he had sometimes spoke before,
Saying, "Boys, I fear when it's too late
This old tree will seal our fate."
The rapid current flowing there
Had washed its roots completely bare,
But as they had often done before,
They thought they'd tie to it once more.
Early in the morning the Captain rose
And left his men in sleep reposed;
And for some wood he stepped on shore
For to prepare their breakfast o'er.
But scarcely had he stepped on shore
When looking at this tree once more,

He saw it start and loud did cry,
Saying, "Wake, my boys, or you must die."
There was none but Wilson that awoke
When with a crash down came the oak.
The Captain stood alone on shore,
He saw them sink to rise no more.
But Wilson made his way at last,
Something gave way that held him fast.
The other three, who never woke,
Were crushed beneath the fatal oak.
For three long hours they searched in vain,
Till at last two bodies they did obtain.
They were Hatfield and Lawton, two boys, brave
But Roberts still sleeps beneath the waves.
Young Hatfield was the Captain's pride,
Long in his family did he reside,
And seemed to him more like a son
Than like a child that was not his own.
By land the Captain started home,
Both night and day he journeyed on,
Taking these two boys to their friends
That they might see their last remains.
When the sun was sinking in the west
These two brave boys were laid to rest;
Their friends stood weeping round their tomb,
No more they saw them in their bloom.
It was but a glance and all was o'er,
Their friends could see their faces no more.
Poor Juliette, the Captain's wife,
It seemed it would almost take her life.
The Captain strove his grief to hide,
But now he wrung his hands and cried
Saying, "This is a bitter cup,
My boys, how can I give you up?"
Poor Robert's friends, in deep despair,
Longed for something of him to hear.

They searched the river for miles around,
When at Wyalusing he was found,
And near the spot where he was found
There may be seen a little mound.
'Twas strangers hands that laid him there
No friends to shed a farewell tear.
Friends and kindred brought him home
And laid him in the silent tomb.
In death now sweetly sleeps the three
That were crushed beneath the fatal tree.
We leave them in the silent tomb,
While many friends are left to mourn,
With kindred friends whose hearts were broke
By the sudden fall of the fatal oak.

—Raft was sunk September 14, 1870

The raftsmen, of course, had their own favorite ballads. The best known of these is perhaps "On the Banks of the Little Eau Pleine."

One evening last June as I rambled,
The green woods and valleys long
The mosquitoes' notes were melodious
And so was the whippoorwill's song
The frogs in the marshes were croaking
The tree toads were whistling for rain
And partridges round me were drumming
On the banks of the Little Eau Pleine.

The sun in the West was declining
And tingeing the treetops with red,
My wandering feet bore me onward
Not caring whither they led.
I happened to see a young schoolma'am,
She mourned in a sorrowful pain
She mourned for a jolly young raftsman
On the bank of the Little Eau Pleine.

Saying, "Alas my dear Johnny has left me.
I'm afraid I shall see him no more
He's down on the lower Wisconsin
He's pulling a fifty-foot oar,
He went off on a fleet with Ross Gamble,
And has left me in sorrow and pain,
And 'tis over two months since he started
From the banks of the Little Eau Pleine."

I stepped up beside this young schoolma'am
And thus unto her I did say,
"Why is it you're mourning so sadly
When all nature is smiling and gay?"
She said, "It is for a young raftsman
For whom I so sadly complain
He has left me alone here to wander
On the banks of the Little Eau Pleine."

"Will you please tell me what kind of clothing
Your jolly young raftsman did wear
For I also belong to the river
And perhaps I have seen him somewhere.
If to me you will plainly describe him
And tell me your young raftsman's name
Perhaps I can tell you the reason
He's not back to the Little Eau Pleine."

"His pants were made of two mealsacks
With a patch a foot square on each knee
His shirt and his jacket were dyed with
The bark of a butternut tree,
He wore a large open-faced ticker
With almost a yard of steel chain
When he went away with Ross Gamble
From the banks of the Little Eau Pleine.

"He wore a red sash round his middle
With an end hanging down on each side,
His shoes, number ten, were of cowhide
With heels four inches wide.
His name was Honest John Murphy
And on it there never was stain
And he was as jolly a raftsman
As was ever on the Little Eau Pleine.

"He was stout, broad-shouldered and manly,
His height six feet one
His hair was inclined to be sandy
And his whiskers as red as the run.
His age was somewhere around thirty,
He neither was foolish nor vain
He loved the bold Wisconsin River
Was the reason he left the Eau Pleine."

"If John Murphy's the name of your raftsman
I used to know him real well
But sad is the tale I must tell you
Your Johnny was drowned in the Dells.
They buried him 'neath a scrub Norway
You will never behold him again.
No stone marks the spot where your raftsman
Sleeps far from the Little Eau Pleine."

When the schoolma'am heard this story,
She fainted and fell as if dead
I scooped up a hatful of water
And poured it on top of her head.
She opened her eyes and looked wildly
As if she was clearly insane
And I was afraid she would perish
On the banks of the Little Eau Pleine.

"My curses attend you, Wisconsin
May your rapids and falls cease to roar
May every tow-head and sand bar
Be as dry as a log schoolhouse floor.
May the willows upon all your islands
Lie down like a field of ripe grain
For taking my jolly young raftsman
Away from the Little Eau Pleine.

"My curses light on you, Ross Gamble,
For taking my Johnny away
I hope that the ague will seize you
And shake you down in the clay
May your lumber go down to the bottom
And never rise to the surface again
You had no business taking John Murphy
Away from the Little Eau Pleine.

"Now I will desert my vocation
I won't teach district school any more
I will go to some place where I'll never
Hear the squeak of a fifty-foot oar.
I will go to some far, foreign country
To England, to France, or to Spain,
But I'll never forget Johnny Murphy
Nor the banks of the Little Eau Pleine."

YODELINGS OF CHAMPION RAFTSMEN

Awaking the echoes in Witch's Gulch at the Dells, the raftsman
of Wisconsin sang:

There lived, I heard them say,
Down by the rolling water,
An old man and his wife
And they had a lovely daughter—
Ri-tu-ri-lu-ri-loddy,
Ri-tu-ri-lu-ri-lay.

Old Katie took the pail
To get a pail of water,
And to the spring she went
A-thinking of her daughter—
Ri-tu-ri-lu-ri-loddy,
Ri-tu-ri-lu-ri-lay.

She sat down on the bank,
To watch the water fall,
As in the spring it dashed
Her eyes began to bawl—
Ri-tu-ri-lu-ri-loddy,
Ri-tu-ri-lu-ri-lay.

The old man heard her wail,
And down the hill he ran
To call upon his Kate,
Who sat writing in the sand—
Ri-tu-ri-lu-ri-loddy,
Ri-tu-ri-lu-ri-lay.

"Oh, what's the matter, Kate,
Oh, what's the matter, woman?
There's something in your pate
That's rather more than common—"
Ri-tu-ri-lu-ri-loddy,
Ri-tu-ri-lu-ri-lay.

"Oh, yes," old Katie cries,
"I have a horrid fancy,
I see these waters rise,
And think upon my Nancy—"
Ri-tu-ri-lu-ri-loddy,
Ri-tu-ri-lu-ri-lay.

"If Joe and Nanc' should wed,
And such a thing there may be,

Of wedding there should come
A pretty little baby—"
Ri-tu-ri-lu-ri-loddy,
Ri-tu-ri-lu-ri-lay.

"And when it just can walk,
And just begins to toddle,
'Twill to this water come
And in this water paddle—"
Ri-tu-ri-lu-ri-loddy,
Ri-tu-ri-lu-ri-lay.

"Oh, yes," the old man cries,
"And then it might be drown
And washed upon the sand,
And afterward be found—"
Ri-tu-ri-lu-ri-loddy,
Ri-tu-ri-lu-ri-lay.

"Then buried it would be,
'Tis common after dying,
Poor sweet little baby,"
And then they fell to crying—
Ri-tu-ri-lu-ri-loddy,
Ri-tu-ri-lu-ri-lay.

There was a young man, too,
To realize this fancy,
The neighbors called him Joe,
His sweetheart called him "Dandy"—
Ri-tu-ri-lu-ri-loddy,
Ri-tu-ri-lu-ri-lay.

And now as it fell out,
These lovers in their walking,
They heard old John and Kate
A-crying in their talking—

Ri-tu-ri-lu-ri-loddy,
Ri-tu-ri-lu-ri-lay.

They came and asked them why
That they did weep and wail so,
And when they heard it all.
How they did weep and wail—ooo—
Ri-tu-ri-lu-ri-loddy,
Ri-tu-ri-lu-ri-lay.

They all went crying home,
Joe, John, his wife and daughter,
And now the ghost does come
And play upon the water—
Ri-tu-ri-lu-ri-loddy,
Ri-tu-ri-lu-ri-lay.

Love and the troubles of love occupied the raftsmen, and were
reflected strongly in their songs:

LUMBER WAGON BLUES

Some women have their troubles
  The men have theirs likewise;
Compare the two with agony
  In the following story wise;
About the milliner's daughter
  Who loved a shanty-boy,
For he was tall and handsome,
  And she would him decoy.

She had a great ambition,
  Her shanty-boy to wed;
His father had some money,
  His mother she was dead;
And Susie thought him handsome
  And said she was his rib;

But all the jolly raftsmen,
Said Susie told a fib.

The shanty boy he listened,
And measured Susie's waist;
He said he ne'er could marry
A girl with a painted face,
For when he tried to kiss her,
His whiskers would stick fast,
And this would cause him trouble
When he kissed another lass.

Then Susie fell to pleading
With all her winning airs;
With waterfalls and ribbons
She manufactured snares.
The shanty-boy galvanted
With ax and saw at last—
The waterfalls and ribbons
And Susie's heart he passed.

He said he ne'er would marry,
He dearly loved his dog;
He'd learn to cook his supper,
And sleep in a hollow log.
He'd let the bold Wisconsin
All o'er his bones to roll,
And take for his companions
The catfish and the snail.

From "The Jolly Raftsmen" by George Nye
(Georgiana Koepcke), published in *The
Knapsack* magazine, April, 1929.

THE RAFTSMAN

I'll tell you of a raftsman right from the pinery
And how he loved a lady, she was of a high degree.
Her fortune was so great it scarcely could be told,
And still she loved the raftsman because he was so bold.

One day when they had been to church and were just returning
    home
They met her old father and several armed men.
Oh, daughter, oh, daughter, oh, daughter, I pray,
Is this your good behavior, or is't your wedding day?

"I fear," cried the lady, "we both shall be slain."
"Fear nothing at all," said the raftsman again.
"Now, since you've been so foolish as to be a raftsman's wife,
Down in this lonely valley I will quickly end your life."

"Hold," cried the raftsman, "I do not like such prattle;
Although I am the bridegroom, I'm all prepared for battle."
He drew his sword and pistol and caused them for to rattle;
The lady held the horses while the raftsman fought the battle.

The first man came to him, he ran him through the main;
The next one stepped up to him, he served him the same.
"Let's run," cried the rest of them, "we all shall be slain.
To fight this gallant raftsman is altogether in vain."

"Stay," cried the old man, "you make my blood run cold.
You shall have my daughter and five thousand pounds in gold."
"Oh, no," cried the lady, "the fortune is too small.
Fight on, my bold raftsman, and you shall have it all."

"Oh raftsman, oh, raftsman, if you will spare my life,
You shall have my daughter for your beloved wife."
He took them to his own home, pronounced them son and dear.
(He took him home unto his house, he made him his heir.)

Come all you rich maidens with money in great store.
Never shun a raftsman, although he may be poor,
For they're jolly good fellows—happy, fresh, and free—
And how gallantly they fight for their rights and liberty.

We have heard that the favorite ballad was this nameless one:

> Now winter has diminished,
> Our shanty life is finished,
> From the woods we are banished
> Just for a little time;
> At near approach of summer
> We will select our timber,
> We will select pine timber,
> And make handsome rafts of pine.
>
> By water we are conducted,
> By it safely directed,
> And if by chance we're wrecked,
> Like brothers we combine;
> Oh, the rapids that we run—
> They are to us but fun—fun
> And we shoot them on the run,
> When we land these rafts of pine.
>
> Oh, when we to market get,
> Bully boys, we won't forget
> Our whistles for to wet
> With brandy, gin, and wine,
> And together we will cruise,
> 'Till our money is all used,
> But we never will refuse
> To go back and float the pine.
>
> And now my song is ended,
> I hope there's none offended—
> My noble voice refuses
> To sing another line.
> From among the ladies nice,
> We'll select one for a wife,
> And like raftsmen we'll rejoice
> When we build our house of pine.

"TO DE RIGHT, HARD"

The old logging days are gone. The rivermen or "rafters" who appeared each spring on the Chippewa and Mississippi Rivers, carrying their cant hooks or peavies and wearing tough spiked boots, are only legendary figures now. A hardy, roistering crew they were, careless of the dangers and risks involved in their work. They brailed the huge pine logs, then coupled them into rafts which, guided by oars, were floated downstream in the swift-running currents.

Lumbermen who owned pine lands sometimes stored their logs in a safe place before having them brailed by their rafters. The Chippewa had a natural reservoir in the Beef Slough, a good place for the reception and manipulation of logs, from which they were later sent down the Chippewa and Mississippi in the form of rafts.

The main channel of the Chippewa, strangely enough, was smaller than the outlet of Beef Slough. Pilots and most river men were aware of this, but sometimes that condition led to amusing incidents. Laurence Kessinger in his quaint old *History of Buffalo County*, published in 1888, relates this story:

In the year 1835 Jefferson Davis, then a young lieutenant in the United States Service, stationed at Ft. Crawford, was sent to the mills on the Menomonie to get lumber to rebuild the fort. The order had been filled, and Davis and the soldiers were coming down the Chippewa under the command of an old French voyager who acted as pilot. At the critical point where Beef Slough sets off to the left while the main river turns to the right, the Frenchman called, "To de right, hard." "What's that," said the West Pointer, "you're going to run this raft right to hell? I tell you to pull to the left where the main river is." It was done, and the lumber was lost in Beef Slough.

Told by Norma Palunek,
Alma, Wisconsin

chapter 4

PIONEER MEDICINE AND EARLY DAY CURES

V ERY OFTEN the pioneer families in Wisconsin had to be their own doctors. The women, especially, became very proficient in treating wounds and common illnesses, and displayed a brand of heroism only conjectured about in our day. The pioneer mother was always available for help when needed by a neighbor, and the beautiful saying about the pioneer mother of Wisconsin, that the trails from her cabin led in every direction, is one of the most cherished of Wisconsin pioneer traditions.

Nina O. Peterson wrote for us a special tribute to her mother, who was one of these early-day heroines:

She was a gracious lady, my mother. She was the symbol of hundreds like her who followed the dim lantern light over paths, across fields and through woods on missions of mercy. She was not a nurse but a pioneer woman who knew what to do and never ceased doing what she could for others. Her old satchel was ever in readiness, her first-aid kit fitted with such articles that she thought might be needed. Her drugs were limited, a bottle of carbolic acid, a can of epsom salts, camphorated oil, and clean white rags and the box of mustard.

Nursing was not a job or a position to her. There never was any money involved, for her remuneration was greater than gold or silver. It was the firm handshake, the grateful voice of thanks, the

112

deep relief in eyes, and the knowledge that baby and mother were doing as well as could be expected or that the fever had broken and all would be well.

I recall on one cold rainy evening, we heard father say "Whoa," at our kitchen door. We ran out. Mother said, "Children, go back inside. Don't get all wet." We obeyed but did not understand why she did not come in.

"Bring me a full change of clothing," she called.

Father was getting kerosene, kindling, and a lamp. He went out to the summer kitchen, which was in a shanty near the house. This kitchen was used during the warm summer months instead of the kitchen in the house. He carried in pails of water and the tub. He gathered the carbolic acid bottle, soap and towels, and going outside, he helped Mother from the buggy. Then he drove out to the barn and unhitched the horse. Mother went directly into the shanty.

In about one hour she came into the house. She had washed her head, bathed, and changed clothes.

"Aggie, did you burn your clothes?" Father asked her when he came into the house.

"Oh, yes, of course. We can't have them around and take any more chances," she informed him.

This time she had been gone from home for three days. She had been up night and day helping nurse a small boy who had been very ill from scarlet fever. She was not afraid for herself, but from her continual asking day after day, "Is your throat sore? Do you feel all right?" we knew that she was worrying about us.

When we were awakened by a knock on the door during the night and heard Mother hurrying about, then footsteps on the stairs, we knew that she was going out in the dark again to help someone. How brave she was, and how much energy she must have had.

The only doctors in those days were many miles away and could only be contacted by driving with horses those many miles. Those neighbors in trouble would send someone for Mother while another of the family would harness their horses and drive quickly for the doctor. By the time the doctor had his horses in harness and had reached the bedside of the patient, hours had passed.

On one of these occasions a child had pneumonia. My mother was called. She followed the lantern light cross-country for about two and a half miles. When she arrived she knew at first glance at the child that she had work to do, and fast work. The room was hot and stuffy. She gave orders. When she opened the window the child's mother remonstrated. A towel was placed on the window to prevent direct draft. An old-fashioned bread and milk poultice was made and the child bathed to reduce his fever. I know Mother did not forget to pray along with her work that night. By the time the doctor arrived the child was breathing easier, and his fever was down. He told them that if Mother had not acted quickly as she did the child would not have lived. What greater pay could one receive for a night's work?

Insanity, also, was one of her problems. She knew how to handle a demented person. The daughter of a family living nearby was insane. Most people were afraid of her whenever she had a bad spell. Her parents could not handle her but ran after Mother to calm her down. The daughter evidently liked the way Mother talked to her, or it could have been the tact my Mother used.

The poor were her concern, too. I have trudged beside her, helping carry a gunny sack full of outgrown clothes for miles along a pasture fence to aid a needy family.

There were many children in one of these homes. The outside spelled poverty, but the inside of the cabin was rich in love and cleanliness. The house was immaculate. The wide rough boards of the floor were scrubbed white. I recall how much happiness the old clothes gave this family. The only remark I ever heard my mother make regarding them was when we were on our way home. "I hope that we will never be that poor," she said, and sighed. "Winter will soon be here. I think I will make them a quilt."

But while the ailing neighbors came in for their share of attention from the pioneer mother, the immediate family was a first consideration. Folk medicine provided a number of possible remedies for this or that, and Neva Argue, of New Glarus, says that in Grandmother's day, she not only had to cook, churn, bake, spin, and sew—she had another chore equally as essential. She must gather and dry the herbs that she knew would be needed for the care of her large family during the long winter and spring months.

Hops had to be picked and dried, a pillow made and stuffed with them, to be used by a restless one to induce sleep. There must be enough hops dried and stored to use in treating future colds. A generous amount of them would be steeped in vinegar and used as a poultice, or laid over an aching ear.

Linden flowers and leaves were gathered and dried, to be made into a tea to relieve coughs resulting from colds. The tea was used also to induce perspiration.

The inner bark of a wild cherry tree was used too, to make a tea to allay a bad cough.

Spikenard tea was an old stand-by given to relieve coughs caused by colds.

Peppermint was gathered in September and carefully dried and packed in bags, to be later used as tea to treat colic and diarrhea.

A tea was made of red clover blossoms. This was drunk to purify the blood, and to also relieve rheumatism.

If one had what they termed kidney trouble, namely, burning and scalding urine, one simply dug horseradish roots, made a tea from them, and drank that for relief. The roots of the wild blackberry bush were used in the same way for a diarrhea prevalent among infants, termed Cholera Morbus. Another old stand-by for the treatment of Cholera Morbus was equal parts of peppermint leaves and rhubarb root steeped together, with a teaspoon of soda added when the tea was cold. This infusion was to be taken a teaspoon or two at a time.

If Johnnie was thought to have worms, Grandma had a remedy for that. A slippery elm tree was found, the outer bark was peeled away, and generous strips of the inner bark were given to Johnnie to chew.

Sores and bruises were thought to heal much faster when bathed generously with an infusion made of cheese-plant.

Cornsilks were gathered and dried, and a tea made of them was drunk when the kidneys were thought to be not active enough.

Mullein was very extensively used in bygone days. If Grandfather had asthma, he smoked nothing but mullein, and inhaled the smoke. Both the leaves and roots were used in this way. Just think of the amount of mullein that must be dried to supply a smoker all winter long!

One staple that was a must in Grandmother's cupboard was ground mustard. A cold in the chest called for a mustard plaster, made by mixing ground mustard, flour, and water together, spreading the mixture on a cloth, and laying it on the chest until the skin became red as fire. Then the plaster was removed, and goose grease was rubbed in to prevent the skin from blistering.

If one had been unduly exposed to the elements, acquiring a wet body or feet, one simply had to soak feet and legs in hot water which contained a generous amount of mustard. This was to draw the blood to the lower extremities and counteract any congestion in the lungs.

Catnip was an essential herb also in every household of Grandmother's day. A tea made of catnip was used for colic in infants, for convulsions and spasms in older children, and as a general tonic for stomach disorders in adults.

If one had a canker sore in the mouth, grandfather opened a gun shell, removed the powder, and applied it to the sore. If the burning and stinging of the power on the sore was of any significance, then it must have been a sure cure.

When one acquired a ringworm, Grandmother, Grandfather, aunts and uncles all pooled their pennies in a dish of vinegar. They applied the resulting solution several times a day to the ringworm, which soon healed up.

If one was unfortunate enough to get stung by a bee, he simply daubed a good mud poultice on it, renewing it as often as necessary until relieved.

To draw a boil to a head, either of the three following poultices was used. A slice of salt pork bound on it overnight, or a mixture of bread and milk used as a poultice, or equal parts of laundry soap and sugar worked together to form a pliable mass, and that then applied to the affected spot.

Sore throat was often treated by rubbing on a mixture of coal oil, turpentine, and lard, then removing one's sock or stocking, as the case might be, and tying it about the throat for the night.

In many families, it was thought that as surely as the first-grader had to have a dinner bucket to start school, just as surely did he have to have a lump of asafetida sewed up in a small cloth bag and worn around his neck all winter to ward off diseases.

The first skunk that fell prey to the trapper's snare was brought home. Not only his skin was saved, but the lard or fat from his body was rendered out and used as an ointment to rub on the chests of young and old alike, to cure colds.

When a member of the family became nauseated, with continued vomiting, Grandmother immediately killed a fat hen, cleaned the lining of the gizzard well, cooked it and fed it to the sick patient to settle his stomach.

Fennel was regarded as an essential herb in Grandmother's day. They made a tea from its fine hairlike leaves, and drank it too for kidney and bladder disorders. To use the seeds of fennel as flavoring in foods was thought to impart strength and longevity, and, as Long-fellow wrote:

> Above the lower plants it towers,
> The Fennel with its yellow flowers;
> And in an earlier age than ours
> Was gifted with wonderous powers
> Lost vision to restore.

But in actual practice the application of home remedies took some special doing. Olive M. Hope of Salem gives her version of doctoring in pioneer days:

The refusal of Mary or Johnny to eat a meal as usual, or a whining complaint that he or she had a sore throat, sent Mother on a trip to the cellar. When she returned, she carried a long strip of side-pork fresh from the brine. Spreading it out upon the table, she sprinkled it well with black pepper, summoned the patient to her side and wrapped the slimy, greasy concoction around the ailing throat, and fastened it there with a swath of scratchy red flannel. Regardless of the season, we were hustled off to bed with a stone jug of hot water at our feet, and covered all too well with heavy comforters and blankets. Should there be any evidence of a cold or "rattling" in the chest, the treatment was supplemented with potions of burning hot red pepper tea or whiskey sling. A cold on the chest also called for a thorough rubbing with "goose grease." In fact, said grease was apt to be applied to any part of the body and was supposed to "open up the pores." We often heartily wished it had not so effectively opened up the nostrils, for rancid goose grease is not the sweetest smell in the world!

One young mother who attempted to practice this home remedy on her infant son erred by using a bottle of skunk oil instead of the goose grease. When the error was discovered and the baby was playfully called "Skunk," his three-year-old brother stammered out the word "Tunk," a nickname which to this day still clings not only to him, but to his son. If there happened to be an earache, father lighted his pipe and blew hot smoke into our ears. Sometimes, as a last resort, heated oil was poured from a teaspoon into the aching member. Well do I remember once, when as a child, I was lustily singing a song for the entertainment of visitors. My vociferous tones were interrupted by a louder soprano scream from another room, where my mother had poured a spoonful of too-hot oil into my sister's ear.

Other of Olive Hope's old Wisconsin family remedies were as follows:

As soon as the sap began to flow, my father went to the woods and brought home strips of bark from the wild cherry trees. From this he brewed a strong, dark tea, in which to soak the oats fed to the horses. This was supposed to give them an appetite and thus prepare them for the hard work in the fields.

As a spring conditioner, we children were given sulphur and molasses, to 'thin the blood' and rid us of the winter impurities.

How did Mother know when we had worms? Why, if we grated our teeth during sleep, if we insisted on "picking the nose," of course we had worms, and in case catnip was ineffective, we were given huge potions of strong tansy tea. At the slightest mention of an ache or a pain, we were given a dose of Dr. Somebody's pills, and oh, how immense they seemed! The very thought of swallowing one made us keep our childish ailments to ourselves. We took Hostetters Bitters, Ayers and Hood's Sarsaparilla, so much of it that I never dreamed I could forget how to spell it—but I have. And, in spite of all the dosages we had, I have survived past my allotted three score years and ten.

FOR WARTS:

Slide a pin through the top of a wart, then hide the pin where no one will ever see it or step over it, and presto! the wart will vanish.

Moisten the wart every day with the juice of the milkweed—same good result.

If the wart is on a lady's hand, one of the opposite sex must take a short piece of black thread, tie a loop loosely over each wart, then hand that thread to the "warty" one. She must find a flat stone, stand astride of it, lift it with her right hand, place the thread under it with the left hand, replace the stone, walk away, and not return to the stone until the wart has gone—which it is supposed to do in time. This charm must always be worked by one of the opposite sex.

Another correspondent on the subject of warts says that to children, warts perhaps are the most interesting skin maladies. The child easily pulls them off, only to find that they return uglier and grubbier than ever. After several decapitations, they still persist until the child has a real case of frustration.

An old rhyme seemed to take the humorous side of this subject. It is:

> The Man-in-the-Moon has a wart on his chin.
> He calls it a dimple, but dimples stick in.
> Whang-Ho, why certainly so,
> It must be a dimple turned over, you know.

Since warts were so frustrating, many treatments have been devised. They are:

Count the number of your warts. Find a string and tie as many knots as the person has warts he wishes to destroy. Touch each knot to a wart, then throw the string away. When the string is rotted, the warts will have disappeared.

Steal your mother's dishcloth. Go into the garden and throw the cloth away. As in case one, when the rag has rotted, the warts will be gone.

But best of all is the Wisconsin remedy which I think goes back to Cornwall or Devonshire, England. It is: Steal a rasher of pork in the waning of the moon. Go into the garden. Touch the pork to each wart. Turn your back to the moon and say:

> "Quail away! Quail away!
> Steal the cat's tail away."

Then throw the rasher over your left shoulder. When the pork has rotted, the warts will be gone.

Dorothy Kundert of Monroe related to us an interesting yarn about old Bill Clarno and his wooden leg:

Old Bill Clarno had lost a leg fighting in the Civil War. The government would have provided him with an artificial leg. However old Bill preferred to cut his own; then it was just the way he wanted it.

His granddaughter (who told me this story) used to have to hold the selected piece of basswood limb while old Bill whittled and carved to shape the wood to fit his stub limb. It was quite a job for the tired arms of a very little girl to hold the wood steady. Finally the "peg leg" was fashioned—tapered to the end, and capped with a bit of leather or rubber. The top was hollowed and filled with milkweed fluff and soft material to form a soft pad for the stub leg to fit into.

"Sometimes Grandpa Clarno's limb became sore and inflamed from the rubbing irritation of walking on the peg leg, however carefully it was carved and shaped, and strapped to the upper limb, with leathers to his waist belt, and another extending up over his shoulder. Then Grandma would have to rub it with Gamma Geelia."

"Gamma Geelia?" I asked. "What's that?" (Hopefully I was always on the lookout for a new herb medicine.)

"Gamma Geelia? Oh, I don't know exactly. We used to make it. Think Grandma got the recipe from an Indian. How did we make it? Oh"—laughing in remembrance—"many's the time I had to collect

Gamma Geelia buds so we could make some medicine. What kind of tree? I'm not rightly sure. They're kinda scarce. Only two I know of now are over on the other side of Pecatonica. Think they're some kind of Pople tree. Grandma sent me with my little basket when the buds were nice and full."

"Did you make a poultice out of the buds?" I asked.

"No, you cooked them. Grandma'd put some lard in the frying pan, get it pretty hot, then put the Gamma Geelia buds in it and cook them 'till the juice came out pretty well; until the buds got quite brown. Then she strained the fat to take out all the hulls and stuff, and poured the fat into little jars she always saved from things she got. It made a real healing ointment. Oh we used it for just everything, but especially on Grandpa's stub limb when it got inflamed. It took the soreness out right away."

Gamma Geelia ... Gamma Geelia ... the words rolled around on my tongue hours after the interview had terminated. Gamma Geelia! Wonder whether it was one of old Cut Nose's recipes. Gamma ... Gamma ... Pople buds ... Gamma—could it have been Bamma? That sounds more like our word "balm." Bet that's it! Balm Geelia. But Geelia! What could that be? She said the tree looked like a Pople tree. Must be a form of poplar tree. Funny how a thing won't let go!

Turning on the bed light ... clock said 2 A.M. Kicking back the covers I hied myself to my desk corner, searched through my Herbalist. Balm Gilead—page 205. Eagerly I tracked—page 205. Yike! There it is—"Populus Candicans" (Balm Gilead). Practically the very words. Without a doubt the folks I had interviewed had never seen the words in print. Passed down by word of mouth the words had been corrupted. However pronounced, here is the exact recipe as listed in the Herbalist:

Populus Candicans
(Balm Gilead)

Description: These buds as well as those of other species of
                Populus are covered with a resinous exudation
                which has a peculiar, agreeable, balsamic odor
                and a bitterish, balsamic, somewhat pungent taste.

Properties: The buds boiled in olive oil or lard make an excellent salve. Internally they are valuable in coughs resulting from colds.

Dose: The buds must be soaked in alcohol to dissolve the rosin before they can be used as a tea. A teaspoonful of the buds to a cup of boiling water. Drink cold, one cupful during the day, a large mouthful at a time, of the tincture, 5 to 20 minutes.

These old folks also said, Mrs. Kundert added, that to heal a wound from a rusty nail, find the nail that was stepped on. Grease it with lard or something fat. Put it up in the warming oven or on a high warm place and leave it there for about ten days. Then bury it well someplace and don't tell anyone where you have buried it. "Don't you put anything on the injury itself?" I asked. "Oh yes. Stick it in some turpentine or coal oil, and put on whatever kind of salve you happen to have." For horses with wire cuts this treatment of greasing the wire was also thought to be effective.

One of my little school children developed an eye infection, apparently from some foreign object in her eye. I could actually see nothing, but asked if her father hadn't best take her to see their doctor. "Oh no, he put a flax seed in it. He says it will be all right." And she was right. Each day I watched it that week. For another day it seemed worse, then gradually it cleared. The inflammation and mattering left entirely. Principle, according to her father, with whom I talked later: Flax seed moves around the socket and pushes out the foreign object, and the oily content of seed prevents it from becoming an irritant to the eye; flax oil acts as healer, also. The wet seed becomes covered with a gelatinous substance that picks up the foreign substance.

To make an ointment for use on a bunch or boil that needs to be brought to a head or healed: Gather some bitter hickory nuts. Crush them, hull and all. Put them on the stove to stew, of course adding just enough water to keep them from burning. When the solution becomes syrupy, strain to remove the floating particles. Melt some lard, add the syrup to it, mix well, pour into a jar and let cool. Rub on affected parts—form more of a poultice in stubborn cases. "Especially good when you've a horse with a bunch on her leg," an old horseman told me.

Residents of earlier-day Wisconsin had a number of other famous cure-alls, some of them mysterious.

Madstones: Madstones were used by pioneers in 1830's to cure dog and snake bites. They were gray-brown, about size of marbles. The stone was applied to the wound to which it adhered tightly until supposedly full of poison, when it would drop off. Then it was soaked in warm fresh milk or lukewarm water until poison came to the top in little bubbles. The madstone was applied repeatedly to the wound until no poison was left. When the wound was thoroughly cleansed, the stone dropped away. An early settler, Wash Ellis, had a madstone, charged $25.00 a treatment and did a thriving business. People came from miles around, Ellis kept more than busy. (P.S. A madstone is a ball taken from the stomach of an animal. Deer madstones are best.)

"Old Yeller": This was a powerful physic, prepared and given in the 1860's by Dr. D. W. Carley of Boscobel. It was justly celebrated.

"Cure-All": A doctor concocted a cure-all preparation, heavy on calomel and a very strong physic. He advertised it and sold it with the phrase: "It'll neither cure ye nor kill ye."

"That damn stuff": A local doctor concocted a cure-all which had an unpronounceable medical name. It remained for the customers to simplify the name. Even today, in a local Platteville drugstore, one may get the article simply by asking at the counter for a bottle of "that damn stuff."

"A Sure Cure for Hoss Colic": Pound into powder three or four old tobacco pipes, and put it into three pints of water. Boil it down to about half, and give it to the horse cool. For this use, then, lay up your old pipes.

Alice Baker of Southern Wisconsin remarks that:

Modern day doctors deprive themselves of many useful remedies. I am sure they do not know the value of oat tea to bring out the pox of either chicken pox or measles.

They, also, do not know that good blood-filled sheep-ticks are good as a last resort for TB sufferers.

Arnica blows (ray flowers of the small Calendula blossoms) in alcohol is good for bruises.

If a mother would guard against a case of acne which her child may have in adolescence, she must, before her baby is three weeks old, give it a good dose of saffron tea. The child, whether boy or girl, will be assured of a clear complexion.

The vinegar jug, of treasured memory on the frontier, is described by Mrs. Edgar Wohlust. She remembers:

A little antique electric jug lamp made from a much treasured black jug, which my ancestors brought here to Wisconsin from their native land, Bohemia, in the year 1851, takes my thoughts back to those days, and again I can hear my grandmother, as she would rock our baby sister, and all the rest of us, the bigger ones, would sit around her and listen to her tell us stories of the days when she came here to settle in Wisconsin. Each tale was more interesting than the other, but my favorite was the one about my little vinegar jug.

There were no glass containers as today; jugs of various sizes were the only containers they had for storing liquids. They contained wild honey, maple syrup, coal oil or kerosene, whiskey, wine, and vinegar, the most treasured liquid of all.

The little black vinegar and whiskey jugs had their place in the special place in the cupboard, always ready for any emergency. Here Grandmother also had goose lard, turpentine, and camphor: these three were used to put on the chest if anyone had a bad cold or cough. Sarsaparilla and sulphur and molasses were given to us in spring as a tonic, and we always found a great deal of work outside to keep us out of the way when Mother or Grandmother came with these. Here also were found neat rolls of white cloth and wool pieces, carefully wrapped in paper to keep them clean and ready should illness or an accident occur.

Grandmother put great store in the vinegar jug. She always said it saved many a life from bleeding to death. When anyone cut themselves real badly with the axe or scythe, the bad cut was cleaned and the bleeding stopped with vinegar. This would prevent infection and coagulate the blood. If very bad, then wheat flour was put into the cut also and it was bound with a clean white cloth, and in an hour the invalid was as good as new again.

To get the vinegar they put so much faith in, the settlers treasured their apple orchards and took care of each precious tree. Also, to them apples were a change from plain everyday food. They were eaten raw, cooked into sauces, apple butter, and into the apple pies the men adored.Windfalls were peeled, sliced, and dried carefully for winter. The men and boys liked to put the dried apple slices into their pockets when they went into the woods to clear land or hunt. When hungry, they would chew on them. They also were made into various sauces, pies, and cakes, if there were no fresh apples available.

Apple juice or cider was used as a drink, also made into applejack. This was made with cider and dried grapes or raisins and left to ferment. It had an intoxicating effect on those who imbibed it too much or too often.

Cider or apple juice was a treasured liquid, as a good deal of it was put into wooden kegs or barrels and left to get sour. When it had a transparent scum, or mother, as it was sometimes called, then it was good. Most of this vinegar was then strained and put up into jugs of various sizes, for future use.

It was used in dandelion salads, boiled cabbage, soups, and many other dishes to give them a tangy taste.

Drinks were made from it, by combining vinegar, sugar, and cold water to taste. This was put into jugs and taken to the fields for the men to drink when they were thirsty. The settlers didn't believe in drinking too much clear cold water, as it was thought if one sweated too much, the body should have a nourishing drink. Cider was also taken to the woods or fields to drink.

It brings a nostalgia to me, how many times Grandmother made a jug full of the vinegar drink, and being the eldest, I had to take it into the fields or woods for those that were working there. She would put the jug into the center of a head kerchief and tie the corners together, and in this way I could carry it better. I was always met by the men. Grandfather would take the jug, and as a treat I would be swung on the shoulders of some stalwart lad and given a ride. Each one would take only a sip, and as they were very warm, they would sit and rest and cool off, before drinking more of it with relish.

I can remember how we children enjoyed the vinegar drink, because Mother or Grandmother made it sweeter for us than for the older folks.

Headaches were cured by drinking a remedy made by mixing two tablespoons of vinegar, one teaspoon of sugar, and one teaspoon of baking soda in a glass or cup of water. How we little ones loved to see it fizzle!

Feverish brows were kept moistened with a soft cloth dipped in vinegar and water, also sponged frequently with this. Sprains and infections were bound with cloths wrung in vinegar and water. Just a simple remedy, yet to the humble hardy settlers it was the only doctor or remedy they could depend on. Even in this modern age, I still use these remedies, as my ancestors did, and I have never lost a patient. And so, on concluding my story, a remark our wonderful President Eisenhower made should be remembered by those of us whose ancestors had a humble part in the settling of Wisconsin. I never had the feeling of being "poor" as a child, although the material and financial lack would have made some people consider my home "poor." My parents had the kind of pride that kept them free from false pride. They filled the home with a happy family atmosphere, plus strength of character, purpose, and faith.

And I'd like to thank my ancestors for their foresight in immigrating to this land of ours. They too had no false pride, had faith in Him above and in themselves. They took the tribulations and drawbacks with staunch hearts; they may not have been rich in the measure of gold or silver, but they gave us a priceless heritage, an auspicious promise of a country where there is freedom of speech, of worship, where every individual regardless of color or creed is treated equal.

Once in a while a really unusual personality was encountered in early-day medical Wisconsin.

Sometime around 1850 a Dr. Dodge practiced as a clairvoyant doctor in New York State. He had lived a normal existence on his adequate income until one evening he visited a traveling hypnotism show. He generously offered to assist the hypnotist in the show, and during the course of the performance the hypnotist exclaimed: "At last I have found a true clairvoyant!" That observation was the beginning of Dr. Dodge's career as a "doctor." He came to Wisconsin with other pioneer settlers and set up housekeeping at his farm home between Albany and Monroe, raising his family and practicing his "medicine."

The charge for a call would usually be three dollars per "prescription," for medical assistance. Answers to questions were one dollar. Sometimes he would answer questions brought by messenger or mail. Accompanying the question would be a lock of hair, besides the fee. The doctor would stare fixedly at a spot on the wall until he went into a trance and would have to be lowered into a chair by his assistants. From his trance, he would speak in a dull, monotonous voice, finding the answers to the problems as a woman "writer" took down every word he uttered. The prescriptions he would have filled in a Monroe pharmacy and sent to the patient. He could tell which shelf and in which jar in the drugstore each particular drug could be found. It came to him in his trance.

Dr. Dodge refused to locate stolen goods, but was very helpful in learning the locations of lost articles by the same method. He even told a child where to find a lost ball. The ball was there. After he revived himself from his trance, he was completely exhausted. He lived extravagantly, and carried on a brisk practice, although most of his "patients" came to him surreptitiously.

On occassion a lock of hair could tell him the nature of an illness. Around 1870 or '75 the small son of Sever and Mary Gothompson fell ill. Every attempt at treating the illness failed, since the diagnosis could not be made by the medical doctors. The boy was very near death when the distraught mother took a lock of his blond hair to Dr. Dodge. The doctor grasped it, went into a trance, and through clenched lips muttered, "Measles—they went in." It was too late for even his help and the child died. Years later, before her death at nearly ninety-five years of age, Mary Gothompson still marveled at his diagnosis. There had been an epidemic of measles at the time.

Almost every old time family has a similar story to tell of the "clairvoyant Dr. Dodge." He was still going into trances as an old man, but each left him a little weaker and more exhausted, until finally they took too great a toll of his health.

Will Towne, a late prominent citizen of Albany township in Green County, was raised in the Dodge home. (Mrs. Harland Gillette is Will Towne's youngest daughter and may be able to add to the stories.) A grandson, Verne Dodge, still lives at Brodhead, and there are a number of great- and great-great-grandchildren of the clairvoyant doctor in his adopted state of Wisconsin, but none has exhibited any of the mysterious powers of this illustrious ancestor.

Told by Frances Burt

Viola Robertson, Northern Wisconsin, made a comment for us on the role of the Indian medicine man and the herbs:

The Indian medicine man had no books to study, and because of certain beliefs and superstitions would have refrained from keeping records or medical formulas even if he had known how to read or write. His medical secrets and cures were handed down from one generation to another; usually from father to son. The Indians seemed to think the more mystery surrounding a medicine, and the longer the secret could be kept in the family, the more powerful it became. Each time it became known to anyone else, it would lose some of its power, accordingly. The medicine man believed it was bad luck to tell anyone else except those he believed worthy of learning his magic in preparation to fulfilling their destiny as his successors.

This might be regarded as pure superstition by many of us today, but at that time it was very sound logic. We have to remember that in that era, life was a constant struggle for the survival of the fittest. Naturally, the healthiest tribe would become the largest and strongest. Truly, that was a time when "might was right" and the best man won. Certainly it could be tragic if these secrets fell into the wrong hands, such as a hostile enemy tribe or even one of their own people who didn't know how to use the secret, or who might inadvertently disclose it or trade it, in an indiscreet moment, for something that seemed more valuable or desirable to him at that particular time.

Choosing the medicine man or witch doctor was not a simple

matter. The candidate had to show by certain feats of magic that the Great Spirit had invested him with a certain quality of rather supernatural power. In other words, he had to be sort of preordained by the Great Spirit, and be able to prove it before he could be considered and accepted by the existing medicine man and the elders of the tribe. He also had to be something of a psychic and psychologist as well. Perhaps his methods, consisting of chants and dances usually accompanied by drums, fires, and smoking of various aromatic herbs, might seem crude to us, to say the least, and certainly not acceptable to our psychologists of today. Nevertheless, his results were often amazingly successful and sometimes instantaneous. The Indians believed and understood what the witch doctor was trying to accomplish, and so undoubtedly achieved better results than our psychologists could have done if they had been there instead.

The medicine man not only administered to physical, mental, and spiritual ills of his people but was also expected to have some control over the weather. In extreme circumstances, he was even called upon to make it rain. In fact, he was expected to make "big medicine" to help almost any situation from crop failures to wars.

Considering all this, it is no wonder the medicine man was held in such high esteem. He preserved the life blood of his tribe and was a sort of divinely gifted High Priest as well.

The Indians had one superstition that was bizarre, to say the least, and we can be thankful it was only used for a cure in extreme circumstances. When scientists explored the ruins of Aztalan (a village built by prehistoric Indians near Lake Mills) they found evidence to substantiate the story that Wisconsin Indians did eat human beings occasionally. They believed they could inherit the strength, wisdom, or physical attributes of their victims in this manner. It was more common to use animals for this purpose, but whether man or animal it was regarded of little value unless the victim was caught and killed by the person wishing to attain the coveted characteristic. They seemed to think that committing the deed alone would in some way make them worthy of possessing whatever they desired. Killing a deer and eating the heart immediately before it was cold was supposed to make one fleet of foot and graceful. Sometimes a very old

person who was considered very intelligent would be eaten to prevent his mental power from dying with him. No wonder Indians
were traditionally men of few words. Perhaps it was wiser not to be
too wise in those days if you didn't relish being sacrificed to further
someone's education. One of our famous health advocates once said,
"We are what we eat." Evidently, the Indian took this literally.

Nature has her laws of compensation. When one ability is missing
or undeveloped, another grows strong enough to hold the fort.
"Necessity is the mother of invention." By instinct, plus the trial and
error method, the Indians were able to take whatever nature provided and make everything they needed. All things considered, the
error part of it was not as great as one might expect. Many of the
herbs, roots, and grasses found here were gathered and prepared by
the medicine man and produced very potent and effective results.
Very many of the Indian medical discoveries have been adopted and
developed by the white man and are still being used today.

With the help of Dr. E. W. Burkhardt, who so generously gave
me much of his valuable time and assistance, I list some of the herbs
and plants that grow wild right here in Wisconsin. These herbs were
used by the first settlers and many of them were used by the Indians
before the white man came. The Indians used to chew the ginseng
root and also dried some for winter use.

Name of Plant	Latin Term	Uses
Ginseng	Panax	Tonic and stimulant
Elderberry	Sambucus	Colds and fever, kidneys
Plantain	Plantago	Kidneys, poultice
Wintergreen	Gaultheria	Tonic and stomach
Touch-Me-Not	Impatiens	Skin
Dogwood	Cornus circinata	General tonic and liver
Wild onion	Allium cernuum	Sinus inflammation
Skunk cabbage	Symplocarpus	Asthma
Violet	Viola oderata	Earache, intestinal parasites
May apple	Podophyllum	Liver and constipation
Belladonna	Atropa	High fever and convulsions
Burdock	Arctium lappa	Falling hair, skin trouble
Yellow dock	Rumex crispus	Coughs, bronchial trouble

Name of Plant	*Latin Term*	*Uses*
Peppermint	Mentha piperita	Tonic, colds, stomach
Iris	Iris florentina	Tonic
Foxglove	Digitalis pur-purea	Heart stimulant
Golden seal	Hydrastis cana-densis	Tonic
Black-eyed Susan	Rudbeckia	Locally for pain
Monk's hood	Aconite	Fever, colds, and inflamma-tory pain
Chamomile	Anthemis	Sedative, tonic, eyewash
Juniper berry	Juniperus	Kidneys, diabetes
Mullein	Verbascum	Earache
Slippery elm bark	Ulmus fulva	Tonic, colds, poultice

HOME REMEDIES MORE COMMONLY USED

Bear fat —Used to massage sore muscles and soften callouses on feet and hands. Also used to soften leather.

Blackberry juice —Used to drink for blood-building and tonic.

Wild grape juice —Used to drink for blood-building and tonic.

Squash and pumpkin seeds —Dried and ground, were believed to cure stomach worms.

Butter, sugar, and ginger —Mixed together, were used for children's coughs.

Lemon juice, honey, and glycerin —Mixed together, were used for cough syrup.

Skunk oil —Believed to make hair grow on a bald head.

Goose grease and mustard —Mixed to rub on chest for chest colds, and also for aching back.

Flax seed —Cooked to take for laxative, and ground for poultice.

There are many citizens living today in Wisconsin who remember Mother's remedies and wonder how, indeed, they lived through them. One of these is Thelma Kiger of Montello:

How I ever survived my childhood has always been a mystery to me. I firmly believe that no child on the face of this earth ever went through the curative treatments that my mother inflicted on me and my brothers and sisters.

Mama brought with her all the superstitions and remedies from her native Sweden when she arrived in America at the turn of the century. When she married and settled down on a farm in central Wisconsin, life became a constant battle against the elements and disease to bring her six children to maturity. To do her credit at this late date, I must admit that she succeeded in doing just what she started out to do.

I never could convince Mama that I wasn't sick. She had an obsession that anyone that looked the way I did had to be ailing. I always "looked pale," she would tell me. Of course, the fact that I had inherited the flaxen hair and fair skin of my Nordic ancestors hadn't a thing to do with it, to her way of thinking. And when Mama got that look in her eye, I knew that I was in for it again—"a purging" or a new "cure" that she had recently heard of.

One fair day, a lady came driving up to our farm home in a horse and a buggy. This caused no end of excitement, for in those days visitors who were not known were few and far between. It soon developed that she was selling books, and to my consternation they weren't books on fairy tales or anything a child could find pleasure in reading. It was a doctor book, at least five inches thick, and in it one could find a remedy for anything from a simple case of dandruff to unheard-of tropical diseases. About one third of the volume was devoted to the care and ills of livestock. Naturally Mama bought it, and I do believe it is gathering dust in her attic at the present time. Through the years she religiously added her own personal cures for various diseases that beset man. I can still remember one notation she triumphantly jotted down in her sacred book. It was an Indian cure for cancer of the stomach. A sufferer was to eat nothing but honey for a period of several months, but I don't think Mama ever tried that one on me.

How I used to dread the arrival of the Watkins man! When he used to rattle up into our farmyard in his old Model T Ford I knew instinctively that I was in for it again. He carried more bottles and pills than I have ever seen since. Mama always bought something. If it wasn't a bottle of liniment for the horse or to use in the chickens' drinking water, I could be sure that it would be a remedy for us children for whatever she thought ailed us. I believe that I hated the worm tablets that he sold the most of all. They were huge, pink wafers that were bitter to my tongue. Naturally he had convinced Mama that I must have worms, and in the event that I didn't, the wafers could do me no harm. To this day, I can still wake up at night and shudder at the taste of those pink wafers.

Whenever Mama became stymied for a particular remedy, she would consult her closest friend, Mrs. Peterson. She was a sweet bosomy lady about Mama's age, with a family of four, so they had a lot in common. Where Mrs. Peterson gleaned her storehouse of knowledge from I'll never know, but I do believe most of it she learned from her own mother, who was known as Grandma Fryk to us. I adored Grandma Fryk. She always had a sack of candy for me when she came to call. So it was self-evident that Mama turned to the two of them for their expert advice, as she considered them both authorities on the subject of home remedies.

There was the time that my brothers and sisters and I acquired the "winter itch." It had swept through our country schoolroom like wildfire, and Mama was desperate. I can still hear her on the telephone.

"Yes, Mrs. Peterson. Your youngsters have it too? Well, what can I do? Yes, I see. I should take a cup of pure lard and stir sulphur into it and apply to the skin after a bath." Every night for a week the washtubs were dragged into the kitchen and filled with steaming water which slopped all over the white, scrubbed, hardwood floor. We were scrubbed with strong homemade soap within an inch of our lives. Then the horrible salve was smeared over our young bodies and we were dressed in clean pajamas, ready for bed. Needless to say, before we even left for the mile walk to school in the morning, Mama had the copper boiler steaming on the wood range and was busy preparing to boil our long underwear and sheets and pillowcases. We had to wear fresh underwear every day until we were cured. Before we left for school, Mama smeared our bodies again with the salve. The fumes that rose from underneath our woolen clothing and scarves were enough to kill any manner of germ, however insignificant. How I pity our poor teacher—what she must have suffered while all her charges were taking the "cure."

Sulphur was a common household remedy in those days. Sulphur and molasses in the spring was a ritual to rid the body of the poisons accumulated during the winter months. Whatever it might have lacked in curative powers it made up for in smell. Mama was forever throwing large handfuls of it on the kitchen range and letting the acrid fumes seep through the house and our clothing. If an epidemic hit our community, she was determined that none of her brood should catch it. So we inhaled the fumes, coughing and gasping for air.

When the smallpox epidemic hit our community sulphur was burned daily, but Mother also took all precautions. She set up a vaccination center at our home, and neighbors came from far and wide with their young to be vaccinated. The country doctor worked from early morning till late at night, and we children were kept busy all day making everyone welcome. I remember fainting dead away when I was vaccinated (I was six). The doctor's needle held more fear for me than the sulphur treatment.

Mama also relied on cream of tartar. That would prevent almost anything. She would stir up a teaspoonful of the white powder in a cup of water, and we would down it valiantly to please her. I think she must have bought the powder in giant containers as we drank so much of it. I never could understand just what we were taking it for.

The food we ate for breakfast on winter mornings also played an important part in our growing hale and hearty. Every morning, Mama took out a huge aluminum kettle from the pantry and cooked up a mess of "grot," or oatmeal, as it is commonly called. To anguished wails that I hated it and could not possibly eat it all, she remained adamant.

"Eat every bit of it!" she would say. "It will stick to your ribs on these cold winter mornings." I vowed at that early age that when

I grew up *no* one could ever force me to eat "grot" again, and I can truthfully say that I have kept that vow.

By the time that I reached the age of twelve, I had begun to hope that I had made the grade and would eventually reach maturity. I was growing fast and was spindly-legged, and though I was still "pale," I felt wonderful. But my hopes were short-lived. Another salesman came to our house. Mama was always so friendly to everyone, and of course, as it inevitably did, the conversation was brought around to the state of my health. The salesman (I have forgotten what he was selling) eyed me quizzically.

"Ma'am," he said knowingly, "that child doesn't look well. I am sure that she is suffering from a liver ailment." At this point, I made a hasty retreat, but it was already too late. Mama had been taken in hook, line, and sinker again. He instructed her how to make a tea of juniper berries which I was supposed to drink every day. I drank it. The expression "bitter as gall" has a real meaning to me. I consumed quarts of the vile brew till I thought surely my insides must be all blackened, and I still didn't feel any different. But after I lived through that ordeal life had its compensations. Either Mama had run out of remedies or she finally gave up. I was left strictly alone, I was on my own at last, and from then on I began to hope that I would live.

Not to give Mama credit for the service she rendered my state of health would be unjust. I grew to womanhood having suffered nothing more serious than slight cases of measles, chicken pox, and mumps. I can never remember feeling ill at any time during my youth except when I was forced to swallow her nostrums. She did her job well and I am grateful. Mama not only kept us well but she had the determination to see that we lacked nothing in her search for our health.

chapter 5

ANTICS AND ANECDOTES

THE laziest man in Wisconsin was a settler named Tim Wooden, who lived in Washington County near Grafton. If he was asked where he came from he would reply that he didn't come at all—just growed up with the country. He got along so well without working that his neighbors believed he had communication with wood-spirits, elves, wights, and the like, who would admit him to their secret treasure caves and say: "Just help yourself, Tim."

One time some Menominee Indians who knew how lazy Tim was decided they would test him to the breaking point. They persuaded him to go with them to Grafton, and when they arrived they told him they were going to have his scalp.

The Indians tied Tim to a tree, piled wood about him, and acted like real savages set to get some fun out of grilling old Tim alive.

The chief, bearing a flaming torch, stepped up to Tim and told him that he was ready to set the wood on fire, but that if Tim would walk to Milwaukee the Indian would spare his life.

"How fur to Milwaukee?" Tim asked.

"Milwaukee twenty mile."

"Sorry," said Tim, "I'm too tired. But if you'll lend me a hoss I'll try fer it. If you can't give me a hoss, just set that pile afire!"

The Indians turned Tim loose.

One day Tim was taken bad sick with the cholera. When his end approached one of his friends stepped up beside his bed and said, "Tim, I reckon you're a-dying."

"Well, I ain't doing anything else," Tim said.

Tim Wooden is said to have died a well-to-do man, a fact which still has folks in Washington County scratching their heads.

BLUENOSE BRAINERD COMES TO WISCONSIN

Bluenose Brainerd came to northern Wisconsin from some locality in Nova Scotia, in eastern Canada. He never did tell from just what town or region. When asked just how he came he said he "came in a balloon." In this wind-propelled aircraft he flew westward for days and days. In Wisconsin he landed in the top of a very tall pine tree. In this lofty retreat he subsisted for a week or more on pine cones and bird's eggs.

He might have remained there longer, but some lumberjacks came along one day and cut down the tree. When he reached the earth he found that he had landed right in a big logging camp. At the camp he got a job as a sawyer.

One spring morning Bluenose Brainerd took his fishpole and bait and went fishing. It was foggy when he left his cabin home, and the fog grew thicker and thicker as he tramped through the woods toward the lake where he intended to try his luck.

When he was about a quarter of a mile from the lake it was so thick that he could no longer make any progress. He was up against a solid bank of fog. Another man would have given up and gone home then, but not Mr. Brainerd. He had come to fish and fish he would. He took his stout rod, fastened a frog to the hook at the end of the line, and made a mighty cast right into the fog. Then he waited, and before long he felt a tug on the line. When he reeled it in he found that he had hooked an old boot. By this token he knew that he had not cast far enough; his line had not reached the lake. Brainerd added another sinker to his line. He cast again and soon felt a fierce pull at the bait. With a quick yank he set the hook and reeled in the line.

Whatever had hold of the bait made a hard fight for it, but he brought it in. This time his trophy turned out to be a section of stovepipe from the roof of some fisherman's shack. Brainerd said that he knew then that he had nearly reached the water. He added a third sinker to the line and put another frog on the hook. This time he made a mighty cast and knew by a muffled sound that his bait had hit the water. Soon he felt a hard jerk, and he knew that he had hooked a "live one." When, after a hard fight, he succeeded in reeling in his catch through the dense fog, he found that he had caught a forty-pound muskellunge, the biggest ever caught in those parts.

Bluenose Brainerd was a good storyteller when he was in the mood and the listeners appreciative. He said that the big moskitos were mighty aggravatin' when he first built his cabin and came to live near the banks of the Chippewa. They were real vicious, and thievin' too. They carried away any grub that was unguarded, stole garments from the washline, and even appropriated vegetables from his garden. Bluenose shot a few of them and killed many more with his ax, but these protective measures made little difference to them, their tribe was so numerous. To continually combat them was exhausting. He desired to be at peace. One day he bought a jug of lumberjack whiskey in town and when he returned invited the entire moskito tribe to a jamboree. He poured the liquid fire into a washtub which he put in his icehouse. When the moskitos came he invited them all to enter this log building. They soon discovered the liquor and went for it. They buzzed about the tub making a noise like a portable sawmill and pushing and crowding each other to get their share of the drink. Soon all were dead drunk. While this was happening, wary Bluenose had closed the door, and he now hauled them out one or two at a time and with a pair of pincers nipped off their bills. Bluenose never had any trouble with them after that. Most of them starved to death.

From *Bluenose Brainerd Stories—Log Cabin Tales from the Chippewa Valley in the Wisconsin North Woods.* Chas. E. Brown, 1943.

PAT, THE GREAT LIAR

In an Irish settlement south of Whitewater, Wisconsin, there lived a notorious liar, locally known as "Pat." At community gatherings, farmers talked about the corn they husked per acre, the milk produced by their cows, the weight of hogs sold, experiences in storms and blizzards, amount of wood cut per day, local baseball games, fishing and hunting successes, and adventures with ghosts.

Pat always had a bigger hog, a bigger pumpkin, a better-producing cow, caught more and bigger fish, shot more game or wolves, had more terrible experiences, and had bigger ghosts chase him.

So some of the boys got their heads together and decided to make up a very exaggerated story to tell to Pat, to see if they could stump him. Here was their story:

"One day we discovered a lot of wild ducks on Turtle Lake. A bay with a grass margin was black with ducks. There were thousands upon thousands of ducks. The ducks were so thick on the water that it was impossible to see a bit of the water in the bay and for nearly a mile out into the lake. We got our double-barrel shotguns loaded and crept cautiously into the grass. When every hunter was in position and ready to fire, one of us shouted to disturb the ducks and to get them into the air. As the ducks rose, all the hunters fired, but no ducks fell. It was impossible to see the sun or the blue sky through the rising ducks. Moments went by, and still no ducks fell. Then, as the ducks got farther apart, the dead ones started to fall into the lake. There was an intermittent falling of dead ducks for a long time, as the dead ones slipped from the backs and wings of the live ones."

Pat listened intently, and at the end of the story he spat his tobacco juice on the ground and said, "I had the very same experience with wild geese, and some of them dropped in Illinois."

More often than not the folk tale heroes of Wisconsin have been real persons magnified by the tale-spinners to demigod proportions. The Wisconsin strong men lead the list of these, with a frontier pistol-shot named Captain Scott right in their wake. We can only pause to whet your appetite for these heroes, the first of whom is without doubt Pierre Paquette.

PIERRE PAQUETTE

Pierre Paquette, born to a French father and a Winnebago mother on the Missouri frontier in 1796, grew to a height of six feet, two inches, his flesh as hard as steel. As a young man he worked the portage between the Fox and Wisconsin for the American Fur Company. He was in charge of some twenty yoke of oxen that hauled the boats across the muddy stretch between the rivers. It was work for a man, but Paquette was equal to the job. He was literally as strong as an ox, and he proved it once when one of his beasts gave out. Paquette immediately yoked himself, and, teamed with the remaining ox, pulled a full load to the Wisconsin's shore. They called him the "Wisconsin Samson."

Satterlee Clark, once the sutler at Fort Winnebago, and the giant's intimate, had seen Paquette the day he had swung a pile driver weighing more than two thousand pounds. Clark had been privileged to crack hickory nuts with a sledge hammer on the muscles of Paquette's naked arm. Henry Merrell, postmaster and a truthful man, said that Paquette could pick up a barrel of pork as easily as another man would lift a ten-gallon keg. B. L. Webb remembered how two men, one at each end, would strain to hoist a single three-bushel sack of wheat from the river boats to his warehouse floor, but that Pierre Paquette had more than once seized a sack in each hand, and tossed them up with utter ease.

Andrew Jackson Turner, the famous historian, contended that "the name of Pierre Paquette was probably more frequently on the tongues of men than that of any other man in Wisconsin." When he was killed in a dispute with the Indian, "Iron Walker," they told throughout the Northwest of his last words, spoken as he bared his chest to the revolver barrel: "Shoot, and see a brave man die."

THE SCOTCH GIANT

The Scotch Giant, Randall, four-hundred-and-fifty-pound teamster, seven feet six or seven feet eight inches tall, amazed the rugged denizens of Mineral Point by swinging a plow over his head with one hand and lifting barrels of whiskey with his fingers. Randall, about whom many pleasant legends cling, could easily carry a dozen eggs in either hand and break not a one.

The Scotch Giant really belongs to Belmont, however. At least, he is buried in Belmont Cemetery.

One time in a barroom brawl the Scotch Giant was tormented by a hanger-on. He became angry, and threw a punch at the pest. The blow missed his victim, but his arm drove right through the tavern wall.

The Giant's job was carting pigs of lead—great wedge-shaped hunks weighing as much as seventy-three pounds each, or more. He was in the habit of walking along with one of these in each hand, using the pigs he carried to brake the wagon wheels when going up a hill.

The Giant was supposed to have eventually traveled with Barnum.

ALLEN BRADLEY

Allen Bradley of Rock Island, the third of the mighty men, measured six feet around his chest, wore moccasins because no shoes would fit him, and his hands were as broad as shovels. He was a man equipped for unbelievable performances. Using only an ax, he could cut seven cords of body maple in a single day. Once he was given the job of salvaging the riggin' from a schooner wrecked on Hanover Shoal. Bradley worked alone. He cleaned her up from keel to truck and, when he was done, loaded the thousand-pound anchor into his boat and carried it ashore in Fish Creek.

A FAMOUS MARKSMAN

Even more honored than the big and strong were the great hunters, the fabulous marksmen, who were the real aristocrats of the frontier. Captain Martin Scott of Fort Howard and Fort Crawford was famous far beyond Wisconsin's borders as a phenomenal dead shot with rifle or revolver. Scott took his reputation seriously; he never touched liquor, for fear that alcohol might impair his skill—a forgivable eccentricity for a champion.

It sometimes pleased the captain to have his friends throw two potatoes into the air; then he, firing from the hip, and seeming but to glance at his targets, would pierce them both with a single ball. From the farthest available distance he could fire at a nail projecting from a fence, and his bullet would drive the nail home as nearly as a hammer. It was said of Scott, as it was of Davy Crockett, that when coons saw him approach, they came down from their perch and surrendered.

Ruthless as he was on the hunt, Captain Scott could be magnanimous on occasion. A reckless fellow once challenged him to a duel. Scott calmly shot away a portion of his adversary's liver, so the story went, restoring the man to better health than he had ever known, and winning the marksman a lifelong friend!

Told by J. Curvin

WHAT? NO MILK?

Wisconsin is perhaps best known nowadays as a dairy state, and the production of milk is a foremost consideration. Much of the early interest in dairying was the result of the endless campaign of William Dempster Hoard, founder and editor of *Hoard's Dairyman*, published at Fort Atkinson, and Governor of the state. Hoard's famous statement that you must "speak to a cow just as you would to a lady," was heeded finally in his day, and indeed, today, many cows are spoken to more gently than some ladies.

By 1887 the propaganda campaign for dairying and dairy products was getting into full swing. At the banquet of the Wisconsin Dairymen's Association, February 9, 1887, at Sparta, the delegates opened the festivities with their favorite song:

> The fruit of the churn is the crown of our table,
> Our Governor [Hoard] tells us "the cow is the queen."
> Her horn is exalted for now she is able
> To kick up her heels at the vile margarine.
> All hail to Wisconsin, her hills and her waters,
> So ample the lover of nature to please;
> And last but not least are the dairyman's daughters,
> Those lovely purveyors of butter and cheese.
>
> CHORUS: The sweet golden butter, the creamery butter,
> The premium butter, the cream of the cheese!

Then the delegates lit into the banquet. Some spread!

Roast turkey, corned beef, boiled ham, baked chicken, pickled
   tongue, and ragout of lamb
Relishes—chow chow, celery, mixed pickles, pickled crabs
Salads—chicken, cabbage, and potato
Breads—corn bread, white bread, rye bread, rolls, graham bread
Jellies—currant, plum, orange, crabapple, lemon
Cakes—fig, lemon, chocolate, fruit, ice cream cake, doughnuts
Cheese—Sheboygan, Lodi, and Burnham Valley full cream
   cheese
Fruits—fancy Valencia oranges, New Messina oranges, Florida
   oranges, California oranges
Coffee and tea
Jersey cream, Holstein cream, and Hereford cream

While fourteen toasts with appropriate replies were proposed,
there was one outstanding omission among the beverages. Milk was
not included.

The University of Wisconsin, unique among state universities, and
outstanding for pioneering programs of many kinds, has its own
folklore and favorite tales. This great university is perhaps best
known for the term "Wisconsin Idea," which has come to mean the
extension of campus-based studies to every corner of the state, and
around Wisconsin's favorite cliche: "The boundaries of the Campus
are the boundaries of the state," have grown many tales of heroic
educational adventure to rival the Odyssey in excitement. However,
the University students have created much lore of their own, and
we will have to limit our accounts to a couple of famous student
tales. The first of these is the celebrated Fortenbaugh Incident of
1887. This version of the story is told by Mr. Leon R. Clausen, once
president of the J. I. Case Company at Racine.

THE FORTENBAUGH INCIDENT

When the Electrical Engineering Class of 1897 were seniors there
was brought to the University a certain S. B. Fortenbaugh as Pro-

fessor to assist D. C. Jackson, who was at the time head of the Electrical Engineering School.

Professor Fortenbaugh's peculiar Boston accent and mannerisms and habits attracted the attention of the students but did not meet entirely with their favor. Furthermore, as we went along through the year it became apparent that the Professor was masquerading somewhat and riding on his reputation rather than on his ability and real knowledge. He made the mistake of underestimating the class and overestimating his own importance and ability. As a result of this, the members of the class naturally were looking for openings and began to study the Professor and has habits.

The Professor wore trousers that had exceedingly wide legs but exceedingly sharp creases, so we recognized this fact by drawing his picture on the blackboard before the class hour, thus advising him that we were conscious of his attire. The pictures usually showed him cutting a dog in two with his creases or having some other misadventure.

Another thing we brought to his attention was the fact that we knew that he sailed an iceboat. We had rather an early spring in 1897, and the ice became honeycombed earlier than usual. The Professor left his iceboat on the ice until it became unsafe to go out to the boat, so it was marooned about two blocks from shore until it finally sank. This was duly recorded on the blackboard in considerable detail, so the Professor would know that we were keeping up to date on the news.

Most of the members of the class had already telephoned the Professor, advising him of the fact that his iceboat had sunk.

A couple of days later was the first of April, and some members of the class felt it would be proper not to show up on April Fool's Day. In other words, we would fool the Professor by not being present that day. All but one of the fellows stayed away; this particular one had not learned of the plot, so he was present. The Professor retaliated by giving the class a written quiz the next day, consisting of three questions, none of which could be answered without the information that he would have given us on the first of April had we been present in class. The only one capable of answering, therefore, was the one fellow who was present that day. The rest recognized the Professor's technique and decided that the best policy was not to attempt to answer but to hand the blue books in blank. This was done, but it had a repercussion which I will refer to later in the story.

One of the most interesting parts of the Fortenbaugh Incident was the Prof's habit of using the word "simply." It appears that he was so much addicted to the use of this word "simply" that he used it incessantly during his classwork and in conversation as well. It was so pronounced that the class felt they should do something about it to call it to his attention, so we agreed that every time he used the word "simply" we would rap two times on a chair with our pencils. The first couple of days the raps were modest and rather restricted, so they did not especially attract the Professor's attention, although he hesitated once in a while to listen for the peculiar sound.

About the third day this tapping on the chairs became a habit with the members of the class. I, personally, made the mistake one day of holding in my hands a piece of trolley wire, which was very heavy, and when it was rapped against a chair it made considerable noise. This immediately caught the Professor's attention and he slammed his papers down on the desk; his face became as red as fire and he delivered himself of a very vigorous statement of denunciation about in this language while he glared defiantly at the class and showed his teeth, and his mustache was quivering with indignation:

"It seems that I am addicted to the use of the word 'simply.' Now I want to say to you that if any member of this class does not like the word 'simply' he *simply* doesn't have to *simply* listen to it. Now we are proceeding."

This defiant pronouncement rather subdued the class for a moment, but after class we decided, in consultation, that we could not let this kind of a challenge pass unnoticed.

Therefore, in the afternoon we agreed that a better method of drawing the Professor's attention to the use of the word should be used, which would not be quite so noticeable as the method of rapping on the chairs with pencils.

We therefore pried up the lecturing rostrum, and underneath it we placed an electric buzzer connected with very fine wires. These wires we carefully placed in the fine cracks of the hardwood floor after carefully cleaning them out so the wires could not be observed and then brushing a little dust back into the very fine cracks.

We carried these wires to the back of the room where they were connected to a battery on top of a cabinet high above the floor and invisible. The cabinet was very heavy and could not well be moved; it was practically a part of the room.

The wires were then carried around the room, in an invisible manner, until they reached a steam radiator alongside of which Victor Bergenthal usually sat during the class hour. This made it possible for Bergenthal to reach around behind the radiator and bring out a length of wire, which he wrapped once around his knee. By simply moving his knee twice, rapidly, up against the radiator, he made the necessary contact so the buzzer would operate twice— "buzz, buzz." After this it was only necessary to wait for the Professor to use the word "simply," and there would be an immediate "buzz buzz" from some unknown place.

It was interesting to watch the Professor after this, because he would use the word "simply" and then pause and listen for the "buzz buzz" which always came, sometimes quickly and sometimes a little bit later, after he had used the word.

This went on for two or three days, and he could not locate the origin of the sound, which finally got on his nerves so much that it was almost impossible for him to carry on the class at all, because he just could not avoid the use of the word "simply." So about the third day he dismissed the class after about twenty minutes, because he could not carry on any longer, and then organized a search, in which he asked one or two other professors to join.

Thus the story got into the hands of the faculty. After carefully searching the room the experts on the faculty finally found the origin of the sound, but they had to pry up the rostrum to get at it.

Professor Fortenbaugh demanded disciplining for the whole class because of the insult to him personally and the lack of proper consideration for a member of the faculty. We learned through a leak that the faculty considered it such a good joke on Professor Fortenbaugh that they would not support his demand for discipline. However, they had stopped the buzzer.

The next part of the incident was that we discovered the Professor was bluffing in his instruction work. He was giving us a course on electrical railways. We found out where he was getting his source materials—much of it came out of a monthly publication, this being the most up-to-date source.

We discovered in this source some mathematical errors among the equations. We also made it a point to be several days ahead of the Professor. We could always approximate what the lessons were to be, and we just kept ahead of him by at least two days.

It was great fun for us to let the Professor get himself out on a limb; in fact, we would sometimes ask him questions to coax him out on the limb. We would especially try to get him to commit himself on matters which we knew to be erroneous, and then we would bounce down on him with the evidence that the statements that he had just given us, or the equations, were not correct. This gave him the jitters, and he would often slam down the papers and dismiss the class so he could take the next twenty-four hours to investigate and attempt to correct himself. It often was very embarrassing to him to come back the next day and admit he was wrong.

The outcome of the whole thing was that we rather spoiled the Professor's semester. He began to take a rather violent dislike to us because of our discovering and emphasizing his weaknesses.

He retaliated at the end of the term. He gave the final examinations, and in making up his final markings he averaged up the students' performances during the three portions of the semester, especially on the three written examinations, one of which, of course, most of the class did not answer. It was obvious, therefore, that no matter how perfect one was in two of the examinations, the zero which most of us had received on the third examination made 66 per cent the best mark that every student except one could make on the semester's work.

Of course, this put us in the position of being short on one course of the credits we needed to graduate and receive a diploma. This constituted a very serious problem, not only for certain of the students but for the class officer and the head of the department, Professor D. C. Jackson.

The question was: What to do? They could not very well have all but one of the graduating class of the Electrical Engineering course refused their diplomas and not allowed to graduate. This would be very, very bad. Some of the students felt bad about it—not getting a diploma—but personally I was not concerned, because the technique of the professor was so obvious.

However, Professor Jackson, who was the class official, desired in some manner to patch the thing up, so he began calling in the members of the class individually. My name, beginning with "C," was one of the first called. He pointed out the seriousness of the impasse and wanted to know if I was anxious to get a diploma and to graduate in a normal manner. I told him that it did not make a particle of difference to me whether I had a diploma or not; that I had received from the University what I came there for and the mere possession of a diploma was of no consequence.

On leaving Professor Jackson's office I advised the other members of the class what I had said and urged the others to take the same position. If we stood together we could at least all be on the same basis and probably bring about a solution.

Finally Professor Jackson called the entire class together and said he was very sorry about the whole matter; he thought it could be adjusted, and if the class would all go to a written quiz to be given by Professor Fortenbaugh, with our blue books in hand, and be prepared to write the quiz, he thought the professor might do something very magnanimous. We immediately saw that this was a diplomatic way on the part of Professor Jackson to save the Professor's face, and it offered a way out, so we all went to Professor Fortenbaugh's class with the understanding among ourselves that we would give the Professor five minutes to say something, and if he did not say something in five minutes we would all get up and walk out.

Fortunately the Professor did say something; in fact he made a very beautiful and sentimental talk to the class and even acknowledged that he had made some very bad mistakes, but he hoped the class would forgive him and that we would remember him favorably in the future after we had left the University. This I am sure we all did, because we all recognized that he was really at heart a first-class fellow and good-natured to a fault, only he did not understand the Western type of student, particularly not the engineering students.

The Professor was not asked to return to the University the following year.

This was the end of the Fortenbaugh Incident.

The Fortenbaugh Incident was less spectacular than the famous rope sweep involving the student militia in the mid-nineties. Mr. Halsten J. Thorkelson, member of the class of '98, remembers this well.

THE GREAT ROPE SWEEP

When the Class of 1898 entered the University of Wisconsin in the fall of 1894, two years of military drill were required of all male students, excepting only law students and those who were physically incapacitated.

One of our younger instructors in mathematics had graduated a few years earlier without meeting this requirement. He escaped the vigilant eyes of both the Military Department and the registrar's office because his first name was Pearl. This naturally was interpreted as feminine in gender. More than one coed whose first name appeared to be of masculine gender was called to account for failure to appear for drill. Such encounters always resulted in the humiliation of the Military Department and not of the coed concerned.

Drill started early in the fall term, our class being one of the first to make use of the newly erected armory and gymnasium. The large hall with gun racks along the walls permitted drill sessions to be independent of the weather, although the outdoors was always favored for battalion maneuvers. The first appearance of the freshmen for outdoor drill on the lower campus between Langdon and State Streets gave the sophomores an opportunity to impress freshmen with the lowly status of their existence. Freshmen usually outnumbered sophomores but were quite helpless when being initiated into the meaning of the various signals which followed the words "Company, attention." If ever a group of men felt like dumb driven cattle, we did when, lined up on the lower campus, we attempted our awkward responses to the unintelligible commands barked at us by newly fledged officers who were probably even less at ease than we were.

When the class of 1898 made its maiden appearance on the lower campus in the fall of 1894, the sophomores made flying wedges and practiced football, rushing on our defenseless groups, bowling us over, and in general being as rough in their greeting as possible. To add to our comfort, they secured lines of hose and soaked freshmen and campus. All this made us hope that our turn at being sophomores might speedily come.

When we became sophomores, however, the Commandant determined to put a stop to the custom of using the initial freshman outdoor drill as the time for interference by sophomores. A rope was tied to posts around the lower campus, thus effectively preventing any rushing attack. With alert if slightly nervous student officers stationed at strategic observation posts near the rope, freshman drill started with a suspicious calm.

In a short time students in the assembled audience untied the rope and stretched it from Langdon to State Street. With one group holding one end on State Street, and another group of students holding the other end on Langdon Street, the lower campus was thoroughly swept from west to east and then from east to west. The results were funny beyond description for everyone, including the dignified but furious Commandant, had to jump over the rope or be bowled over. Whole companies were toppled like tenpins as with hilarious regularity the rope swept back and forth to the continued applause and shouts of encouragement from the audience. The Commandant, as he indignantly yet gingerly moved from station to station along the edge of the parade ground, asked the officers who had been assigned to observe operations if they recognized any of the offending students. Without any collusion each officer returned identical replies: "No Sir, I do not know any of the parties. I think, Sir, they are all law students."

The Commandant, who believed wholeheartedly in discipline, unfortunately viewed the incident as an insult to the flag. The faculty, which did not on the whole take such a serious view of the matter, felt the obligation of supporting their colleague and took summary action. They dropped about a dozen students from the

University. About half of those dropped had had nothing whatever to do with the affair, but there was no convenient method of establishing their innocence. After somewhat extended negotiations, the students who were the representatives of the classes of 1898 and 1899 agreed to see to it that in the future freshman drill would not be interfered with if the students who had been dropped were reinstated. This was done, and for over half a century this agreement has been well kept.

Wisconsinites love anecdotes. Most any smaller town in the state still has a spot where a few yarners like to swap tales of many kinds. We would be very bold to say exactly what are the favorite anecdotes of Wisconsin, but we would like to present a few that we believe are close to being favorites.

THE DEACON'S HOSS

Old Deacon Fraser was a near neighbor of Ben Hooper's in Green County, living about a half mile away. He had a horse that he had brought from the East and of which he was very fond. One day Old Bolly strayed from his pasture into the woods and could not be found. After every attempt to find the "hoss" had failed, the Deacon called on his neighbor for help in recovering the animal. Ben was willing to assist his friend and went into the woods to hunt for the "critter." That evening he came to the cabin with the "hoss." The Deacon was very grateful and asked Ben how he found Bolly. "Wall," said Ben, "I just sott down and thought where I would go if I was a hoss. Wall I did, and he wuz."

A DUTY

At Fort Atkinson, Frank Cole, once owner of the Badger Lunch, lived with his wife in a nine-room apartment over his lunchroom. He was a compact, sturdy man, with white, clipped hair, who talked extremely well, and had read some books. Above all, he'd learned from talking and from listening. Here's one of Frank's stories he liked to tell about his friend, Maxwell Goodrich's grandfather. Mr. Goodrich observed that every once in a while in the old days, in order to prove manhood, a citizen would get drunk, whether he liked to drink or not. Mr. Goodrich encountered a normally dry citizen driving into town and looking pretty disconsolate. "Where are you going?" asked Goodrich.

"I'm going into town to get drunk," replied the citizen. "And God— how I dread it!"

A QUEER TALE

It happened that in an early day, a Methodist circuit rider came to a crossroads in the state of Wisconsin where stood a typical country lad—barefooted, pants rolled up, one suspender, and shirt bosom open. The preacher was mounted on about the poorest horse that had ever been seen in these parts. Addressing the boy, he said, "My son, which one of these two roads will take me to Stoughton?"

The boy paid no attention to the question. He had never seen a respectable man mounted on so sorry a steed. The minister repeated the question, and the boy, looking up, queried, "Who are you?"

Back came the answer, "I am a follower of the Lord."

"Well," said the boy, "it won't make any difference which road you take. You'll never catch him with that hoss."

Told by Mrs. W. R. Hoard, Sharon, Wis.

CAMPMEETIN' TESTIMONY

One time about fifty-four years ago the parties that lived on Parkers Point were cooking for the dry roll crew. There was a church across the river two miles away. Some of the crew went to church with the cook and her husband. One fellow had too much to drink. When church was about over the minister asked if anyone wished to testify. The drunk man got up and said, "I want to testify for Libbie Parker. She's an awful good cook."

Told by Mrs. Charles Holcombe

BALANCING THE BOOKS

A local businessman, when questioned on his procedures, passed off the following:

"Vell, de first nickt I open store I counts de monies and finds him nix rickt; I counts again and der be tree gone; and vot you tink I does den? Vy, I did not count him any more, and he comes out shoost rickt ever since."

Grant County Herald—May 13, 1875

A GOOD SUIT

The following was taken from the souvenir program of the 24th North-American Saengerfest held in Milwaukee, the week of July 21 to 25, 1886.

This is a sample of German-American humor, for it was written in the "Schoenste Language," a quaint German idiom partly English. It was a humorous advertisement, a speech by a tailor named Louis Silverstone titled: "Milwaukee Five Hundred Years Ago."

The last sentence was as follows:

"I hope for old memory sake of five hundred years ago you vill all, strangers and citizens, get cut up een new suits of clothes by me, and vhen ve meet again in five hundred years from now, and sqveze drough der golden gate, I vill make you all a suit for nodding and throw you in a pair ov pants besides, and still be your ould friendt and tailor."

Told by Albertine Schuttler

A MADISON CHARACTER

Pinneo, whose first name nobody could remember, called himself a "shingle weaver." He had come to Madison in the 1830's after coasting up and down the western rivers, and had built himself a shelter of sorts near Lake Mendota, where, in partnership with a bibulous Vermonter, Johnathan Butterfield, he manufactured shingles for the ready market of the growing town.

Neither of these worthies took business too seriously. With the revenue from each completed order of shingles, they would sally forth together on a monumental bender, the progress of which was followed with considerable public interest. Pinneo, with his natural flare for spontaneous theatrics, easily outshone his partner on these frolics. He was a born clown. He wore in foul weather or fair nothing but a red shirt and a pair of coarse homespun breeches. His feet were always bare, and his toes were as hard as a turtle's shell; he was proud of his ability to pull up great quantities of grass and roots with them. But for all his peculiarities, the town liked Pinneo, since he was an affable fellow and "always had a laugh and a joke for everyone."

Pinneo's wonderful sense of the absurd paradox moved him one day to mount an old white horse without bridle or halter and race through the streets of Madison. Extended in one hand was the jawbone of "some defunct quadruped." "Look ye!" he shouted to the amazed spectators. "I am Samson, in quest of the Philistines! Out of my way!"

When the Reverend Philo inaugurated church services in Madison, the first to be present in the congregation was Pinneo. He listened attentively to the opening portion of the service. Then the minister launched into a plea for men to lead better lives in the new country, and specifically to forswear the Demon Rum. There was a stir in Pinneo's vicinity as he rose deliberately to his feet, and nodding his great head somberly, intoned, "That's so, Mr. Philo, indeed that is so! Butterfield must be saved! Hold on, Mr. Philo, till I bring him in." With that Pinneo stalked grandly out of the room. He did not return.

Told by J. W. Curvin

THE FIRST OF THE SOLONS

The first one to represent Washington County in the State Legislature at Madison was "nomen et omen" Solon Johnson. He took his seat on June 5, 1848, a short time after Wisconsin had risen to the level of a state. From the life of this gentleman two anecdotes have come upon us, which throw spotlights on his character as well as on life in general in those days.

Solon Johnson was gaunt, and measured six feet five in his socks. In his ways he was somewhat eccentric, but that did not hinder him from being kind and noble-minded. In his extenuated body he carried a kind of penned-up gayety which occasionally broke loose in the most waggish way. After he had been elected—his abode was in Port Washington, the former county seat—he went to Milwaukee and bought himself a new suit of clothes, in which he intended to make his debut in the halls of the Legislature. He had always been rather negligent in his dress, and his fellow citizens would have craned their necks to see him in a dress suit and with a silk hat. Solon presumed the like and carefully packed his suit away. He intended to don it on the day of his departure for Madison. Until then, the purchase should stay a secret.

But somehow, as it is often the case, the secret leaked out. Someone was put on to Solon's purchase, and soon the whole town knew about it. A meeting was called and a scheme devised how Solon could be made to show and "wet" his new garb. "General" Wooster Harrison, a jocose Yankee, known in those days all over the eastern part of Wisconsin, was entrusted with the execution. The ruse worked to perfection.

Harrison went to Solon and found him in his room, where the following dialogue ensued:

"Good morning, Your Honor."

"Good morning."

"I have called on you," began Harrison with measured and impressive speech, "to pay—to pay—well, you know, Solon—pardon me for addressing you by your given name, but, believe me, my motives are prompted by the purest of friendships."

"I can assure you," replied Solon, "that no apology is necessary."

"My object in calling," continued Harrison, "is to compliment you on your success in attaining to the very high and honorable position of representative of our new State in the maiden Legislature. The responsibilities are great, as the laws formed at this session will serve as precedents for all coming generations, and we feel confident as to your ability to represent judiciously the interests of Washington County."

"You do me great honor," replied Solon, touched by the homage of his friend. "I know not how to express my gratitude towards my friends for this manifestation of their loyalty and their good wishes, and I shall try and prove myself worthy of the great confidence they have imposed in me."

"And now," continued Harrison, "that my humble mission is at the end, I have one request to make. I know you will think me foolish, but then you will pardon the whim. What I wish, my friend, is to see you dressed up in your new togs. I have heard that they are worthy of the high office you are to represent, and I am in a great anxiety to see how you look in them."

"Well, I have a new suit," admitted Solon, somewhat flattered, "and although it is not as grand as you may have imagined, I will comply with your request."

With that he began to invest himself with his new "toggery," while his visitor prodigiously complimented him as every piece was fitted to its proper place. When he had everything on, his toilet finished, and his friend standing before him in simulated ecstasy over his appearance, heavy knocks fell on the door below. Then followed a commotion in the hallway, and somebody shouted up with excited voice:

"Where is Mister Johnson? I must see him at once."

Meanwhile Solon had opened the door of his room, and a messenger, panting and livid, rushed toward him.

"Are you Solon Johnson?" he gasped.

"I am; what can I do for you?"

"A friend of yours has been seriously hurt and desires to see you at the hotel at once."

"Who is it?"

"I don't know. I couldn't get his name; they told me to get you with all possible speed."

"You had better go at once," suggested Harrison, feigning innocence.

There was no need for a second bidding. Solon took his hat, and in his new clothes accompanied the two men to the hotel. He found a large crowd gathered there, asked to be led to his friend, and inquired as to the seriousness of his injuries. In response, a roaring laughter rose from the crowd, followed by three cheers.

Solon grasped the situation. "Harrison, you old rogue," he exclaimed, "this is another of your diabolical tricks."

Another roar from the crowd confirmed his apprehension. "Well, boys," he added, "you have earned your treat. Landlord, they all drink at my expense."

Three more cheers were given to the representative of Washington County. He had been made to show and "wet" his new suit.

Soon after the Legislature had convened, Solon Johnson introduced an important bill, on which he wanted to speak. Before, he had given a sumptuous dinner, at which considerable wine was drunk, and he had paid more homage to Bacchus than was good for him. He hardly had entered the hall when he began addressing the Assembly. This being out of order, the speaker reminded him of the parliamentary rules.

"Order, or no order," exclaimed Solon, "I wish you to understand, Mr. Speaker, that I am here to represent the interests of the great county of Washington, and, if my bill is not passed, I will tear this house down over your heads."

Some of his friends succeeded in calming him. He was brought to his room, where he could meditate over the fix his indulgence had put him into. His bill afterwards was passed, and so were a goodly number of others which he introduced and urged for passage "with great vigor and fair ability." Taken in all, he was an able, though somewhat rash, representative.

Told by Carl Quickert

THE GREAT GRANT COUNTY WOLF FIGHT

The rugged primitive life in Grant County was not without its amusements. A favorite form of entertainment was the wolf-fight, one of which is described for posterity by an active participant in the scene:

I don't remember the year. (It was 1838—Ed.) We didn't take any account of time when we ranged at will over these fenceless prairies. We didn't cut the year into weeks and Sundays, but took it as it came. Anyway, the time it was about the first court: Harvey Pepper was Sheriff; Judge Dunn was on the bench; I was foreman of the jury; old yellow-black Paul was plaintiff; and Colonel Jones, who went to Congress and perched himself on top of Sinsinawa Mound— he was the defendant. Jones owned Paul as a slave down in Kentucky, and when Paul got to Wisconsin he quarreled with his master and became obstreperous, and Jones drove him off.

Paul then went through the country fiddling at what they called "stag dances." Females then were scarce and very dear and hard to get, so the boys would dance alone on the sod floor, and Paul would "fiddle" for his whiskey, and when he ran too far out of knees and elbows he would go back to Jones and saw wood, and Jones would supply him with old clothes.

After some years, Paul concluded, as courts and lawyers had made their appearance, he would sue his old master for wages and have a final settlement in this free country. We heard the evidence. The yellow darkey hadn't a bit of proof in support of his claim, but eleven of the jurors went in steep for the plaintiff, contending if Paul recovered wages it would make him a free man. I asserted he was free anyway, wages or no wages—that we were sworn to go according to law. Some of the jurors said, "D——n the law; when it comes in one door, justice runs out the other." Pepper, the Sheriff, locked us up and, to make the purgatory complete, said he was sworn to allow us no meat or drink except water.

Imprisoned in this ten-by-nine cell, we quarreled long and loud. I stood out for the defendant against the eleven who were determined that Paul should be paid for our shindig music and that Jones was the man to do it. I told my eleven brethren I was used to starving, and would die at my post rather than violate the law. They talked of fighting but I was ready for 'em.

We should have hung there until this time, probably, but for a couple of huge, gray timber wolves that old "Wolf-catcher" Graham had brought into the town plat, securely caged in his wagon. Everybody then attended court, and everybody brought his dogs. The old wolf-catcher set up a loud cry, saying he would let out a wolf against all the dogs in creation, if the people who desired the sport would pay him $20 each for his wolves and allow him the scalps. The money was raised quicker than you could count it. We would have almost paid the national debt to see a wolf-fight. The first wolf—and he was an old settler, I tell you—was let loose in the yard, right under our window. We ran to it and climbed on each other's shoulders. Such snapping, barking, growling, and bristling you never heard or saw. Dogs and wolf were piled up almost to the upper story, in a living, biting, snapping, rolling, tumbling, and boiling mass. Some of the dogs were thrown hors du combat, but others took their place. The revolving mass turned around the corner where we couldn't see them, and then my eleven associates cried: "For heaven's sake, Free, do agree, so we can get out of this cursed hole and see the fun."

"Boys," said I, "I have been raised with wolves. I won't budge an inch for any arguments dogs and wolves can furnish."

"Well, Free, just say that Jones shall pay one dollar, and we will come down to that."

"Never a cent."

We heard the uproarious laughter and shouts of the outside world. It was too much for the boys. The friends of poor yellow Paul yielded, and cried out "We agree; write out the verdict, Free."

I wrote out the verdict for the defendant; but lo! we were in a worse condition than ever. The Judge, Sheriff, and all hands had gone to the entertainment. No time was to be lost. A chair was picked up, a window smashed, and as Judge Dunn heard the glass come jingling to the ground, he screamed, "Pepper! Pepper! Let those men out; they will tear down the courthouse!"

These words sounded like the trump of jubilee. We handed our verdict to the Sheriff, and rushed downstairs like a flock of frightened sheep when the dogs are after them.

But the scene of the fight had changed. In the dog and wolf revolution, the latter actually entered the sacred halls of Pepper's tavern, where all our fair female population were gathered and gossiping. Such a scattering, screaming, fright, running upstairs, and jumping on beds was never seen or heard of. But the poor wolf, as if he understood the tenderness of the female heart, galloped upstairs too; on the bed he jumped with tongue protruding, and with be-seeching looks, prayed for mercy. But up rushed the dogs dripping with blood; now mad with fury and blessed with victory, they scaled the parapet. A universal and deafening hubbub ensued. Men rushed in with clubs, seizing a dog or two by the tail and tossing them out of the window, and sometimes punching the wolf, that by this time had learned that the generous dimensions of female apparel offered him the safest retreat. But notwithstanding the poor wolf's surrender and meek behavior after he entered the forbidden halls, he was slain without mercy. There is not a living man or woman or animal that witnessed that scene but if they are still alive remember it to this day. I am satisfied that the jury never would have agreed in that case had it not been for Graham's wolf.

THE FIGHTING FINCHES *

In the years before the Civil War the Finches, a lawless tribe of pioneer border bandits, terrorized Rock and Jefferson Counties from Lake Koshkonong northward to beyond Waterloo and from eastern Dane County to the banks of the Rock River.

The Black Hawk War was the cause of the Finches coming to Wisconsin. They were hard fighters and went where the fighting was. The trouble was that they stayed in Wisconsin after the War was over.

The Finch country was largely a huge swamp area with Lake Mills, Fort Atkinson, and Jefferson the chief seats of the Finch influence.

They came to Wisconsin from St. Joseph, Michigan, and St. Joseph was delighted when they left, for a "Finch War Dance" with the aid of stout redeye whiskey could supply as much terror as an Indian raid.

In fact, the Fighting Finches dressed themselves as Indians, and staged many "Indian raids" in Wisconsin. One of their immediate decisions made after their Wisconsin arrival was that there "weren't no place in the country for nobody 'ceptin' a Finch."

A Norwegian settler was badly beaten up by the Finches and his land confiscated by them. The settler brought his trouble to the old Injun fighter, Governor Dodge, first Governor of the New Wisconsin Territory. Dodge bellowed to Sheriff Bird "Exhaust the power of the county, sir! And if that don't do, I'll call out the militia, by God, sir! If that Finch tribe is goin' to run this Territory, I'll dam' soon find it out, sir!"

So the Sheriff and a helper headed down to "Finchland." One tale goes that they were wise enough to pick out a "little Finch"—a kid, in fact, one they thought they could handle. They found him out cutting wood, grabbed him when he wasn't looking, and hurried off toward Madison to show the Governor that a Finch could really be caught.

* Federal Writers Project, Folklore Section.

Soon the Finch tribe heard the news, and mounting their sturdy (stolen) hosses they took off after the Sheriff. They didn't quite catch up to him, but the Sheriff thought they were going to, and that was almost as bad.

The Governor is said to have congratulated the Sheriff on his capture, but did make the remark that "the Finch was a little too small to keep, so toss him back in!"

The Finches had an elaborate hangout in what is now known as the London Marsh, south of the Chicago and Northwestern Railroad tracks between Lake Mills and London. No sheriff could follow the Finches into this place. At night settlers could see moving lights through the trees. Out of this swamp the Finches were never routed.

FINCH HORSES

No one will never know just how many horses the Finches and their henchmen stole during the years of their raidings, but the number must have been considerable. No doubt they were blamed for many lost horses which other horse thieves had carried away and for the loss of other stock missed by the settlers of Jefferson, Rock, Dane, and Dodge Counties.

The Finches knew how to change the appearance of the horses by staining or bleaching them and by grooming their manes and tails. For their stolen horses they seemed to have found ready markets. Rolling Prairie, east of Beaver Dam, was a favorite trade center, and some markets were found even as far away as Chicago.

The horses which they themselves rode were the best specimens of frontier horseflesh. In a horse race once held at Janesville a Finch pony outdistanced all others.

Because of their widely heralded misdeeds and hard riding the Finches were feared by many settlers who never really knew them. Pioneer mothers are said to have quieted their children at night by saying, when there was a rush of wind, "Be quiet. The Finches are riding by." That was enough to quiet the naughtiest child.

A country blacksmith, who shod a horse for a stranger who came to his smithy, refused to take any pay for his work, for he thought that he recognized his customer as one of the Finch band.

A FINCH HORSE TRADE

Of sturdy pioneers one hears so much,
"Honest, hard-working, thrifty," and such.

Sometimes a man who was hardly a saint
Would rustle horses, then disguise them with paint.

A farmer west of town owned a valuable pair.
One morning the better horse was not there.

"Lost, strayed, or stolen," the news went around,
And the beautiful animal could not be found.

Spring's work coming on, he must have a team.
There came to Black Earth some "dealers," 'twould seem.

He went to the barn where the horses were sold.
There were the "traders," so rough and so bold.

They had a fine horse, not the least bit shy,
So much like the "lost one"; this nag he would buy.

"Almost identical," but no white strip on her face.
As he led her home she seemed to know the place.

When she shed her hair later on in the year,
Sure enough! The white strip did reappear.

(It is believed that the horse thieves who visited Black Earth at this
time might have been the Finches.)

THE CAMP MEETING

Once a traveling preacher was officiating at a camp meeting near
one of the Jefferson County settlements. As usual, a rough platform
had been built of logs, and seats had been provided for the congregation by felling tree trunks and laying other logs upon these.

People had driven with their teams and had come on horseback,
some from considerable distances, to be at the revival. Among those

gathered there were a number of roughnecks who had come for the sole purpose of "raising hell" and annoying the preacher and those gathered to hear the word of God.

While the meeting progressed, a stranger rode up on horseback, tied his mount to a nearby tree, and came in and sat down on one of the rear seats. He was a handsome fellow, and the eyes of some of the girls present were soon upon him. Soon the rowdies, all more or less drunk, began to create a disturbance. Thereupon the stranger arose, walked over to them, and drawing a pistol from his belt, quickly cowed them. He marched them to the front of the platform and forced them to kneel during the continuance of the meeting.

It is said that several "got religion" right then and there. After the close of the meeting the stranger rode away. Some of those present insisted that they recognized him as one of the Finches.

THE CHARIVARI

A party of pioneers (men and boys) were preparing one night to serenade a newly married couple residing somewhere north of Lake Mills.

The Charivari was not an uncommon occurrence in the countryside in the early days. The young people had assembled in the neighborhood of the log cabin and were banging away and having a "rare old time" with their tin pans, kettles, guns, "bull fiddles," and other terrific noise-making devices when three men on horseback suddenly rode into their midst, firing pistols. Someone recognized them as the Finches, and the entire serenading company fled with the greatest of haste into the timber.

It was afterward said that the newly married neighbor was a henchman of the Finches and that they had learned of the proposed serenade and had come to his rescue.

It was a long time before any serenades were again held for newly wedded couples in that "neck of the woods."

THE WRESTLING MATCH AT THE FORD

Jack, or John, Finch was widely known for his prowess as a rough-and-tumble wrestler in days when every country district had its champion. He was one of the least obnoxious of the twelve fighting members of his family. He had a farm in Rock County and was not known to have been involved in any horse-stealing raids.

Jack was a man of great strength and had downed most of the fighters of the country around in wrestling matches and in trials of strength. He once placed on his shoulder a great hand-hewn mill beam and walked away with it. No other two or three men could do more than lift the beam off the ground.

A story of Jack's wrestling exploits has come down to us. One day when he had ridden down to the place known as the Indian Ford of the Rock River and was about to make the ride across, he saw a man whom he recognized as a rather renowned wrestler of the Sugar River country in Green County. The two men had met before but had never been pitted against each other in a match. Jack Finch hailed the other man, and after a few minutes of conversation, called back and forth across the stream, a challenge was given and accepted. The two men tied their mounts, each on his own side of the bank, and waded out to meet the other in midstream, where the water was almost waist deep. Spectators who arrived and viewed the fight said that it was a mighty struggle.

They quickly came to grips and struggled back and forth in the water. The stones in the bed of the stream were slippery and the footing uncertain, but the two were well matched. Neither was able to throw the other man. Several times they disengaged and took new holds. It was a fair fight. After more than an hour of fighting the two men shook hands and decided to call it a day. Each untied his mount and went his way.

THE EARL VELVET

Early in the 1840's, with settlements springing up between Milwaukee and Madison, important trade routes were established between these two communities. Along these routes were driven the freight wagon trains, many times carrying valuable loads of merchandise to outposts in the Wisconsin wilderness.

A. R. Earl, farmer, millwright, carpenter, and joiner, one of the most important pioneer landowners in Aztalan Township, had been told that the next wagon train was to bring a bolt of velvet imported from England for Mrs. Earl, the former Louisa Waterbury. One of the Finch boys overheard the remark, and when the wagon train reached Aztalan, or Jefferson (the stories conflict), the light-fingered Finch located the shipments headed for that community and under the very nose of the purchaser he made off with the Earl velvet. He was probably aided to some extent by the equally light-fingered members of his clan and, no doubt, by cleverly plying the wagoners with drinks. There was much to suspect but nothing to prove, and the Finches acquired merely another smirch on a checkered record.

The incident might have died with nothing but a cloud of suspicion to mark its passing had not some of the women of the Finch family, most of whom were excellent horsewomen, suddenly "blossomed out" in velvet riding habits of the material and color consigned to the wagon train for Mrs. Earl. Hot words were passed, it is said, and threats of reprisal were made, but the anecdote ended without definitely stating if anyone around Aztalan besides the Finches were owners of velvet riding habits in those days.

Years after the Finch clan had become a more or less distorted memory in Jefferson County, settlers would warn their children never to try "finching" something that wasn't theirs. (This is an interesting word, used probably as a provincialism of the word "filch," flavored unwittingly by associating it with the name "Finch.")

PATSY FINCH, HORSEWOMAN

Patsy Finch (her name is thought to have been Patricia) was reputed to have been one of the most attractive among the beautiful Finch women. She was, like others of her female relatives, a very skillful and fearless horsewoman and could ride bareback as well as in a saddle. She had flashing blue-black eyes and long black hair, which streamed out behind her as she traveled down the road on some errand. The settlers liked her, and despite the bad reputation of some other members of her family, no one ever molested Patsy.

Often her rides were little errands of mercy to aid some sick member of a settler's family. With the young men she was a favorite and was in great demand at country dances where young and old tripped to the tunes of "Money Musk" or "Comin' Thru The Rye."

Some of the lads wanted Patsy for a helpmeet and sought her hand. She finally disappeared from her home neighborhood in Jefferson County and was seen no more. Conjecture was that she married a reputable Milwaukee merchant of means and raised a nice family.

THE MINOCQUA BANK ROBBERY

The bank robbery of Minocqua has never been solved, and just how much money was taken has not been accurately recorded. Interest in the event always has centered around the incidents of that day rather than how much was stolen. Probably the thieves gained only a few hundred dollars, since the robbery occurred in the days when the town was very young and before anyone had very much money, even if they had faith enough in the bank to deposit it there.

The accounts of the robbery say that three men were involved. They rode into town on the train which had just recently been coming that far north. They strolled down Main Street to get the lay of the land, then turned and pulled handkerchiefs over their faces. Their guns were drawn. One man walked to each end of the block and told everyone to stand back, keep quiet, and not make any trouble. The third man was to hold up the bank while the other two kept the crowds at bay.

The bank robber walked into the bank and then seemed to get cold feet. Out he came again and told his pals he was going across the street to the saloon and have a drink first. The idea seemed satisfactory to his pals, who were having no trouble at all with the populace. Citizens had gathered in amazement behind the holdup lines, but the men in charge cooly told them not to interfere.

Meanwhile, one resident had gotten into position with a deer rifle in the second-story window of one of the buildings. As the bank robber came out of the saloon where he had been cordially served his drink, the man called down to the town mayor, saying he had a bead on the robber and asking if he should shoot. The mayor told him to hold his fire as they wanted no bloodshed. So the bandit entered the bank unharmed, demanded the money, and came out with it in a big gunny sack.

The men walked toward the railroad threatening everyone they saw with their pistols. When they reached the tracks they jumped on a hand car which they had apparently taken the trouble to get into position earlier. Working the handles up and down, they manuevered the car down the tracks toward the south.

Then the men of Minocqua took action. A group of them had obtained guns, and now they got into a horse-drawn wagon. They drove as fast as they could down the road to the south to Hazelhurst, only a few miles away. They drove up to the depot, put the team behind it, and took their positions behind the outhouses. As the hand car came down the track they opened fire. A number of shots were exchanged back and forth as the robbers rolled past and disappeared to the south. So far as is known, there were no injuries. No word of the bank robbers was ever received in the North Woods. But the bullet-holes made by the shots of the bandits remained in the boards of the outhouses, to be pointed out to visitors in the area for many years to come.

Told to Margaret Kelk by
Otto Krasselt

TRAPPER JOE

Sunrise Island in Lake Sis-n-bog-ama was truly a spot of magnificent enchantment. There were several other islands in this beautiful lake of Northern Wisconsin, but this was the one that Trapper Joe had known as home for five years.

His neatly built log cabin, with its walls covered with the pelts of the past winter's catch, could not be seen from any point on the shoreline, for it was standing back among the big, spreading pines.

The buds of the poplars were opening and the partridge ceased feeding upon them. Glorious spring was in the air; the lake was open and free of ice.

Trapper Joe washed his tin dishes and whistled as he laid them on the stove to dry.

Mark, his tracking hound, gave voice to two short bays, sniffing with his nose pointed toward the distant shoreline. A moment later a loud splash sounded from the same direction, and the two other dogs joined the bayings of the hound.

The season was growing late for trapping, but Trapper Joe had left four otter traps set right in the place from whence came the sound of the big splash. So, hastening to his lightest canoe, he ordered Mark to enter, gave it a hard push toward the opposite shore, jumped in, and paddled swiftly.

As he neared the place from where the splash seemed to come, he became more cautious, letting his paddle idle in the water, his eyes strained to shore. The canoe was gliding on from the force of the final stroke when Mark growled fiercely. An instant later a hand reached up, grasping the side of the frail craft, upsetting its contents; then the hand slowly relaxed and sank into the dark water, but not before Trapper Joe had seen it.

The dog swam around frantically while Joe righted the canoe, and as Mark climbed in, Joe's foot came in contact with the owner of the ghostly hand that had upset him. Going down after the body, he abruptly touched bottom, the water scarcely coming to his shoulders. When he came up he was holding what appeared to be a boy. Grasping the canoe, he made for shore with the double load.

Pulling the skiff up on shore, he laid the other burden on the dry grass. As he did so a clanking, metallic sound drew his attention, and there, firmly clamped on the boy's ankle, was one of his large traps. The blood was freely oozing from the wound it had made, so Joe was assured there was still life. Hurriedly he removed the iron jaws, tipped the canoe free of water, laid the boy gently in, called the dog, and paddled home.

The warm, leaping flames in the fireplace forced open the eyes of the chilled victim. The first words came in the Chippewa language: "Who dwells in this teepee of trees?" Joe understood.

Taking his hunting knife, he cut away the drenched moccasin, ripped up the leg of the fawn skin pants, rolling it above the knee. And a brown hand came down to prevent him from pushing it further. This act he did not notice, but when his unaccustomed eyes beheld the contour of the exposed limb a thrill of admiration colored his face, and he quickly looked into a pair of wonderful, deep blue eyes overflowing with modesty.

Carefully dressing the damaged ankle, he went to a chest and selected a fine wool union suit, placing it on the bed in an adjoining room, and when he returned the patient was sitting up. "Come, put on some dry clothes and sleep," he said.

A reply came quickly. "How can I, a motherless girl, partake of a lone man's teepee? Or are you really the friend your eyes speak?"

"Yes, you will find that Trapper Joe is truly a friend!"

Up and down the short pathway in front of his door he paced. The darkness was never more in harmony with his thoughts, nor was his voice more pleading to his friends, the pines, than on this bewitching night. For he was to lose his prize in the morning, and the night was far too short to solve his problem. Too soon came the fleeting rays of the sun over the tops of the lake-surrounded forest, to glorify the birth of a new day.

The cabin door opened, and stepping to his side was his night's inspiration. Her voice was low and sweet in its expression of thanks: "Indeed you are a noble friend, great trapper of Sunrise Island, and I need you more. Listen closely, my story is quickly told; then you will take me far away. I was a wee papoose when my grieving mother gave me to the Chippewa Indians. And though my parents were both white, I have naught but the traits of these brown people. Last night while standing in front of my teepee, wondering where the moon would sleep, it was past the hour of waking when the son of Wild Wolf, our great Chief, came from out of the darkness, clasped me in his strong arms and, voicing his passionate love, carried me toward his canoe. As he neared the shore of the lake a thorn from a tree pierced his foot. Throwing me to the ground, he moaned with pain as no brave should! So I bounded away into the lake to hide my trail, but a heavy trap gripped my foot to hold me back. I would not cry out, for pain does not burn my courage. When I would try to swim the heavy trap drew me beneath the water, but there at least I could hide. Then you came, my friend, with the same blood as I, and I thank you from my doubly beating heart. Now I must haste away before Wa-ke-a comes. Will you take me to the farther shore where dwells the Godly Father Pirot, that he may instruct me?"

The request was mentally granted by Trapper Joe, but his heart was pounding with the thrill of the trapper. Had not his trap retained this valued prize? And so he voiced it to the girl: "Your name I shall call Ne-na-na, because you came to me from the bottom depths of the lake. Now I ask, will Ne-na-na return with me after calling on Father Pirot, as my wife? I have never before known love; can it be so?"

Blushing, she took a seat in his swiftest canoe. "Yes"—and she smiled—"I will never be trapped by a better trapper or brave."

By Comrade Howard
King, Wisconsin

GRANDMOTHER COLBURN

Grandmother had been sound asleep, but awoke with the certainty that a noise in the lean-to had disturbed her. No question about it, someone was out there, and that was where the barrel of salt was kept. Salt wasn't easy to get. Grandfather would have to go after the marauder. "There's someone in the lean-to, Alonzo," she whispered.

Alonzo didn't respond, and she reached one arm over to his side of the four-poster to give him a nudge. But Grandfather wasn't there, and now she was wide awake enough to recall that he had gone over to sit up with Neighbor Turner who was ill. Well, she wasn't going to lie there and let a thief get away with whatever he fancied. So Grandmother got up and lighted a candle. She was quiet about it, but the light must have shone through a chink in the door and warned the prowler, for when she entered the lean-to nobody was there. But someone had been there without a doubt, for leaning up against the barrel of salt was a pair of buckskin breeches, a string tied around the bottom of each leg, and each leg filled with salt from the Colburn's salt barrel.

Grandmother looked at the breeches, then at the salt barrel, which was now about half full. She went over to the door leading outdoors and buttoned it. Then she came back, picked up the buckskin breeches and dumped the contents of one leg back into the barrel. After that, she carried the breeches over to the door, opened it, set them outside, came in, and buttoned the door once more and went back to bed.

THE WHITEWATER KISS

The village of Whitewater was coming along nicely in the fall of 1840. A tavern had just been completed. Reverend Daniel Smith had just founded the Congregational Church. Thanks to the militant action of Governor Dodge, the Indians no longer scared anyone—much. The immigrants, now blessed with a store, a new post office, a blacksmith shop, and a schoolhouse, prepared to face the winter. It was a year of abundant harvest; cellars were full of garden treasures, of hazel and hickory nuts. Each week brought nearly every family tidings of the outside world in copies of the *Milwaukee Sentinel.*

So it came to pass that the pioneer mothers and fathers, believing that by cultivating the fine arts their youngsters would help prevent coarseness and vulgarity from gaining a foothold in society, circulated this petition: *We, the undersigned, convinced that a well-conducted dancing school will develop the more refined feelings and graces of our natures, and at the same time afford amusement to the young, do agree to pay the sums set opposite our names toward defraying the expenses of said dancing school, to be held at the house of Freeman L. Pratt, in the village of Whitewater—the school to be conducted according to the strictest rules of propriety.*

The necessary money was soon raised. The Murrays of Beloit, both gentlemen of cultivated tastes and good morals, were engaged as teachers. The dancing school was a great success. The Pratts furnished refreshments—temperate, to be sure, but in a style "most grateful to the palate." Perhaps a few of the young men would now and then absent themselves from the circle upon some pretext or other. The account books at Stanton's store bore evidence of one mild orgy: *Eggs, liquor, and cigars, 13 cents.* But such indulgences provoked no incident.

As winter gave way to spring, the dancing school committee decided, as a crowning glory to the enterprise, to give a grand ball. The scholars and their invited guests assembled. The Murrays provided their most inspiriting music, the Pratts their most delectable repast. Mirth and glee filled the winged hours, and civilized merriment reigned supreme.

But suddenly the tide of mirth was stayed. A venturous youth, impressed by a mischief-loving spirit, did dare, with encircling arm, to press upon the lips of a fair lady present an unmistakable kiss!

A shuddering silence. The music stopped. Dancers drew back from the gross fellow. Would no one of the company take the obvious step? Yes, one would—an elderly gentleman, possessed of that nice sense of chivalry, propriety and fitness that characterized the old school. To him this public kiss was an outrage, an insult to the house and company; and furthermore it was in direct violation of the rules of the school. He ordered the offender from the room. The young man stood firm. Then the old school gentleman seized the profligate by the collar, and with the assistance of some few others of the more virtuous guests, gave him what the vulgar might call the "bum's rush."

Now the young man resented such crude treatment, and after nursing his injured pride for a time, entered complaint against the prime movers in his expulsion, for assault and battery. He retained as counsel Judge Noggle, who was opposed in the case by the Hon. James H. Knowlton. A jury having been summoned and sworn, the trial commenced.

Knowlton claimed that since it had been agreed that the dancing school should be conducted according to the strictest rules of propriety, and that kissing a lady in a ballroom was against all rules of decency, therefore the defendants were not only entirely justified in serving as informal bouncers, but they deserved for so doing high praise as guardians of public morality.

It was now time for Noggle to reply for the plaintiff. He rose splendidly to the occasion. First he pointed out that the defendants were not the sole managers of the dancing school, and had not the sole right to determine concerning the propriety or impropriety of any act for their committee. He further, and most emphatically, contended that a kiss was not improper.

"Kissing," the liberal Noggle proclaimed, "was the first thing taught us by our dear mothers. Kissing has been practiced, furthermore, in savage, barbarous, as well as civilized lands, in all ages, in all climes. Kissing has never been and never will be forbidden by laws either civil or moral. Gentlemen of the jury, I submit, finally, that each of you has kissed, and that each of you has been kissed!"

After this powerful plea, of course, the jury at once returned a verdict in favor of the young man. It did more. On that brave day in 1841 it "judicially decided the legality of a kiss," a point which from that time has remained unquestioned in Whitewater, and has long since become incorporated into the common law of the vicinity.

Told by Prosper Craveth

THE KISSING BUG

The kissing bug is one of the chief pests of Wisconsin. It is known outside the boundaries of the state, but has appeared to thrive best in Badger territory. The bug was said to be first introduced here by Gophers coming to fish in the Wisconsin lakes. The bug is hardly larger than the point of a pin, and is thought to be carried by adverse winds. Hardly a community has escaped an epidemic of kissing bug bites. When these occur the result is always dangerous, for those persons bitten will rush about in a circular pattern, kissing any object or person in view. When entire communities are bitten the ordinary occupations of the people must cease and for a short period only frantic kissing is carried on. Strangers to Wisconsin have often been surprised and confused, when, coming into a town infected by the kissing bug, they are immediately kissed. Research scientists at the University of Wisconsin are trying to determine the effect of the kissing bug on student life and interests. A sample force of students has volunteered for testing.

chapter 6

INDIAN PLACE LEGENDS *

Wisconsin Indians had many stories, myths, legends, about the springs, streams, lakes, prairies, woodlands, rocks, hills, and valleys of the region. In the centuries of their occupation of their homeland, and as a result of their life experiences and culture, a wealth of tales and legends became attached to many of the scenic landmarks of their environment. A knowledge of most of these is now lost to their descendants, who have long been segregated by the government on Indian reservations or confined to tracts of land long removed from the lands of their ancestors. The tales presented here represent the whole state, and give a taste of the breadth and beauty of the Indian imagination.

LAKE MICHIGAN
(Sauk Indian Legend)

In creating the world Getci Munito placed a lot of small lakes where Lake Michigan (Kotcikum) now lies. These were of all sizes —some very large and some very small. After a while these lakes began to quarrel with each other—each wanted the best place for himself. This went on for some time. Then they finally decided to

* Collected by the Folklore Section of the Federal Writers' Project of the Works Progress Administration, edited by C. E. Brown.

get together in a council to settle their disputes. The outcome of this meeting was that all the lakes, large and small, were merged into one great lake for the common good, and now, so the Indians say, we have Lake Michigan. This lake, although generally peaceful and quiet, sometimes gets very rough and wild. This occurs when some of the large and small lakes merged into the great lake become restless and turbulent because they wish to be free again.

WISAKA RACES THE BUFFALO

(Mascouten Myth)

The world had already existed for some time when Wisaka was born. He lived alone with his brother Yapatao and their Grandmother Masukumigo Kwao, the Earthwoman.

Wisaka roamed all over the earth's surface killing many great serpents. At length all the surviving serpents gathered in a council. To this meeting they invited the Grandmother.

"Grandmother," said the Underworld Serpents, "your older grandson is abusing us badly, and we want to destroy him in some way."

"It is useless to try it," answered the old woman, "Wisaka is immortal. Yet maybe you have the power to kill his younger brother."

So the serpents planned to kill the brother in revenge.

They challenged Wisaka to race a young buffalo. This was to get him out of the way. The race course was to encircle Kotcikum (Lake Michigan). As soon as the contestants had rounded the opposite shore of the lake, the serpents attacked Yapatao, and Wisaka could hear his younger brother calling for help. Then Wisaka ran all the faster. As he drew near home he could hear his younger brother calling again, "Oh, my elder brother, Wisaka, they are killing me!" Wisaka ran very fast. He passed the buffalo, but when he arrived at home it was too late; they had already killed his younger brother. They had skinned him and carried his hide away. Then Wisaka went into mourning. He blackened his face and attacked and killed the underworld monsters.

The track made by Wisaka and the buffalo in their race around Lake Michigan could once be plainly seen. At one time the Indians followed it as a trail in going to their villages or on war or hunting expeditions.

THE RED BANKS
(Green Bay Myth)

In the beginning Earthmaker created four men. These four brothers were Kunuga, Henanga, Hagaga, and Nanyiga. These first four he made chiefs of the Thunderbirds. He opened the heavens in order that they might see the earth. He gave them a tobacco plant, and he gave them fire. The earth was to be theirs to live upon. The four brothers flew down to earth and landed in the branches of a tree. The place was at Within Lake, at Red Banks on the shore of Green Bay. They then lit on the ground and began walking toward the east. There they selected a camp ground. There they started the first fire. One brother went to hunt for food. He took the bow and arrows which Earthmaker had given them and he killed and brought back a deer. Not having any cooking vessels, they roasted the meat over the fire on sharp sticks.

At this camp ground the Thunderers were joined by other clans. These obtained fire from them. The first to join them were the War clan people. They came from the west. Then came the Deer clan, the Snake clan, and the Elk clan. The Bear clan, the Fish clan, the Water-spirit clan, and the Buffalo clan followed them. All of the other clans came. Together they formed a tribe, the Hochungara (Winnebago). They began to intermarry. The men of the upper clans married women of the lower clans. They cut poles and stripped bark from the trees and with these built wigwams. From clay mixed with slippery elm bark they made cooking vessels. They formed a village. The members of the upper clans were the chiefs. They organized a council lodge in which the members of each clan had their place.

In the beginning the Thunderers were very powerful. They made the valleys and the hills. With their clubs they made dents in the hills. They planted the tobacco, and with its crushed leaves, which they threw into the fire, they made offerings to Earthmaker. And Earthmaker gave to the Hochungara his blessings.

THE LOST GIRLS
(Sturgeon Bay Legend)

A Menominee Indian family were living near Sturgeon Bay. In this family were two girls. These girls liked to play on the sandy shore of the bay and to swim in its waters. One day their father went to call for them but could neither see them nor make them hear his calls. He found their footprints in the sand leading to the water. A big hairy snake lived in the waters of the bay. He had seized the children while they were swimming and had carried them them away to his den under the water. The father was very sorrowful.

He resolved to ask the assistance of Manabus. For six days he fasted and prayed. At the end of his fast Manabus appeared to him in a dream. He told him not to worry more, that he would rescue and return the little girls.

Manabus summoned the Thunderers from their homes in the north. These great birds were the enemies of the hairy serpent. They dove into the water and found the white clay-plastered wigwam of the monster. They broke down the entrance to his den and killed the big snake. The children were within. They were safe; the serpent had not yet eaten them. They were returned to their father's wigwam none the worse for their experience. Their parents were overcome with joy at their return and offered their thanks to Manabus.

Later the Indians could see a great cloud over the bay. That was the Thunderers carrying away the hairy snake. (Menominee)

PORT DES MORTS
(Death's Door Legend)

In peace and plenty the Noquets had long lived on the shores of the islands of the Potawatomi chain at the head of the Green Bay Peninsula. Hunger they knew not. The lake was full of fish; in the wood was an abundance of deer, bear, turkeys, and pigeons; and flocks of ducks and geese frequented the lake and bays. Of all the islands, Washington was the great game preserve. Never did the great forests on its back refuse food to the hungry man. Hence, one day when a band of Potawatomi who resided on the neighboring point of Door County invaded the land of the Noquets while the latter were away, the spirit of trouble spread his mantle over the peaceful isles.

The Indian wanted a deed to the land, though he held no abstract purporting to show how it had passed from hand to hand down from the original grantor; nevertheless, his rage was quite as great as, if not greater than, would be that of his white brother if he found someone calmly appropriating for his own use the home he called his own.

The injury and insult must be wiped out. Fortunately or unfortunately, there were no courts and lawyers. The poor redskin had recourse only to bloodshed. War was declared by the simple process of the Noquet warriors embarking in canoes for a raid on the Potawatomi. But the medicine men were failures, or else the braves neglected, in their haste, to propitiate the manido, for they had only gone a portion of the four miles which separated them from their enemies when a breath of wind struck them, the forerunner of a hurricane which swept the waters in green masses over the frail craft.

Of all the brave band which went forth, not one was ever seen alive. To the wives, the mothers, the fathers waiting on the shore, no word came back. Day by day they gazed over the strait. And then their warriors came home to them. The bodies were found tossed up on the beach of Detroit Island, and friends and relatives could do no more than hurry them to hastily prepared graves. Here, in an open space, so the story goes, they were interred.

THE WATER MONSTER
(Lake Winnebago Legend)

A very large fish (some say a sturgeon) lived in Lake Winnebago in the early days when the Winnebago had their villages on its shores. This monster had a great appetite for moose, elk, and deer. He lay in wait for them in the river channel where they were accustomed to swim from one side of the stream to the other. Then he dragged them under the water and devoured them, horns, hide, hoofs, and all. Of course no Indian would cross the channel at that place.

After may years of such killings this huge fish was found by some Indians, floating on the surface of the water near the shore. He was quite dead, and in searching for the cause they found the large branching antler of an elk protruding from his stomach. He had eaten the elk, but because of its extraordinary size he had been unable to digest its horns.

The Indians believe that some of the descendants of this monster are even now inhabiting Lake Winnebago.

BUTTE DES MORTS
(Legends of the Hill of the Dead)

Legends giving different locations as to the place where the "great battle" was fought between rival Indian tribes are related by descendants of the early settlers of Butte des Morts. Most of these stories are probably true. Not one, but several battles have been fought in this territory between various tribes. The abundance of easily procurable food and other comforts supplied by the forests, marshes, and waters made this region highly attractive to the aborigines. Situated as it is on a through route of travel, and known far and wide as a land of plenty, it is inevitable that there would be controversy among the rival tribes, followed by battle.

Mas-pah-quo-to-noh—Hill of the Dead—has always been revered as sacred ground by the Indians. Here were held elaborate and long-drawn-out ceremonies, and much medicine was made. Here were held the dances and feasts by which they celebrated seasonal events or inaugurated tribal activities. The stately mournful booming of the dance drum or the jolly rhythmic beat of the rattle and water drum led the cadence of their songs.

Each nation, in turn, buried its dead on or near this hill. The bodies of those who perished away from home were brought back to Grand Butte and interred with fitting ceremony. Bundle burials show that the dead were not always brought back the same season. The fact that they were eventually brought back and buried here indicated conclusively the veneration in which this ground was held by these people. M'Nepoose was here! M'Nepoose would watch over his children!

The Hill of the Dead, here referred to, was situated near the shore of Butte des Morts Lake, west of Oshkosh.

BIG FOOT'S TRACKS

(Lake Geneva Story)

Big Foot was the chief of the Potawatomi village located in 1831 where Fontana is now situated, at the western end of beautiful Lake Geneva. This lake bears his name on some early maps. The name "Maunguzet" (Big Foot) was given to the chief by a relative.

On one occasion Big Foot was out hunting in the wintertime. The snow on the frozen lake surface was about eighteen inches deep, and the chief was wearing snowshoes to facilitate his progress. While trudging along he came upon the tracks of a deer. It was running and was being chased by a wolf.

The running deer followed the shore of the lake, and the hunter followed its tracks. After traveling quite a distance he came to the fallen deer. The wolf had killed it but had abandoned his prey because of the approaching hunter. Big Foot returned to his Lake Geneva village with the deer across his shoulders.

His brother-in-law, who was also out on the lake on some mission, came upon the large deep tracks which Big Foot had made and followed them to the Indian village.

When he learned that these were tracks made by the chief he jokingly gave to him the name "Maunguzet" (Big Foot), and this name ever afterwards clung to Big Foot. (Potawatomi)

THE WATER MONSTER OF LAKE KOSHKONONG

Many years ago the Mascouten, or Prairie Potawatomi, had villages on the shores of Lake Koshkonong. A water monster of great power and terrible form dwelt in its depths and made havoc with every Indian canoe. No Indian dared to attempt to cross the lake from shore to shore even in mild weather, because of fear of this destructive denizen of its waters. No white men came to grief; the lake passage was unlucky for red men only.

Near the narrows of the lake rises a high rocky hill, and near it there is an island on which the Indians camped when trapping muskrats. On the west side of the hill there was a place where no Indian could cross. All who attempted it were sure to be drowned.

Once there were two Potawatomi brothers who concluded that the story of the water monster was false. One day, starting in opposite directions, they set out to navigate the lake in their canoes. All the Indians watched them in fear. They expected that they would never be seen again. Soon a big wind arose, and it was so strong and fierce that it even blew the ducks that were flying overhead into the water. The Indians in the camp sang sacred songs for the well-being of the two boys, but night came and they did not return.

The two canoes were later found capsized. After some time several white men told the Potawatomi that they had found the bodies of the boys floating in the lake. There was white clay in their nostrils and ears, a sure sign that the Lake Koshkonong monster had caught them and drowned them. Some Indians are afraid of the waters of Lake Koshkonong to this day, believing that the water monster still prowls about its shores.

Before the Potawatomi came, Indians of the Sauk tribe lived on the shore of this lake. They had enemies, probably the Illinois, who once trapped a number of them on an island. They were unable to escape, as the island was partly surrounded by a large swamp. The Sauk were here exterminated by the arrows of the enemy, and some also perished through starvation. This happening gave the lake a bad name.

THE SPIRIT RACCOON
(Lake Mendota Legend)

Many centuries ago two Winnebago hunters near the ford of the Yahara (Catfish) River at Lake Monona saw in the sandy soil the tracks of an animal, unmistakably those of a raccoon. They were of unusually large size. The hunters followed them to a wooded point on the eastern shore of Lake Mendota, at present known as Maple

Bluff. Here the raccoon had found a hiding place in a hollow log. One of the Indians fitted an arrow into his bowstring and was about to shoot when the animal called to him in human language and besought him not to shoot. It informed him that it was a spirit animal and that a dire calamity would befall him if he killed it. The Indian wisely desisted. The other hunter had no such scruples. He said that he did not care whether it was a spirit raccoon (which he did not believe) or not; he was going to kill it, as he was very hungry. So he shot and killed the animal. He skinned and cut up the raccoon, then built a fire and roasted its flesh. Of this he ate heartily, his friend refusing to partake of this feast.

The day being warm, the two Indians lay down under a tree and slept. After a while, the Indian who had eaten the flesh of the spirit raccoon awoke. He was very thirsty and descended to a large spring once located at the base of the bluff. Kneeling at its rim, he began to drink its water. The more he drank, the more thirsty he became. Finally, his thirst became so intense that in desperation he waded out into the lake. As soon as the water rose above his middle, his dreadful thirst ceased. It returned again the moment he ventured into shallower water or tried to go ashore. In the lake he was obliged to remain until night came, and he then sank into its waters. He was transformed into a fish. His hunter friend stood on the lake bank but was unable to help him.

For many years Indians camping near this bluff have heard after dark, in the deep water, the splashing of a great fish—the unfortunate Indian—followed by the beating of a war drum and the singing of his war song.

From this legend Lake Mendota obtained its Indian name, Wonkshekhomikla, "where the Indian lies."

There is another version of this story in which the animal discovered in a hollow tree was a catfish instead of a raccoon.

THE BATTLE AT DEVILS LAKE
(Winnebago Legend)

A quarrel once arose between the water spirits, or underwater panthers, who had a den in the depths of Devils Lake, and the Thunderbirds. These animals were called Wakhakeera, and the Thunderers were called Wakunja. The great birds, flying high above the lake's surface, hurled their eggs (arrows or thunderbolts) into the waters and on the bluffs. The water monsters threw up great rocks and waterspouts from the bottom of the lake.

This terrible fight continued for days. The falling eggs tore down the trees and split off great pieces of rock, and the tumbled-down and cracked rocky surface of the surrounding bluffs stands as evidence of this great struggle.

The Thunderers were finally victorious and flew away to their homes and nests in the North. No Indian dared to approach the lake for a long time. The water spirits were not all killed, and some are in Devils Lake to this day.

It was a custom of the early Indians to make tobacco offerings to the spirits of this lake, depositing tobacco on boulders on the shore or strewing it on the surface of the water. The Winnebago (Hochungara) name for this lake was Tawacunchukdah, sacred lake. There are a number of Winnebago myths and legends concerning Devils Lake.

THE BIRTH OF THE BUFFALO CLAN
(*Winnebago Myth*)

Devils Lake was the place of birth of the Buffalo clan of the Winnebago tribe. Once very long ago a great commotion came to the waters of this spirit lake. The waters churned and boiled, then a dark object appeared in its middle. It was a very long time before it came to the surface. Then it swam ashore. The waters now became quiet. It had horns, a tail, a hairy hide, and four legs—it was a buffalo. It shook itself, it walked about, and it ate grass and leaves. It became a man; it was the father of the Buffalo clan, Tcega.

The Buffalo clansmen had a particular function of acting as public orators and as intermediaries between the chief and the tribe. This clan and the Water-spirit clan were brother clans, serving each other in various ways and on various occasions.

THE SIOUX WAR PARTY
(*Green Lake Legend*)

A long time ago, oh, more than a thousand years ago, a war party of Sioux Indians came up the Wisconsion River from Iowa in canoes. They carried their canoes overland from Puckaway Lake to Green Lake and camped overnight at the Sugar Loaf. There were many Sioux in this war party, and they decided to attack the village of their enemies, the Winnebago, on the opposite shore. In this village the men were away on a hunt. Only the old men, boys, and the women were at home. The Sioux hoped to obtain many scalps, prisoners, and much plunder by attacking the Winnebago town.

In the morning, in full war paint, they embarked in their canoes and singing their war songs, paddled toward the south shore. When near the middle of the lake, their canoes commenced to go round and round, and then they went down.

The water spirits, who had a den in the bottom of this lake, were good friends of the Winnebago, who had made tobacco and other offerings to them. They did not wish to see them slaughtered. They caused the great whirlpool which overturned and sucked down the Sioux canoes filled with bloodthirsty warriors.

After that the Winnebago found dead Indians and smashed canoes and stone axes, flint arrows and copper knives all along the shores of the Lake. (Winnebago)

THE WISCONSIN RIVER
(*Winnebago Legend*)

The bed of the Wisconsin River was formed by an immense serpent. He was a manitou and had his home in the great forests near the Big Lake. His powers were very great, and all of the other animals were afraid of him.

Once this great serpent started to travel from his home in the northern forests toward the sea. In crawling over the land his great body wore a deep groove, or channel, through the forests and prairies. Into this bed the water flowed. When he moved his tail great masses of water splashed from the channel through the forests and formed lakes. Many lakes and ponds were made in this way. All animal life fled before him as he traveled. Other less powerful serpents made haste to get out of his course, and they fled in all directions before him. Thus came the beds of the smaller streams which now pour their waters into the Wisconsin. In places where the water pours over falls there were rocks in the path of the great serpent, so he crawled down over them. The water below is deep. It now rushes over the rocks, making the same loud noise which he made.

Near the Wisconsin Dells he encountered a great body of rock. Finding a crack in this, he thrust his head into it and rent the stone wall by the contortions of his powerful body. The queer shapes of these rocks are due to his struggle to get through them. Where the banks of the river are very wide he rested. Below the Dells he changed his course of travel to the west, finally reaching the Mississippi River.

The Winnebago name for the Dells was Neehahkecoonaherah, "where the rocks strike together."

MAIDEN ROCK

(Mississippi River Legend)

Wenona was the beautiful daughter of Red Wing, a Dakota chief, whose village was on the banks of the Mississippi River. Many braves of the Dakota tribe came to woo this fair maiden. But Wenona had given her heart to a young Chippewa chief, White Eagle, whom she had met on the top of the great towering Mississippi River bluffs.

Her aged father would not listen to her pleadings for permission to wed this young lover. He was a member of an alien tribe whom the Dakota hated fiercely and with whom they were almost constantly at war. Red Wing said that he would rather kill his daughter than have her become the wife of a brave of the Chippewa nation. He promised to have his warriors track down and kill the Chippewa lover. He had selected for her husband Chief Kewaunee, an old man of the Dakota tribe.

While White Eagle waited for Wenona on the top of the high

bluff her father was arousing his warriors to hunt down the hated Chippewa. Wenona fled to warn him of his danger. White Eagle was overjoyed to see his loved one. She told him that she had pleaded with her father to be allowed to become his wife and had failed and that he was sending his warriors to kill him. Her father had betrothed her to Old Chief Kewaunee.

As White Eagle was entreating her to flee with him to his own people, the Dakota warriors had ascended the bluff and were surrounding the lovers. A deadly arrow shot by one of the Dakota warriors pierced the heart of White Eagle, and he fell at Wenona's feet. Gathering his body in her arms she held him while his life blood gushed away. Then Wenona went to the edge of the bluff, and before anyone could stop her she cast herself from its edge down to the rocks below. She preferred to go to the spirit world with her lover rather than share the wigwam of Kewaunee.

Her father, who really loved her, recovered her crushed body from the rocks. He mourned her loss until the end of his life. In remembrance of Wenona's sacrifice a bluff and a village on the Upper Mississippi today bear the name of Maiden Rock.

THUNDER MOUNTAIN
(*Potawatomi Legend*)

Now regarding the Thunder Mountain in the western part of Marinette County: Thunder is a large bird like an Eagle, only much larger. And when this bird was created it was made to have power in order to defend us from the great serpents, who wanted to kill and eat the human race. It was also to moisten the earth for vegetation. Thunderers, we call these great birds. One of them is called Chequah. And the mountain we call Bikwaki, so Thunder Mountain is Chequah Bikwaki.

Many, many years have gone by since the Hill received its name. In the beginning of its Indian history the Thunderbirds used to make their nests here and sit on their two eggs until their young were hatched. Some Indians many years ago in the summer time visited the Hill and were surprised to find several pairs of young

Thunders. It was always the custom with Indians to offer tobacco for friendship and safety.

And later on in another visit by the Indians a pond was discovered on the top of the Hill. And it was dangerous. The Serpent who lives under the Hill had caused this pond to be so that he could sun himself when the sky was clear. And on a sunny clear day he was sunning, probably asleep, when a lone Thunder discovered him and decided to catch him alive and carry him off. So the Thunder came down from the sky and caught the Serpent. The Thunder would carry him high. The Serpent, struggling, would carry the Thunder back down on the pond.

At that time an Indian hunter who was passing happened to look to the top of the Hill and to his surprise saw the two struggling, and went up to witness the great fight. He was noticed by them, and the Thunderbird spoke and said, "My friend, help me, and shoot the Serpent with your arrow, and I will make you a great man!" The Serpent also spoke and said, "Help me, and shoot the Thunder, and I'll promise you my friendship to the end of all time!" The Indian did not know which one to help, so he shut his eyes and shot an arrow toward the fighters and shot the Thunder. That shot weakened the Thunder and he fell down and was taken under the Hill as a prisoner. The Thunderbird is still there, and the Hill is called Chequah Bikwaki. Whenever there is going to be a thunderstorm lightning is seen flashing from the Thunder Mountain.

THE WINDOW OF WAUCHESAH

(Thunder Mountain Legend)

Little Hill, or Little Mountain, is a high mountain of solid rock on the Peshtigo River. Its Menominee Indian name is Wau-che-sah. Surrounding it is a region of small forest openings and barren plains. The Thunderers, coming from their homes in the west, set fire to these plains by the flashes of lightning which issued from their eyes, and they keep the region burned over as they desire it to be.

At the beginning of this hill and ledge there is a small lake, a deep fountain of clear cold water. This lake the Indians believe to be a

window of the mountain. In the lake there is the den of a Great
White Bear, the king of all bears. Through this window the bear
observes what is going on in the world and keeps an eye on his
enemies, the Thunderers. (Menominee)

THE BATTLE OF THE PIERCED FOREHEAD
(Menominee River Legend)

It is known that a battle was fought on the present site of Marinette
and Menominee and that it was a sanguinary struggle. Mr. Louis
Bernard, a Menominee Indian residing in Menominee, whose fore-
fathers were involved, tells this story of the fight:

It was springtime. All nature was waking from the long winter's
sleep; the grass was green, trees were budding, and the birds were
nesting. In the forest the young deer followed close to its mother
and the black bear cub romped about the mouth of the winter den.
In the water the fish were running upstream to spawn. And with the
first return of the fish came the great sturgeon, the prize food fish
of the Indian.

They were speared, netted, and trapped until each band had an
abundance for immediate use as well as fish to dry. But this year
a band of Indians, living on the banks of the Menominee, had built
a stone dam across the river. It had been well constructed and the
sturgeon were stopped so that none got past it up the stream. Under
the direction of the chief, who had planned the dam, his band reaped
a rich harvest.

While this arrangement was very satisfactory to his people, to the
other bands farther up the river it was very annoying. They waited
patiently, thinking that when the lower group had secured enough
fish for their own use, they would demolish the dam. Days passed
and still no sturgeon came upstream. The run would soon be over,
and unless the dam was torn down there would be no sturgeon for
those in the upper villages.

It so happened that the Indian band located next above the dam
builders had for its chief a brother of the chief of the lower tribe,
for all were Menominee. As time passed, this man considered that
for the welfare of those in his band he must take some means to

secure sturgeon. He called to him his son, aged twelve years, and instructed him:

"My brother, your uncle, is chief of the band below us. You shall go to him and give him my message. Say to him that I, his brother, send my greetings and would tell him that in my camp there is much hunger. For the meat of the last season's hunt is now gone, and as yet we have made no catch of the great sturgeon. Tell him that I, his brother, ask him as a favor, because his band is fat and sleek and has caught and put by many sturgeon, I ask him again to open the dam and let some of the great fish swim by. This I bid you tell him."

The lad started on his trip. It was not hazardous, nor had he much to fear. Was he not going to his father's brother, his own uncle?

When he came to the camp on the lower river, he spoke with boys of his own age and let it be known that he had a message for the chief. This information reached the ears of the chief and he summoned the youngster to appear before him.

"What would you with me?" he inquired, as he sat on his couch in his cabin. The boy stood before him and dared not speak until he was thus addressed. He was now free to deliver his message. This he did, speaking the words that his father had told him. When he was done he stood in silence waiting for whatever reply his uncle might wish to send back to his brother, the boy's father.

The chief sat still for some moments, then as though suddenly resolved, he leaped up, crying, "This is my answer" and grasped the loose skin of the boy's forehead in one hand, drawing it away from the skull. Then with the other hand he seized a flint knife and with one stroke skewered the weapon in the skin.

"Thou shalt take this, my answer, to my brother, your father!" he cried.

In shame the boy crept from the camp and started on the homeward trail. The pain of the wound was not great, but his anguish of spirit and shame at the insult was unbearable. Nor dared he remove the knife. It was a message and not for a boy of his age to tamper with. At the most he could but wipe away the blood which ran down into his eyes and mouth. But the knife remained.

Though the distance between the two camps was not great, and he could easily have reached his father's tepee before dark, he lingered long on the way so that when he came to it, it was long after sunset. Taking advantage of an opportunity, he crept under the edge of the lodge and lay down on his bed. As he lay among the skins there came to him his mother, who inquired if he were too tired from his journey to eat something. No, he was not hungry. She went away. Later she returned. Was he sick that he lay so close among the fur? No, he was not sick. All the time he kept his face hidden.

Then came his father, and shortly the whole miserable story came out. At the sight of the knife in the skin of his son's forehead the rage of the chief was great. Nothing could wipe out this insult save the blood of his brother and all of the members of his brother's band.

At once runners were dispatched to other bands farther up the stream, asking for their aid in an attack upon the dam builders. And the asking was not in vain. Shortly a great number of Indians gathered and moved down the river toward the camp of the chief who offered the insult.

They did not hurry. The attack was well-planned. By canoe they came down as far as what is now the Old Boom House, and here they disembarked under cover of darkness, for they journeyed at night. Then they stole up the hill where are now the golf grounds. Here they planned an ambuscade; with the first coming of light they set upon the other band and in a long hard fight killed every member of the village and avenged the insult of the Pierced Forehead.

PINE LAKE

(Forest County Legend)

In Pine Lake, near Hiles, there is a line of submerged rocks. The story of these rocks is that when pursued by an enemy, probably the dreaded Sioux, the Indians of this region would come to the bank of the lake and cross on the hidden stones.

Being beneath the surface, the enemy would not see them. Reaching the lake shore, the attackers were dumbfounded to be unable to find any trace of their intended victims. It was as if the water, the air, the wood, or helpful spirits had swallowed them up or borne them safely away. For them a veil of mystery surrounded this lake.

NANEBOZO AND THE BEAR
(*Legend of Crawling Stone Lake*)

Nanebozo was walking in the woods near this well-known lake when he was chased by a big black bear. He had once angered this bear by whacking him over the nose with a stick when he sat asleep under a big tree. The bear remembered the injury and was determined to have his revenge when he again met Nanebozo. His opportunity to do so had come. As Nanebozo ran toward the water, his only avenue of escape from the angry bear, he gathered up an armful of stones. As he stepped into the water he dropped or threw them before him, one after the other, using them as stepping stones. Over these stones the baffled bear dared not follow Nanebozo, who thus safely crossed to the other shore and escaped his pursuer. Here he "made a nose" at the bear.

Some of these stones still remain in position in Crawling Stone Lake in Vilas County and mark the flight long ago of the Indian culture hero, Nanebozo. (Chippewa)

OLD LADY LAKE

Smith Lake, a short distance north of Hayward, the old people among the Chippewa Indians know as "Old Lady Lake." Some Chippewa, who were traveling northward over a trail from the present locality of Hayward, had in their party a very old Indian woman. She was very infirm, and there appeared to be no doubt that she would be unable to stand the hardships of trail travel, so when they reached the shores of Smith Lake they made her as comfortable as possible and left her to die. No one ever knew what became of her. For many years after that Indians traveling over the trail saw, or thought they saw, the spirit of the old lady when they passed the shores of ths lake. The spirit harmed no one, but the Indians were never desirous of lingering long in the vicinity. (Chippewa)

THE THUNDERBIRD AT THE POST
(*Chippewa Legend*)

The Indians believe that thunder is the voice of an immense invisible bird that comes at times to warn them that the Great Spirit is displeased with something they have done, and that it always comes when the country is already storm-vexed, as the time is then opportune for this mighty bird to add its voice to the naturally saddened feelings of the people, thereby making its presence more effective. The lightning they believed to be flashes from the eyes of this enormous bird, and when the storm is fierce and the flashes are vivid it is taken as a warning that their bad deeds are many and that their retribution must be great. When an Indian is killed they believe it is a judgment sent by the Great Spirit through the agency of this mysterious bird.

They call this bird Chenemeke. When they see distant flashes of lightning and do not hear the voice, as they believe it to be, of this great bird, they know it is at a distance, but they still believe that it is teaching a lesson to a distant people and will soon be with them. But should a storm pass by without the voice and the flashes coming near them they are happy again, for they feel relieved, believing that the bird is not angry with them. They firmly believe this bird to be an agency of the Great Spirit, which is kept moving about to keep an eye on the wrongdoings of the people. When a tree is stricken and set on fire, the lesson which it wishes to impart has been given, and the rain is sent to prevent the fire from destroying the country.

There is a point of land in this part of the country that the Indians call Pa-qua-a-wong, meaning a forest destroyed by the great Thunderbird. It is now almost barren, the timber which was once upon it having been destroyed by lightning. The Indians believed that the stormbird had ruined this forest to show its wrath, and that the people might profit by the lesson. A hunting party of Indians was once caught on this barren land in a thunderstorm and took refuge under the trunk of a fallen tree which had been sufficiently burnt on its under side to give them shelter. One of the party, in his hurry to get out of the rain, left his gun standing against the log. The lightning struck it, running down the barrel and twisting it into odd shapes and destroying it; and the owner of this gun was thereafter pointed out by the whole band as the person upon whom the storm bird desired to bestow its frowns.

MARBLE POINT

On Marble Point on the shore of Lake Superior there is much game, but the old men will never go there except to get special charms for the Midewewin ceremony. Here are supposed to live the "Little People" of Marble Point, who are much respected and of whose power there are many tales. The stones found here are all very round, supposedly made so through the work of these Indian fairy folk, and the atmosphere of the whole region is one of sacredness. One may not cut a tree or kill an animal without incurring the displeasure of the "Little People" and perhaps receiving swift punishment. (Chippewa)

WINNEBOUJOU

(*Brule River Myth*)

Winneboujou, the giant blacksmith, sometimes spoken of as Hiawatha, was an all-powerful manitou. His forge was near the Eau Claire Lakes in northwestern Wisconsin. He used the highest flat-topped granite peak for his anvil. The region where he worked in the southwestern part of Bayfield County is that of the Smoky Mountains, a wild and rugged country.

There he shaped the miswabik, or native copper of the Brule River region, into various useful weapons and implements for his children, the Chippewa Indians. He was especially adept in shaping copper spear-points and fishhooks required for the catching of the giant senesuggege, or speckled trout. This fish abounded in the clear spring waters of the Lake Superior section of the Brule.

Much of Winneboujou's forging was done by moonlight, and the ringing blows of his pewabik (iron) hammer were heard by the Indians as far down the Lake Superior waters as the Sault Rapids.

These booming noises still echo down the length of the Brule Valley and the waters of the St. Croix River.

On clear moonlight nights these ringing blows are plainly heard. The glow of his forge fire lights up the entire sky.

The sound of the giant smith's hammer was considered a blessing or lucky portent by the Chippewa and was dreaded by their ancient enemies, the Dakota or Sioux. A Chippewa Indian, hearing the noise of Winneboujou's smithing, became possessed of strength and industry.

Winneboujou's summer home was on the Brule River near its source. It was necessary for him to keep an eye always on Ahmik, the Beaver, a rival manitou who might, if not watched, slip across the onegun (portage) to the St. Croix River and then, by way of the Mississippi, reach the gulf. (Chippewa)

THE APOSTLE ISLANDS
(Chippewa Legend)

Winneboujou was hunting in the Brule River country. He had for weapons his powerful bow and a quiver filled with arrows slung over his back. In the big woods of the Brule he saw the fresh tracks of a deer which he followed. It was a large animal, and Winneboujou, looking over the treetops, could trace its movements as the deer ran. The forest was so dense that only now and then could he catch a glimpse of it. Then he shot an arrow to the spot, but the tree trunks and foliage always prevented his striking the fleet animal.

Winneboujou followed the deer all the day and shot away all of the arrows he had in his quiver. So he threw away his bow. When the hunted deer reached the shore of Lake Superior it ran into the water and swam away. When Winneboujou reached the shore the deer was already far out in the water. He became so angry at his failure to get the deer that he grabbed up handfuls of rocks and threw them in the direction which the deer had taken. These, falling into water, became the Apostle Islands, lying where we see them today.

MANITOU MENSIS

(*Spirit Island Legend*)

Spirit Island, in the upper St. Louis River near Superior and Duluth, gets its name from the story of an Indian romance.

A beautiful Chippewa maiden and a strapping young Sioux, daughter and son of two rival chiefs, were desperately in love with each other.

This head of the Lake Superior country was for many years the neutral hunting and fishing grounds of the Sioux and the Chippewa nations. It was also the scene of many a battle between warring bands. It is said that over a thousand invading Sioux were captured or killed in the last decisive battle of the St. Louis River.

The young Chippewa maiden rescued her Sioux lover during this battle, and they both fled in a birchbark canoe to this Spirit Island. After counting his Sioux scalps, her irate father-chieftain pursued them in the early morning but found only their canoe and smoldering campfire. Both brave and maiden had completely and absolutely disappeared, leaving only two pairs of moccasins side-by-side at the foot of a couch of cedar boughs.

The redman's logical solution was that Nesagia Manitou, or Love Spirit, had taken them away in his gegic jemon, or sky canoe, to a hunting ground of never-ending happiness and peace.

Ever afterward their weird Indian love songs could be heard at night by anyone who ventured on the island. No Indian would camp there, as they held the place sacred and regarded it with awe. Many Indians will never land or camp on it even now. A comparatively few years ago a small flock of angora goats were put on the island to summer there, but all swam ashore to the mainland and were so wild and fearful that it was a long time before they could be caught and tamed again. (Chippewa)

chapter 7

WISCONSIN CIRCUS LORE *

THE CIRCUS COMES TO TOWN

Before a circus comes to town there is an almost infinite number of arrangements that must be made. First, the general agent chooses the location, checking first on industries, payrolls, outlying districts, and public officials. The town must be in a thriving part of the country, and yet the circus must not come so often that it will become tiresome to the public.

When the town has been chosen along a well-thought-out route, the railroad contractor makes arrangements for the railroad moves. If the circus is a large one there will be several sections of the train, and these must move with speed so that no section will be sidetracked or held up when transferring from one railroad to another.

Next the general contractor arrives to contract for the license, lot, water, ice, grain, feed, fuel, and straw. The date is then set, and soon the advertising, or billing, car arrives, and before long the public learns for the first time that the circus is coming. If the circus is a large one a "checker-up" arrives a few days before the show, but if

---

* The material in this chapter was collected by the Folklore Section Women and Professional Projects of the Federal Writers' Project, Works Progress Administration, Madison, Wisconsin, 1937. While the big circuses no longer roam the United States, the days of the circus will never be forgotten; and circus lore will go on forever.

it is a small one he may do his checking up early in the morning on the day of the performance. It is his duty to see that none of the posters or lithographs have been removed from the windows, buildings, or billboards. If the advertising has been in the least defaced, passes granted to the owners of the windows or buildings will be cancelled.

The publicity agent is another who enters the town before the show arrives. He takes care of the newspaper publicity. The larger circuses have press representatives who go ahead of the show in addition to those with the show, also directors for radio publicity.

The last man to arrive before the circus is the "twenty-four-hour man." It is his duty to make all final arrangements. First he goes to the railroad agent to see that the circus trains can be "spotted" as near the lot as possible. It is necessary, too, to avoid unloading on a main line where fast trains might interfere. Next the "twenty-four-hour man" goes to the chief of police for permission to haul over the streets and to get the best possible route, one that will avoid bad streets and hills.

After checking up on the provisions that have already been contracted for and seeing that they will be delivered on schedule, the "twenty-four-hour man" marks the telephone or electric light poles with arrows to direct the drivers to the lot.

At midnight the show leaves its last stand and is on its way to the next place of exhibit. It is loaded on several trains, each section leaving at half-hour intervals. The last section, known generally as the "cage" but called the "monkey section" by the roustabouts, is comprised of the elephant cars, camel cars, and animal cages—also the cars used by the performers, musicians, and the managers.

By the time the "monkey section" arrives the first trains, with their heavy wagons, chariots, horses, and properties, have been unloaded. The first train unloaded is the commissary department, which includes the refrigerator, kitchen, canvas, and water wagons. They are immediately taken to the lot where the superintendent of canvas has already designated the part of the lot they are to occupy.

While breakfast is being prepared, the other trains are being unloaded, and at the circus grounds the boss canvasman is "laying out the lot." He has a diagram of the grounds, and he and his assist-

ants have measured the distance where each tent is to be erected
and have iron pins placed where each stake is to be driven. The pole
wagons arrive and the center poles are unloaded at the places they
are to be raised.

The stable wagons have also arrived, and the cloth stables have
been placed by the "stablemen." The heavy duck mangers are placed
inside, and as soon as the horses have cooled off after their work
they are fed.

The last train is switched into position, the "runs" (gangplanks)
are placed at the end of the last flatcar, and the unloading is begun.
The "razorbacks," who load and unload the cars, have a system of
almost military preciseness.

First the elephants and camels are unloaded. The long runway
is taken from beneath the car and placed at the bottom of the side
of one of the elephant cars. The hobbles are removed from the feet
of the elephants and one by one they file down the runway. Next
come the camels, water buffaloes, curious cattle, and other animals.

While all this activity is going on at the lot, the "razorbacks" and
"polers" are busy unloading the trains. Unloading the heavy cages
requires skill and dexterity. First the "razorbacks" remove the barbed
blocks of wood that fasten the wheels of the cage to the flatcars and
place large iron slabs from car to car, making a continuous runway
across the long line of flatcars. A rope is attached to the rear of the
cage next to the end of the train from which the unloading is to be
done, a pole is inserted, and taking hold of it, two men known as
"polers" guide it down the runway, while a third, with the rope at the
rear wound around an iron bar attached to the car, prevents the
cage from running down too fast. Yet he controls the force of its
descent in such a way that as it reaches the ground there is impetus
left to carry it out of the way, where harnessed teams are hitched
to it and take it to the showground.

After breakfast the show its put into final shape. Poles are erected,
stakes driven, canvas unloaded, animals cared for, horses curried,
their tails and manes washed, and provision wagons of all descriptions deliver various supplies. A sledge gang is busy, six men driving
one stake at a time. The sledges strike in such rapid succession that
it hardly seems that one sledge could be withdrawn before the next

one descends. In a short time the tents are up and occupied by the performers, musicians, and sideshow people.

In the dining tent, or "cookhouse," each table is in the same position each day and every member of the personnel has his customary place. Each table has its own waiter, who has a box on the ground at the end of the table in which is kept the dishes for serving.

All meals are served on a regular schedule and are announced by a flag hoisted to the top of the cookhouse. When the flag is lowered no more meals will be served.

The part of the circus lot given over to the "private" lives of the performers contains several tents. At the farther end of the lot is the dressing-room tent. To the right is the wardrobe tent, in which is kept the wardrobe used in the tournament or "spec." To the left is the band tent, and a short distance away is the dog-wagon—home of the performing dogs. Between the guy-ropes of the dressing-room tent, clotheslines are stretched and filled with washing. Back of the dressing room are the large tank wagons providing water for the necessities of the performers.

The dressing-room tent is made up of three parts. At the right is the women's dressing room; at the left is the men's. The space between has four rows, or lines, of stalls for the horses which compose the ring stock—the horses used in the big show. This space is called the "pad room." Saddles and trappings are also kept here. The half of the big room next to the entrance is used to assemble all the various features and acts that are to follow next on the program.

In the men's dressing room the principal equestrians' trunks, ranged in even rows, one after another, follow the line of the large partition wall until the cross-partition is met. Then the line follows the curtain wall and occupies the long side of the room back to the rear wall of the big tent. In the angle marked by the junction of the two walls sits the equestrian director, who is in charge of the dressing room and is responsible for the peace and order of the riders. An additional row of trunks faces the two rows, leaving a passage about six feet wide through which the performers go to and from their places. In front of each trunk is a folding camp stool which the trunk's owner sits on while he is dressing for his various acts.

The circus trunk is each performer's individual spot on the circus lot. The standard trunk has a flat top, is twenty-eight inches long, and has a split tray. When the top is raised, one part remains in the cover, partitioned off from the tray that is just below. Besides this trunk, performers are allowed a smaller trunk for their hats. The trunks are for the purpose of carrying circus wardrobe, not street clothes. On top of each trunk is printed the owner's name. On the lower left-hand corner may be found the letters L.D.R., meaning the Ladies Dressing Room. On the right hand corner of the cover is a letter and a number. If the letter should be C and the number 6, that would mean this trunk is the sixth in the third row. On the opening day of the circus the trunks are given their positions by the equestrian director and are placed there every day by the property man.

There is a circus custom, which has become a circus law, that the clowns have their trunks at the extreme left of the line. To get to them one must pass all the way along the aisle. When this is necessary it is permitted, but custom has decreed that it is never necessary for an acrobat or a bareback rider, whose trunks are located near the entrance, to pass along this aisle between the trunks at the end of the line. "Clown Alley" is sacred to clowns, contortionists, comedians, etc., and woe be unto the gymnast who walks along it. There is no warning whatever, but every clown in the "alley" jumps upon the intruder and throws him out bodily.

THE CIRCUS MUSEUM AT BARABOO

Many of the objects which were so famous and so necessary to the great circuses may now be seen at the Circus Museum at Baraboo. Baraboo was the home for many years of the Ringling Brothers Circus, and the Ringling boys got their great start in Baraboo. John Kelly and many other friends of the circus made the museum possible, and in it is preserved the lore of this great American institution. The stories that follow are true Wisconsin stories about Wisconsin circus animals.

ROMEO

Romeo was an elephant brought from England by the Mabie Brothers to Delavan, Wisconsin. He was not the largest elephant ever to be displayed but at that time was considered the longest. Romeo made his debut into Delavan society sometime around the year 1870 and had a reputation for being a "bad actor," due to his proclivities for occasionally getting loose and causing no little disturbance.

Romeo was a real lover, even though he was Delavan's worst citizen and a killer of men. He obeyed the laws of the beast world and defied all the laws of man and was positively obstreperous. He killed three men and would have killed more but for "acts of God" which intervened.

Romeo needs no introduction to those few remaining who lived in Delavan in the sixties and seventies. He was the trained elephant of the Mabie Brothers Circus, which wintered annually on the shores of Delavan Lake, known now as Lake Lawn. His mate and constant companion was Canada.

One time in a town in Iowa, relates an old-timer, the circus train, traveling overland, was crossing a bridge. Canada broke through. She already had begun to fall when Romeo grabbed her. The circus hands assembled to give Romeo a hand. Various ways of saving both elephants were devised in vain. Meanwhile, Romeo clung to his loved one to keep her from falling all the way down.

Trainers decided that they had to make Romeo let go. After he had supported practically her entire tonnage for almost an hour, Romeo was compelled to release his hold and let Canada fall to her doom. She landed with a terrific thud and, severely injured, had to be dispatched at once.

From then on, Romeo went through life with a grudge against all mankind except his trainer.

On one occasion the circus cook made several pies, and when they were baked he had them put on a rack made for the purpose on the window ledge where they were left to cool. Romeo, smelling the warm food, lifted the latch of the door in the barn and made for the pies. Everything might have remained peaceful, except for the cook, if the pies had not been hot. Romeo, in his haste to devour as many as possible before being caught, burned his mouth and in his pain and anger began to stampede. His trainer tried to calm him, but Romeo was mad and in no mood to be pampered, so he treed the trainer. Then Romeo set to work to pull down the small tree and teach his keeper a lesson in minding his own business.

On the property and connecting two buildings was a drop-trap built for the purpose of catching animals who wandered from their private quarters. The trap would hold the weight of a man, but a heavy animal crossing would drop several feet into a pit. It was across this that one of the men encouraged Romeo to chase him. The elephant fell through the trap as anticipated. They raised him by means of pulleys, and when he was back on level ground once more he was punished with hot irons until he squealed. This experience kept the big pachyderm tractable for sometime after that.

One time Romeo went on a rampage and broke out of his enclosure. News traveled rapidly that Romeo was loose and that it was not safe to travel to Lake Geneva by way of what is now Highway 50. It chanced, however, that a doctor received an emergency call. Instead of following the detour, he decided to take a chance at not being discovered by Romeo and went by the main highway.

The irate Romeo spied him and took after him with all speed. "Doc" whipped his horse to full speed. As he neared the inlet bridge the elephant was lumbering along only a few feet behind him. The physician whipped his horse into a final spurt. Romeo started to follow but stopped abruptly as he saw the planks of the bridge, and the doctor reached the other side in safety.

The incident aroused the community, and the Mabie Brothers finally agreed to send for Romeo's trainer. He came, and it was decided that the way to get Romeo was to make him chase somebody through a stable door. Someone volunteered. He was given the trainer's calico horse to ride. To stop Romeo from smashing through the exit after them two boards were laid in the way to give him the idea of unsafe flooring and cause him to stop. The plan worked perfectly and Romeo was neatly made a prisoner.

QUEEN IN THE CEMETERY

Queen was a female elephant owned by "Popcorn" George Hall. As a rule female elephants are docile, but at times Queen would go on a rampage and cause a great deal of damage.

One time in Albany, New York, Queen wandered away from the

circus grounds. A futile search by circus hands was made of her old haunts where she had previously gotten into mischief. Her keeper also searched unsuccessfully for a time, but he finally discovered her having the grandest time. She had wandered into a cemetery, where she was amusing herself by tearing up gravestones. This, however, was not her last spree.

She had caused so much trouble at different times that "Popcorn" George finally changed her name and sold her to a man in Illinois. En route she squeezed her keeper against the side of the car and killed him.

After Queen left Hall's circus she killed three or four men and was sold twice again, each time under a different name.

BIG CHARLIE

Charlie was a huge elephant weighing about three tons and thirteen feet tall. He was bought from Ringling Brothers by "Colonel" George Hall. At the time he was purchased he was the "lead" elephant of the herd.

Usually Big Charlie was gentle and friendly. His best friend was his trainer, Mabel Hall; in fact, she was the only one who handled him from the time of his purchase until his death, in Evansville, Wisconsin, some years later.

There are many stories told of Charlie's misdeeds. One time the great pachyderm got a splinter in his foot and suffered so from the effects that a veterinary was called to remove it. During the operation Big Charlie took him, wrapping his great trunk around the man's waist, and threw him some distance away from him. As far as the veterinary was concerned, the operation was finished at that moment. He vowed never to go near the elephant again and he never did.

On another occasion a keeper entered Charlie's quarters, and the animal resented his being there. Grabbing the man with his trunk, he forced him against the side of the building, then pinned him in with his tusks, which he dug into the siding of the building. The keeper, however, before he could be crushed by Charlie's mammoth head, slid to the floor and escaped.

One time, before Colonel George Hall's circus took to the road, an exhibition was given at the park in Evansville, the home of the circus. Big Charlie was chained in the park, but he decided he would rather be home, so he pulled his stake and set out for his own quarters across town. The keeper tried to reason with Charlie, but to no avail, for he had definitely made up his mind that he didn't like the park. The keeper, fearing that the animal would become angry and charge, grabbed hold of Charlie's tail and held on. On through town went Charlie, gathering speed as he lumbered along; and still hanging to his tail was the keeper.

Around the circus quarters was a fence, and as Charlie, in his unrehearsed act, arrived, there was nothing for him to do but tear off the gate and enter. As he went past the house in which the help lived, the keeper let go of the tail and made haste to get into the house. Charlie, feeling the weight lifted from his rear appendage, stopped a moment to contemplate his next move. Near him was piled some cordwood. From this he picked up a good-sized piece and flung it through the kitchen window of the building, breaking not only the glass, but the frame and sash as well.

Feeling that he had evened his score with the keeper, Charlie went straight to his own building and at once forgot his grudge. When Colonel Hall and his trainer arrived Charlie was again friendly and gentle and acted as though nothing at all had occurred.

As the years went on, Big Charlie became more unmanageable. One time he threw his trainer, Mabel Hall, and caused her many weeks of painful injury. This was the first time the elephant had ever shown unfriendliness toward her, and so for the first time she became frightened of him. Hall wanted to change Charlie's name and sell him, but the elephant had grown so hard to handle that everyone thought it advisable to kill him before he caused more damage. Charlie was made to wear brass balls on the end of his tusks to keep him from goring those who handled him and also to keep his beautiful tusks from being split.

They tried to do away with the elephant by giving him strychnine in a potato or an apple, but it had no effect on him aside from making him slightly uncomfortable. Old Charlie began to be suspicious of this dainty fare and refused further appetizers.

He was finally given potassium cyanide in a sweet potato, a delicacy he could not resist, and in two hours he was dead. His grave was dug a short distance from the circus quarters, and after his tusks had been removed he was buried.

COCO'S PRANKS

Coco, a little elephant which the Ringlings acquired with the Barnum circus, was a ringleader in nightly pranks, and the cunning he showed was amazing. All elephants, when caught out of order, resume their places as quickly as possible. But Coco was not satisfied merely to be found in his place. He would slip his stake in just where it had been when he pulled it out and would even coil his chain around it. Then he awaited developments with the utmost composure.

Coco's superior intelligence was soon recognized by his trainer, who taught him to mount a tub seven or eight feet high and stand on it on his hind legs. One day when he was being broken into doing this act, Coco slipped and fell from the top of the tub. He lay on the ground dazed, and the men feared for a moment that he had been killed by the fall. But suddenly Coco jumped up, and without waiting for a command he astonished them all by mounting the tub and doing his stand perfectly.

LITTLE CHARLIE

Charlie was a baby elephant which the Ringling circus had imported with fourteen others from the Hagenbeck-Wallace farms in Germany to be trained by Hampten for a series of baby elephant acts. From the time he was unloaded, however, he was observed to be sick, but he was the gamest little elephant on the lot. When the other babies were running around the arena, trunk clasping neighbor's tail, little Charlie couldn't bear to stand on the sidelines. Sick as he was he would rush in, seize a tail, and run around the ring once or twice, falling out when he became too exhausted to continue.

With Charlie, discipline was needed to counteract his self-imposed rigor, and he was kept from overdoing, but he soon died despite the care given him. In his short life he won the hearts of all the elephant men.

MODOC THE BABY RASCAL

There is a belief among the Negroes of the south to the effect that elephants are reincarnations of departed African monarchs and that their wisdom, sagacity, instinct, or whatever it is that gives an elephant so wise a look, come from a spirit that has taken up its dwelling place within the huge pachyderm.

Some of the things elephants do show they must have some means of communicating with one another.

Modoc was a baby elephant weighing only six or eight hundred pounds. He liked to eat and would consume his weight in oats if they were accessible to him. Food was kept away from all the animals, however, and given to them only at mealtime. One night when the elephant house was dark, the superintendent of the big herd heard a subdued rasping noise, apparently coming from the further end of the herd. He sneaked around in back of the herd and peered cautiously over some bales of straw where Modoc was chained, and there he saw Modoc lifting his stake out of the ground. It could be seen in an instant that the little rascal had had the stake out before, for all he had to do was to lift it up and out it came easily. He slipped his foot chain down over the tapering end of the stake and was free. The superintendent suspected whatever activities were about to go on had happened many times previously, but he could not understand how the young elephant was always found chained in the morning, so he decided to watch the thing through.

About twenty feet or more from Modoc's place were piled some sacks of grain weighing about one hundred pounds each. Picking up his floor chain very carefully with his trunk so that it would not rattle or jangle on the floor, he began a most painstaking, sinuous, gliding motion across the space that separated him from the grain. When he arrived, he laid his chain down and picked up a bag of oats with his trunk. His journey back was even more cautious because he had to drag his chain without making a noise. When he reached the herd he went to great big Babylon, who stood like a bronze statue, her massive sides looming up like the walls of a house in the gloom. Modoc stopped and Babylon took the oats. They got into the bag in no time and began their feast. Modoc filled his mouth and munched away like a man eating dry crackers on a wager. He seemed to know that his big companion in crime would eat most of the oats if he lost any time. Babylon took almost half of the bag the first time, and poor Modoc, with his mouth so full he couldn't speak, looked at her with watery eyes as much as to say, "Oh, what a hog!" and gulped oats down at the risk of choking to death.

The superintendent went back to his sleeping room and purposely made a noise. He immediately heard the shuffling of sly little Modoc as he shambled back to his place. He picked up his stake, put it down on the ground, and would have put it through the ring in the chain if he had had time. When the superintendent came along, Modoc was leaning against the wall fast asleep. He gave him a gentle prod, and he awakened suddenly, looking at the superintendent with a sleepy stare. He was ordered to open his mouth but refused to do so. Finally he obeyed, and there were the oats. His keeper didn't do anything to Modoc but went over to Babylon, who was playing possum too. He had trouble in waking her and more trouble in making her open her mouth. She did, however, much to her chagrin. Her mouth was full, not only of oats, but she had the empty sack closely rolled up and packed in too! For punishment she was ordered to sit down and open her mouth while her keeper made a motion as to pass a great pair of forceps into it. She had had a painful operation sometime before and was very fearful of the forceps. She shut her mouth and cried like a baby and was so thoroughly frightened that she never trespassed again, but that rascal Modoc continued to get loose and get into mischief whenever he could.

SNYDER THE CLOWN

One of the favorite baby elephant acts in Ringling Brothers Circus was one that a German trainer taught to Snyder, who later grew to be the famous killer and was shot. The act was done with a special little bed which had been made for him. He was trained to get into it, lie down, and pull the sheet and blanket over his head. In a few seconds he would begin to slap himself, kick off the covers, get up, and run about in frenzied fashion. Then, going back to the bed, the baby elephant would remove a large wooden "bedbug," drop it on the floor and step on it. This stunt was very popular with circus audiences.

The usual baby elephant stunts were to have the animals trot around the arena and come to a halt at the entry, each one raising his right foot and putting his trunk on the back of the one ahead of him. They were also trained to walk in line, each one holding on to the tail of the preceding one; this was the parade procedure.

INGENIOUS BALDY

Baldy, the largest elephant ever known in captivity, has half a car to ride in himself. The elephants are usually loaded by means of a huge gangplank, or runway, fastened to the door sill of the car and reaching to the ground, a distance of thirty feet. Up this incline the elephants walk and take their places in the car. Baldy found that he could get into his car much easier in his own way than in the way that had been provided, but not being able to talk, there was nothing he could do about it. He couldn't explain that the roof was too low and that he bumped his head every time he went in. Despairing of being able to explain these things, he reasoned out a plan. He simply stepped off the ganglank one night, put his huge head under it, and shoved it out of the way. Then, before keepers could imagine what he was about to do, he walked to the car door, raised his forefeet in the air, planted them firmly within the car and slowly climbed in. By removing the gangplank he had all the height from the ground to the door sill gained. He could then put his head in first, then his forefeet, and then scramble in at ease without bumping his gigantic head. Since that time he has always loaded himself into the car in his own way.

The spirit of emulation is strong in an elephant. The smaller members of the herd saw Baldy get into the car that way and they all wanted to try it. It wasn't necessary for them, but nevertheless they wanted to do it that way. The only trouble was that they were not big enough to do the trick, so they were satisfied to take the big plank back again after they had tried it once.

The elephant herd walks up the runway by its own volition and invariably takes its place in the line. If the leader is not there, the others, having arrived from the lot, will wait until he comes. As soon as he goes up the walk, the others will follow him like so many sheep.

From Route Book 1897.

BALDY TO THE RESCUE

Bessie Rooney, the ten-year-old sister of Mike Rooney, the rider, came near being hugged to death by a bear when Baldy, the largest of the elephant herd, knocked the big brute down and saved the child's life.

The bear, who was known as Growler, had a vicious temper. He was chained near the elephants. The little girl had made friends with the elephants and was romping with some of them when Growler seized her and closed his paws around her slender form.

Baldy, who had been an interested spectator, brought his trunk down with crushing force on Growler's head. The bear was stunned by the blow and released the child, who had fainted. The elephant picked her up and placed her out of harm's way.

THE WALTZING ELEPHANTS

Mr. Charles Hampten's predecessor with Ringling Brothers had trained a group of eight older elephants to do a waltz step around the arena together. As they grew older, however, and as younger animals replaced them, the stunt was abandoned and they were used only to march in the parades.

One day just for fun Mr. Hampten took the old waltzing group into the arena and gave them the old commands for their stunt. Much to his surprise they remembered all of it, began to waltz, and enjoyed it so much that they kept going around and around the circle, loath to stop. Finally the delighted Hampten put them back with the herd and, on seeing the old trainer, told him of the accomplishment. He was amazed that the old animals should have remembered the act after the many years that had elapsed. He asked Hampten to bring them out again that evening, and when he, too, saw how well they remembered their act he was delighted and decided that they should be allowed to repeat it as often as they wished.

THE ACHING TOOTH

The circus veterinary has to be a very versatile person, picking up many tricks in the treatment of wild animals as he cares for them. But much of the treatment bears some resemblance to that to which human beings are subjected. Even the teeth of the elephants are filled or pulled, but with forceps as large as ice tongs and augmented with power. One time one of the Ringling Brothers' big bull elephants was observed to have a seeming appetite, but great hesitancy in eating. Examination revealed a swollen gum surrounding a rotten tooth, which the veterinary thought would have to come out. An elephant hasn't many teeth; however, each tooth is about the size of a man's fist, or larger, so they are very hard to pull. The elephant often resents the treatment and goes on a rampage.

Therefore, this particular time it was thought best to fill the tooth. Huge instruments, which required both hands to handle, were brought out, and the elephant was taken out of the menagerie tent so that his uneasiness would not alarm the other members of the herd. He seemed to know that something was to be done to relieve his pain, and after a few kind words from his keeper he was told to sit down on the ground almost in a recumbent position, and he obeyed. Then he was commanded to lift his head and raise his trunk, but he dropped it when he understood that he was to open his mouth. His pitiful little trumpeting told how he was suffering and begging his keepers not to add to his pain. After much coaxing and petting he opened his mouth and the veterinary cleaned the cavity very carefully. It would have held a good-sized lemon easily. The nerve was almost exposed, and the pain must have been almost maddening, but although he trumpeted shrilly at times and whined almost incessantly, he never offered to strike his doctors with his trunk, nor did he show any inclination to flinch from the ordeal.

Amalgam was put into the tooth as rapidly and gently as possible till it was filled, the inflamed gum was washed with a soothing carbolic lotion, and the job was done. The big pachyderm seemed to realize that his troubles were over, for he trumpeted his joy in a very different note as he trotted back to his place in the herd.

ELEPHANT TRICKS

When the elephants retire for the night the herd spreads out to such an extent that often there is not room for all to lie down. When this happens, the one left standing waits until his neighbors are asleep. Then he reaches out a sly foot and stamps on the ear of the one nearest him. Up jumps the terrified elephant, and perhaps one or two others are roused by the sudden commotion. This gives the guilty party his chance to grab a bed for himself and let someone else be "it."

On Sunday nights the show stays on the lot, and invariably some mischief results in spite of the watchfulness of the attendants. Sometimes two or three elephants pull their stakes and sneak over to the cookhouse, where they eat all the bread they can find and any orangeade that may be left in the barrel. If they are caught in their stealing they run back to their places with guilty haste, and they usually get punished.

The night attendants make a bed for themselves by shaking out seven or eight bales of hay which are to be used the next day and spreading their blankets upon it. They go to bed hoping that the elephants will sleep so they can too. But more than likely they will soon be awakened by feeling their "mattress" slowly oozing out from under them. As soon as he sees he has been detected in his hay-stealing, the culprit shambles back to his place in the herd.

One time, "hustlers" who accompanied the Holland and Gormely's Circus through Iowa slept in the end of the animal car and had some queer experiences the first four nights. An elephant kept putting his trunk through the doorway and pulling the quilts off and shoving the boys onto the floor. His chain was shortened after that, and the boys slept undisturbed.

THE AGE OF ELEPHANTS

Contrary to the popular conception, elephants do not attain a much greater age than do human beings; they rarely live longer than eighty or ninety years, though instances of their living to be a hundred and twenty-five years old have been known.

The life cycle of the elephants also corresponds in general to that of the human being. Youth extends to about twenty years, middle life to about fifty or sixty years, and old age sets in thereafter. One old elephant in Ringling Brothers Circus became unable to lift her trunk to her mouth, so the keepers stood by and lifted it for her when she had filled it with water or had picked up a mouthful of food. Like humans, the elephants become stiff and slow as they get older. They are then used only for parades and pensioned off, as it were, for the balance of their lives.

The way to tell the approximate age of an Indian elephant is to observe the ear at the top where it turns over. Every inch that the ear is folded forward represents about thirty years' growth.

ELEPHANTS FEAR MICE

In India, the natural habitat of the circus elephant, there is a small animal resembling our mouse, which feeds on the berries of the same lowland bush from which the elephants graze. The tiny rodents, unlike the mice of America, have barbed claws, arrow-tipped like a bee's stinger. When the unwary elephant thrusts his trunk into the bushes and contacts one of these small "mice," the terrified little animal will often run up the inside of the trunk. His barbed claws sink deeper into the sensitive tissues of the elephant's nose. The frightened pachyderm rushes about trying to blow the obstruction out, but it is stuck fast. It rots and then causes the death of the elephant if he has not already killed himself in his insanity. Because of their fear of this small Indian rodent and their terror of anything getting into their trunks, elephants are said to be afraid of mice.

"OUR ANNIE"

When Al Ringling gave the Madison Zoo its elephant, one of Ringlings' bull trainers, "Baraboo Red" Hampten, was called over to the railroad siding near Coney Island to load the animal selected for shipment. It had been decided to give the zoo a middle-aged female named Alice. She was separated from the herd and boarded into a boxcar where Hampten left her for the night. The next morning the trainer was called again to come down and see the damage Alice had wrought. As is often the case, she had become lonesome for the herd and had smashed the side of the car and returned to the other animals. Thereupon it was decided that it would be more practical to ship a smaller elephant, and so a young female of sixteen years, named Annie, was successfully loaded and sent.

This was in July, 1918. Annie's life story is not one of color and glamour. She was never trained for the sawdust ring, but had a more prosaic duty of pulling stakes and pushing wagons. Yet, in the years she lived in Vilas Park her gentle manners and good humor gave amusement and joy to a legion of annual visitors.

When Annie arrived at her new home she was put in the same building with the lions and tigers and at first resented their growls and roars, but in time she became accustomed to her new surroundings and even became less lonesome for the herd as the attention of the public took her interest.

At times Annie would lose her good nature and become just a little less friendly toward her admirers. At such times she would be given an oil bath in two gallons of oil to soften her skin and make her more comfortable. But though this treatment was soothing it made her cold, and she would shiver for a day or so afterward. In 1924 the zoo solved the problem of keeping Annie completely happy at all times by building a summer yard for her. Here she could dig into the dirt to her heart's content. Every day she would give herself a complete mud bath and rinse herself off with the fresh running water that was installed for her special use. Since that time her skin became softer than the oil treatments made it and she did not have to run the risk of catching cold due to them.

The only time Annie ever caused her keepers any inconvenience or trouble was one spring when she was to be moved to her summer yard for the season. There is a step down of about ten inches from her winter quarters to the ground and Annie refused to take it. She was coaxed and teased to leave but would not budge. Finally she was forced out, inch by inch, with the help of a block and tackle. It was believed that she had stumbled on the step the preceding fall when she was being taken inside and she had not forgotten.

During the winter months Annie had a voracious appetite and thought of nothing else but food. The zoo bought her food in large amounts, and the cost of feeding her was about sixty-five or seventy cents a day. Each day she consumed one hundred pounds of timothy hay, one-half bushel of carrots or sixteen quarts of ground oats, ten or twelve loaves of bread, and all the peanuts and crackerjack the public would feed her. In the summer time the public took her attention from her stomach and she ate a little less.

Despite Annie's few human frailties, she was, in the words of her keeper, "One of the quietest and most agreeable elephants in any zoo." Annie died in February, 1948.

Menagerie Stories

DOONEY THE LION

Dooney was a lion cub raised on a bottle by "Popcorn" Hall. He slept behind the stove just as peacefully as any domestic cat and grew to be a beautiful and enormous animal as well as a very friendly one.

A man by the name of Devendorf, who was one of the circus personnel, became one of Dooney's special friends. One time when the circus was out on the road it did not return to Evansville for two years. When it did come in for a winter season Devendorf went down to see Dooney. He stopped near the cage first to talk with a keeper. As he did so he heard a great howling and fuss coming from Dooney's cage. When he went up to the lion, which had recognized his voice before seeing him, the huge cat seemed overjoyed. Devendorf went inside the cage, and the lion put his paws on the man's shoulders and licked his face in affection.

In the cage next to Dooney's were three vicious inbred lions. As Devendorf backed out of the cage one of these ferocious animals reached out and clawed him, literally tearing off his trousers.

Dooney was later sold to the New York Zoo.

TIGERS ON A LARK

One time when the Hollands were with the Hagenbeck Circus they were riding in the parade directly behind a cage that held two Bengal tigers. Suddenly a wheel came off the tiger wagon and spilled the two big beasts into the streets. Since tigers will attack animals first, all those driving horses drove away to shelter as fast as they could.

A short distance from the parade grounds a washing hung on the line. The two tigers walked over to the line and lay on their backs clawing the washing until there was nothing left of it. Then one tiger spotted a woman standing in a window watching the performance. He walked over to the house, put his paws on the window sill, and stared back at the frightened woman.

Trouble was anticipated in recovering the animals. All roustabouts available were given a side wall of canvas to hold, and gradually they surrounded the tigers and closed in on them. They guided the canvas back to the wagon, and the beasts walked into their cages without further ado. The wheel was replaced and the parade continued with only twenty minutes lost.

BISMARK ON A SPREE

What would have been only a funny incident, had it not been for the imminent danger that attended it, resulted from the combination of Bismark—a big black bear—and a quart of brandy.

Shortly after the animals and trappings of the circus had been moved from the trains to Tattersalls in Chicago, it was discovered that Bismark was rolling about the bottom of his cage in apparent agony, moaning and groaning like a human being. The veterinary was called, and he diagnosed the case as a severe attack of colic and prescribed brandy and peppermint. In the meantime the bear had been taken out of the cage and chained to an iron girder in the menagerie building, where he could be more easily treated. The assistant who was to administer the medicine misunderstood the directions and gave the entire prescription at once. The bear immediately seemed to be much relieved by this heroic treatment and lay contentedly with his nose on the ground for a few moments. Then, without the slightest warning, Bismark let out a mighty growl, leaped from the ground, jumped forward, his tremendous weight breaking the chain, and went cavorting against a cage. Then he picked himself up and went on a wild, staggering run around the side of the building, knocking against everything in his way and all the while setting up great howls of joy.

The noise soon brought everybody to that part of the building where Bismark was holding his celebration. Since it was hopeless to try to capture the inebriate in such a condition, the attendants armed themselves with clubs and, after the bear had reeled about for more than a half hour, managed to worry him back and forth against the side wall until he sought a corner and went to sleep. After he had gone to sleep he was rolled up in a tarpaulin and deposited in his cage.

During the drunken spree the bear acted very much like an intoxicated man. He leered cunningly and hiccoughed, and only by the dexterous use of their clubs were the attendants able to keep the big brown toper from hugging them. One of Bismark's circus tricks was to carry a gun while walking on his hind legs, and this trick he performed with a pole during the course of his spree.

"POP" LOSES PATIENCE

In "Popcorn" Hall's menagerie were three ugly tigers. One time one of these big cats got loose and took refuge under the cage. This was during the winter when the cages were housed in a building. An attempt was made to get the tiger into a "run-box" and thence back into his cage. This was at first of no avail, and besides, everyone was afraid to move for fear the cat would leap. Finally Pop lost his patience and demanded his shotgun. It is an old trick of trainers to frighten lions and tigers by firing a blank cartridge or gunpowder into their eyes to temporarily blind them. But Pop didn't take into consideration that shooting off gunpowder might start a fire in the building. It took some argument to keep the angry owner from firing his gun. Finally, three keepers managed to corner the animal and force it into the chute and back to the cage.

LEOPARD ESCAPES

One time a leopard owned by the "Colonel" George Hall circus escaped. Several people saw him, and soon an armed posse of local men was formed to run him down. Pop Hall warned the men to be careful since they did not know the habits of the cat. The leopard finally took a tree in a woods near Magnolia, Wisconsin. The woods was on the property of Old Man Hess. He was a cantankerous old soul and resented the intrusion of man or beast on his property. Despite warnings, he took his axe with the intention of chopping down the tree and the animal. He hadn't gotten far with his chopping when the leopard leaped from the tree and landed on him, clawing him severely. The cat was finally shot. As soon as Old Man Hess recovered he brought suit against Hall but was not successful.

THE TIGER AND THE LAW

One time when Mr. Al Priddy was traveling with the Hagenbeck Circus and showing in Brooklyn, New York, he was asked to bring a circus animal with him and to speak to about 4,500 school children. So he went to the manager and said, "I'd like a tiger, please." "All right," said the manager, "help yourself."

Priddy took a twelve-months-old tiger cub in his arms without bothering to put a collar on it. He walked to the gate, and seeing a small coupe waiting there, he assumed it had been sent to pick him up. So he got in with the cub on his lap and waited for the driver. Soon two men came out. The driver spied the cub and climbed forthwith into the rumble seat. He had originally intended the circus man and the cub to sit there. The other man had not yet seen the tiger and said to the car owner, "Do you want me to drive?" The other assured him that he did.

When the driver spied the cub he was too frightened to move. He asked Priddy if the cub was perfectly safe and well in hand. Priddy said everything was all right with him and the cub; and he asked the driver if he had the car well in hand, meaning that he should mind his own business and drive on.

They started off, and when they had gone about two miles a parade appeared with its band playing lustily. The cub became excited, and with its paws up on the dashboard and its head out of the window it growled in satisfaction and delight.

At that moment the driver stopped his car just where he was, almost in the middle of the street, and made some excuse about getting some cigarettes. He was gone a long time, and after a while the clatter of hoofs was heard approaching the car. The horse stopped and, looking out, Priddy saw the biggest Irish cop he had ever seen in his life. The cop roared, "Don't ye know ye can't park here? Why don't ye get movin'? All right, drive over to th' police station!" In answer to the policeman's threats Priddy tickled the stomach of the young tiger, who spread out its paws and hissed and growled in the direction of the law. In less than a second the horse's hoofs were heard fading in the distance.

PYTHON AT LARGE

Old "Popcorn" Hall of Evansville spent one winter in bed as the result of a broken hip administered by the wrath of Charlie, his elephant. Among Hall's circus stock was a twenty-three-foot python and a marmoset, which he kept in the house where it was warm. The snake was kept in a box behind the stove and it awakened about once a month to eat. On such occasions it was fed a few pigeons.

One time the local doctor came to see how Pop was progressing. During his call the python awakened, and since he received no attention he set about to create some. The doctor, hearing a noise coming from behind the stove, saw a blanket rising up over the top of the box. Soon the blanket stretched out over the edge, and in a moment the head of the python emerged. The doctor made haste for the first exit and in doing so knocked over the monkey cage. Monkeys are frightened to death of snakes, and this little marmoset set a speed record in alighting on Great-grandpop's picture, where he chattered insults at anyone who would lend an ear. The room was vacated except for Pop, the python, and the chattering marmoset. And the circus man, not being able to move, could do nothing but call for the keeper, who, when he found the python loose, refused to assist in reincarcerating the wanderer. The scene that followed continued to be hectic. Pop was swearing at the keeper and telling him that the ! ! ! ! snake was harmless, that Lou (his wife) had handled it hundreds of times and had never been bitten. The monkey, who had transferred himself to the chandelier, was screaming and chattering as loud as he could.

With threats and imprecations Pop finally induced the man to get the snake into its box. When the helper picked it up the snake struck its head against his hand, and, thinking he had been bitten, the man threw the snake into the box and ran out the door screaming after the fast-departing doctor.

JIGS THE APE

Jigs was a great ape owned by the Al G. Barnes circus. One time one of the girl performers going past Jigs' cage noticed that he was holding his hand on his jaw, apparently in pain. She told the trainer, who promised to take care of Jigs right away. The next day, however, Jigs was still holding his jaw when the girl passed and she again notified the trainer. The following day, seeing the ape still in pain, the girl went to the blacksmith shop, got some pliers, and extracted the tooth. From then on Jigs was devoted to the girl.

Often during the morning Jigs was let out of his cage and allowed to roam about the lot. He always made directly for the girl who had helped him, and as she sat writing letters or mending her costume Jigs would climb into her lap and enjoy himself. One day the girl was dressed in street clothes, and when Jigs hopped onto her lap she pushed him off. The ape fell to the ground, squealing and crying. He soon collected himself, and realizing why he could not sit upon her lap on this occasion, he disappeared. He soon returned with a newspaper, which he spread upon the girl's lap, and then jumped up with a clear conscience.

Other Stories

ZULA THE WILD MAN

One season when the John Robinson Circus was showing in Georgia, it had a giant colored fellow made up as Zula, the wild man, with a ring in his nose, big earrings, red rings around his eyes and lips, and with his hair standing on end. He had two huge teeth hanging down. These had been made from toothbrush handles. Except for a leopard skin, he was naked.

The "wild man" rode on a crude conveyance drawn by a huge water buffalo with horns protruding from each side of its head. As the parade descended a hill the cart, having no brakes, continually bumped the buffalo, causing him to move faster and faster until he broke into a gallop. One of the men in the parade yelled, "Stop him!" The colored people watching the parade thought the wild man and his strange beast were running amuck and began to stampede, falling over one another in their effort to get out of the way.

CAPTAIN SIGBY'S HORSE

Captain Sigby was one of the greatest horse trainers in the show world. At one time he trained ponies for the Seible Brothers Circus at Watertown, Wisconsin, and later trained horses for Joe Greer. At one time he gave Greer a high school, or trained, horse which for years put on the most unusual act ever seen in the ring.

One of the animal's accomplishments was picking cards off a rack, the numbers being called by the trainer. Here the horse depended on the trainer's finger for his cues, and so delicate was his nervous mechanism that the movement of the finger one inch to the right or left sent him the length of the rack.

This amazing animal also rang chimes, playing three tunes by pressing his nose on pads. He played the last three notes in one tune faster than the trainer could give the cues. His next feat was working a cash register, picking out with his teeth the money called for and carrying it to his trainer.

The most unique trick in his repertoire, however, was telling colors blindfolded. His trainer would pass among the crowd and ask the horse whether the coat he had picked out was red, black, blue, or white. At the right color the horse would nod his head. The inflection of the trainer's voice gave the animal his cue.

ZAZEL, "THE HUMAN BULLET"

History repeats itself in the circus business as well as in anything else, according to a scrapbook, musty with age, owned by Mr. and Mrs. George Holland of Delavan, Wisconsin. The book contains a double page of clippings about Zazel, who did the cannon act back in the eighties. The present cannon act of the Ringling Brothers and Barnum and Bailey Circus is very similar—it is still sensational to see a woman shot into the air, catching a bar at the top of the tent.

Many were the wisecracks told and asked about Zazel at that time. An inquisitive visitor at Barnum's circus asked whether Zazel "powders in a cannon." He was questioned, "Why?" To this he answered, "Because she comes out with a puff." Another wisecrack was, "Does she complete her toilet in the cannon?" The answer was, "Yes, she must. She comes out with bangs."

The success of this daring act required that the person in the cannon hold himself still, or else the body might double up in there due to the force of the explosion.

"BIG BEAUTIFUL BOY"

Babe, a horse owned by Marshall Field & Company in Chicago, was often referred to as "big beautiful boy." He used to take the money wagon back and forth from the wholesalers to the retailers and to the bank. He was bought when very young and spent his life in the Loop, hearing nothing but the roar of traffic and seeing nothing but tall unfriendly buildings about him.

While George Holland and his wife, Rose Dockrill, were showing a horse act at the Great Northern Theater in Chicago, then known as the Great Northern Hippodrome, they saw Babe on the street. He was such a beautiful, finely built fellow that they followed him to Field's. The next morning Holland went to Field's to see if he could buy the horse for his act. The driver said he was not for sale, at the same time taking out the daily apple that he had brought for his pet. Holland persisted, going to the store every morning for several days.

Finally, the Vice President said he would talk to him. Asking Holland how much work the horse would have to do, he learned that he would be ridden by Mrs. Holland and that the act lasted only ten minutes, showing twice a day. That night the executive went to the theater to see the equestrian act and was so pleased that he promised to sell Babe. He sold the animal at a ridiculously low price and during the transaction said that he had planned to replace Babe with a truck and that he didn't want his "big beautiful boy" to work hard.

Babe's first trip out of Chicago was to Carthage, Ohio, just outside of Cincinnati. Here Holland took him out of the railroad car to walk him around so that the might get accustomed to space. Because of the great space and the glare of the sunlight, which the animal had never before known, he became so frightened and bewildered that his legs spread out so that he literally walked on his stomach. Every muscle in his body quivered. The animal was wringing wet, and Holland thought Babe would die of heart failure before he could get him back to the car again.

With continued patience and kindness Babe was eventually trained, and he made his initial performance at the Toronto Fair. The Hollands expected him to be frightened and forget this act, for he was a high-strung horse. But as the curtain rose, Babe stood perfectly still, watching it disappear from sight. He did his act as perfectly as a correctly timed machine.

Babe was the only horse Holland ever knew that would raise his head to watch things. He would stand for hours watching the fireworks at the fair; or he would see in glass transoms the reflections of people walking and would watch them go by; or if he happened to be led past the hotel in which his mistress was staying, and she called to him, he would look up, tracing her voice until he found her.

In the ring on one occasion Babe fell, throwing his rider. Holland was pinned under one of Babe's legs, and to avoid crushing his master Babe held his other leg in the air until someone arrived to rescue the trainer.

Three years after Babe had been purchased by Holland he was struck by lightning while playing at a fair in Watertown, Wisconsin. The fair was supposed to have ended on Friday and the horse act was to have moved for the next stand, but because of the popularity of the equestrian attraction the manager persuaded Holland to remain and give a performance on Saturday.

During breakfast the next morning a terrific storm came up, and as Mr. Holland looked out of the window he saw a bolt strike, knocking the chickens head over heels in the farm yard. A few minutes later the groom came running from the stables—Babe had been struck by lightning!

FRANK'S ANIMAL CIRCUS

For years George Hall, Jr., featured a talking pig act. He was the only trainer to have such an act, and so well did he keep his secret for training the pigs that not even his sons could learn it.

Finally one of the sons, Frank, made up his mind that he was going to have a talking pig act too, and he went ahead and trained his hogs. His father knew nothing of it until he attended his son's opening stand. He asked Frank how he learned to train pigs, and Frank confessed that he had learned by watching his father through a knot-hole in the barn. Training domestic animals became a specialty of Frank's after that.

There were two acts performed by domestic animals in Frank's Animal Circus. In the first were two hogs, a sheep, a goat, and an airdale dog. The highlight of the act was the goat walking a tight-rope high in the air. She would walk all the way across and back, then walk out to the middle again and make a complete turn. In the same act the hogs jumped hurdles, the goat rolled a barrel, and the sheep and goat seesawed. For the grand finale all the animals climbed a tall ladder and slid down a chute.

The second act was performed by four dogs and three ponies. It opened with equestrian dogs jumping from the ring onto the backs of ponies. Next the ponies jumped hurdles, the dogs jumping bars and landing on the ponies' backs while they were on the dead run. Both of these acts in Frank's Animal Circus were considered very unusual.

THE PARADE PASSES

W. C. Coup's circus was scheduled to appear in an eastern city. The press man had gone before, putting up gay, glamorous bill-boards and streamers, which declared to big-eyed, wonder-filled little boys that upon a certain day the circus was coming to town.

Not the least to be excited and thrilled was a wee lad who had counted much on seeing the circus. In fact, he had not only counted the days, but his pennies too, for a long long time; and now only a few days were left to count! Many a lollypop he had gone without, but wasn't this glorious event worth it? There would be the tigers, the elephants, the ponies, and the band, to say nothing of the trapeze artists and the clowns. And best of all there would be the parade!

At last only a week remained, and then— But alas, all his dreams came tumbling down; the pennies were no longer needed. He was sick abed.

So keen was his disappointment that he wrote a letter to W. C.

Coup, manager of the circus, and asked if he might have just a picture or a billboard to "kinda make up for missing the circus."

W. C. Coup, upon receipt of the heart-tugging letter, ordered the entire circus parade to march two miles out of its regular route so as to pass by the home of the sick lad.

Wisconsin Circus Owners and Performers

BARABOO

AL RINGLING

Al Ringling was the oldest and most loved of the Ringling Brothers. In Baraboo, the town which had seen him evolve from a small boy holding "pin shows" on a Saturday afternoon to the greatest power in the circus world, his name was highly respected. Al believed that the roughest canvasmen helped him make his shows a success; and he never turned away from them lest, in so doing, he might be guilty of an injustice to one of the innumerable roustabouts who, for thirty years, helped to make the Ringlings known throughout the world.

One time in the early days when Al and a performer were traveling together, they came to a small town on the shores of the Mississippi in northern Wisconsin. They had given a performance the previous night and it had not been very successful financially. They were unable to pay their hotel bill, so the proprietor attached their baggage, one trunk. A boat was about to leave and the actors wanted very much to be passengers on it; but unless they could take their necessary stage properties, which were housed in the trunk, it was useless to think of it. The proprietor, suspecting their desires, kept an eagle eye on them. Suddenly Al conceived an idea and asked, "Wasn't that awful about the man being murdered here in town last night?" The old eagle-eyed one said he hadn't heard the news. "You'll find out all about it in the paper," Al told him. As the old proprietor entered a nearby room to get the paper, the two artists grabbed their trunks, ran posthaste, and made the boat.

THE FIRST SHOWING IN BARABOO, AS TOLD BY AL RINGLING

"I started out a small hall show with a few people and playing small towns, and a times it was something of a struggle to get from one town to another. At that time I would send a man ahead two or three days before the show to post small dodgers about four inches wide and six inches long. He would leave about a dozen in each of the stores. This was the only billing the show got.

"Along in the season we showed Oregon, Wisconsin, and from there we were going to Baraboo. Well, we landed Oregon with little money and after the show had only enough to pay for our hall and hotel bill and nothing to get to Baraboo on. I did some talking with the agent, who finally agreed to let us 'go on our trunks,' the trunks to be held by the railroad company until the money was paid. There was no possible way to get the trunks until the doors opened for the evening, and then we had to take chances on the receipts. I opened the doors early and had a dray near the entrance, and as soon as we had taken enough I went to the depot with the old horse and dray to get the baggage. Of course we were late in opening, and the boys were stamping their feet and whistling. As soon as the baggage arrived we announced there would be a delay because of the baggage not arriving on time, but of course I didn't tell them the real reason."

JOHN RINGLING

John Ringling was once reputed, according to Dun and Bradstreet, to have been worth $90,000,000. He was the advance agent of the show and knew every little town and hamlet in the United States. He was a shrewd investor, and among his enterprises was a road connecting two belt-lines through Texas. This road ran through oilfields which Ringling developed. He built the town of Ringling along this road.

One time when John Ringling happened to be in the town of Ringling, he was sitting around the hotel lobby talking with eight other men. Staying at the hotel was a prospector who came to John and said that he was down and out, but had an option on an oil field, which he would sell for $1,000. John did not have much faith in the worth of the field but got busy and talked each of the men into buying a share at $100. The $800 was offered the prospector, who signed over his rights to the field. In less than six weeks this field was sold for $1,000,000.

HENRY RINGLING

Henry Ringling, one of the younger brothers, took Otto's place as treasurer and head ticket man when that brother died. Mr. Foley of the Great Northern Nursery Co., Baraboo, returned to that city one fall and found the weather to be unusually cold and a frost threatening 42,000 small apple trees about two feet tall. If they were to be saved for early spring delivery it was necessary that they be dug up instantly and put into a sheltering warehouse. Only that afternoon remained, and he had only a team or two. They could not possibly operate the heavy mechanical digger, which had to be drawn under the trees to a depth of eighteen inches, thus severing still deeper roots. It so happened that day the circus arrived in town, its winter quarters. Mr. Foley went to Henry Ringling and related his troubles. Henry loaned him all the heavy working horses and laborers he needed. Before night every one of the 42,000 trees was safely sheltered in the warehouses. The next day Mr. Foley returned to Henry's home and asked for the bill. Henry asked that a box of twelve-cent, not five-cent, cigars be given to the laborers who had helped to take in the trees. "Take 'em down to the boys; that'll do," he said.

DELAVAN

WILLIAM C. COUP

It was W. C. Coup of Delavan, Wisconsin, not Barnum, who first conceived the idea of the three-ring circus. Coup began his circus career by working with small circuses. Later he joined the Mabie Brothers Circus of Delavan, obtaining sideshow privileges. In 1868 he went with the Yankee Robinson Show, becoming assistant manager.

In 1870 Coup was inspired to put on a mammoth circus larger than anything that had been attempted. This great undertaking could not be accomplished without financial aid and the name of a well-established circus executive and owner. Thus it was that he wrote to Barnum, then in semiretirement in Bridgeport, Connecticut. Barnum was sixty years old at this time and did not feel inclined to organize a great traveling attraction. But Coup worked upon his vanity and gained the desired result.

Receiving Barnum's letter of encouragement, Coup went to New York and as general director and manager put together the greatest circus ever seen under the largest spread of canvas.

The show opened in Brooklyn on April 10, 1871, and that season it broke all records to date for profit, making $400,000. Coup's idea being a success, his prolific brain gave birth to more ways of expanding the show's business, and he made arrangements with leading railroads to run excursions from towns within a radius of seventy-five miles of New York and cities in the New England states. Now attendance possibilities were tremendously increased, and for the first time the railroad entered the story. Thus had Coup put his finger unerringly on the disadvantage of wagon show transportation. It was impossible always to go from one large town to another, and he reasoned that if receipts in towns of all sizes varied from $1,000 to $7,000 daily, the intake in larger places was often three or four times as much. He thought that if they could put the show on rails they would be able to make the larger towns and could then expect the smaller surrounding towns to come to them.

When he had interested railroad officials in the proposition, the idea was given a trial, and New Brunswick, New Jersey, was fixed upon as the first loading place. Sixty-one cars were contracted for. The first attempts were almost a failure because the cars were not uniform in size and many were not large enough to hold the heavy wagons. Barnum wanted Coup to abandon the innovation, but Coup insisted on going through with it. During that first week Coup declared that he never took his clothes off his back from the first day until the show reached Philadelphia. All during this hectic week the railroad departments did everything in their power to put this new type of transportation across. Soon special cars were built and the circus was revolutionized.

After two record-breaking seasons of Barnum's Greatest Show on Earth, Coup planned a great indoor Hippodrome in New York City. He secured an option on a site between Madison and Fourth Avenues and Twenty-Sixth and Twenty-Seventh Streets and sold stock in what he called the New York Hippodrome, later to become famous as Madison Square Garden. The New York Hippodrome opened April 27, 1874.

The next spring Coup was obliged to take a continental trip for his health. When he returned he found that Barnum had allowed two different showmen to use his name; this confused the public and proved bad for business.

Coup's next enterprise was to build the New York Aquarium in partnership with Charles Reiche, a famous animal dealer. The two men could not get along, however; and finally, failing to agree, Coup lost his entire holdings on the toss of a coin and calmly walked off the property.

For several years Coup ran his own shows with some success until 1882, when, with his W. C. Coup's Monster Shows, at the time one of the largest on the road, he ran into terrifically bad weather. Then on August 19 a railroad smashup placed him in a bad way financially. From this blow Coup never fully recovered. His shows degenerated until he ended his brilliant career by running a ten-cent museum on the small-town sidings. In 1891 he retired to his home in Delavan and later died in poverty in Jacksonville, Florida, in 1895.

Barnum's name lives for posterity because he took credit during his lifetime for everything glamorous and symbolic of the showman's world, the sawdust ring. He thrived on publicity. He was such a unique, picturesque character that those about him, no matter what their status, paled alongside the color of his conversation, his perseverance through repeated failures, his kindly deeds, and lovable personality. Coup, on the contrary, avoided personal publicity, and for that reason his name is unknown except to students of circus literature, which is now mostly out of print and unattainable by the general public.*

ELISE KENNEBEL DOCKRILL

Elise Dockrill was acclaimed by Barnum and Bailey the "Empress of the Arena." She was the greatest bareback rider the world has ever known and was born in France, where her family traveled with the Franconi Circus. She learned to ride when she was very young

* Adopted from *Railroad Man's Magazine*, published by the Frank A. Munsey Company, New York.

and soon became the star performer with the circus, traveling all over Europe. In 1870 she married Richard Dockrill, an Irish lad from Cork, Ireland, who was a bareback rider traveling with a circus in France.

The young couple combined forces and became known as the "Great London Show." Two years later they brought their show to America and joined P. T. Barnum just a few days before the great fire that burned the museum and animal quarters to the ground. At this time Richard Dockrill's special feature was the exhibition of ten remarkably trained stallions. Mme. Dockrill drove four galloping horses at one time, riding bareback or standing astride them.

While the company's stock was being loaded on board ship at Brest, France, one of Elise Dockrill's favorite horses had its back broken, and on the way over, the crated horses were washed overboard by the high seas. With the burning of properties and costumes and the severe loss of the horses, the young riders were badly handicapped at the start in a new country.

They took a position with the John Wilson Show in San Francisco, where they remained until Barnum had reestablished his circus. They returned to him and Mme. Dockrill became a headliner, while her husband was equestrian director.

In 1880 the Dockrills set out for South America with a show of their own. For finances they took $100,000 in currency in a small trunk. Though the show was well received, their expenses exceeded their profits, and they returned with the little trunk empty and the whole circus personnel ill with yellow fever.

During a performance in Venezuela, programs were printed on white satin, in honor of the president's attendance. Mme. Dockrill went successfully through her sensational performance, dashing through paper balloons and over banners, winning thunderous applause for her skill. The act ended with her springing on and off her horse as he galloped at full speed around the ring. Making her final jump from her horse, Elise suddenly crumpled to the ground. She had stepped into a small depression made by her horse and had dislocated her knee. It was never again strong enough to support her during strenuous bareback riding.

The Dockrills came home, and Richard again became equestrian director for the Barnum & Bailey show and later for several others.

During the time Elise Dockrill was a feature of Barnum's circus, she received $500 a week throughout the year and had one half of P. T. Barnum's private car for her own use. She also had a carriage, team, and driver at her disposal at all times and stopped at the best hotels.

Mr. Albee of Keith-Albee vaudeville circuit, now RKO, said in tribute of Mme. Dockrill, "I traveled with Mme. Dockrill many years and she was the Bernhardt of the circus."

The life story of this famed woman could be told from press clippings of her performances before European royalty, her triumph with P. T. Barnum's Circus, and her great success in South America.

Richard and Elise Dockrill claimed Delavan as their home, and they rest there now in the Spring Grove Cemetery.

> Adopted from the *Milwaukee Journal*,
> April 13, 1930

EVANSVILLE

"Colonel" George Hall

About eighty or more years ago the Howe & Cushing Circus arrived by wagon in the little city of Manchester, New Hampshire. When the circus arrived young George Washington Hall was on the lot waiting for it, and all that day he watched every move of the mysterious nomads who traveled by night and showed by day. That night when the circus left for its twenty-mile haul to the next town, George was stowed away under a roll of canvas.

Thus began George Hall's circus career, which continued through seven decades. He acquired the title "Colonel" Hall, it is said, down in Mexico during a revolution many years ago when his show was attacked by rioters.

To the circus men of his day and the succeeding generations Hall was, and is, known by the endearing title of "Popcorn George." It was a title justly earned and one of which he was proud. His first work with the Howe & Cushing Show was with the "candy butcher." George used to take huge baskets of freshly popped corn around the tent and sell it. Even Solon Robinson, then one of the editors of the New York Tribune, ate some of the popcorn from George's basket. He praised it and told the youthful vendor to look him up if he ever came to New York.

Horace Greeley, of the same paper, also ate of it and gave sage advice and encouragement. When summer was over young George went to New York. He sought out Mr. Robinson, borrowed ten dollars, and became a popcorn vendor in the metropolis. On some days the corn would not sell. He tried various expedients, but some way he always managed to have a supply left at night. Finally the brilliant idea of making it into bricks evolved itself through necessity, and he took one of the first bricks to Horace Greeley, who ate, enjoyed, and wrote of it in the great *Tribune* of those days.

He was thirteen years old then and might have become a leading merchant of New York had he remained there, but his one season with the circus had unfitted him for home life, and when the call of the sawdust came in the spring he found himself again trouping.

The young man was promoted and became a "barker" for the sideshow. Later he exploited the free show in the "big top."

Winter saw him again in New York manufacturing his popcorn bricks in an attic which he had rented and selling them on the streets and in offices. His first loan from Solon Robinson had long ago been repaid. He had paid it by delivering one of his bricks daily to the *Tribune* office, and one of his choicest possessions was the receipt in full signed by Mr. Robinson.

Hall belonged to the days when the circus was distinct from the menagerie show and was a one-ring affair. The lighting was effected by tallow tips set in tin cups with tin reflectors about the ring. The circus carried seats for patrons and gave a ring performance. The menagerie did not, but the genial "Professor" explained the wonders in each cage or elevated stand. A menagerie act completed the performance.

In 1860 Hall came to Wisconsin and ran a sideshow for one season. Then for several years he worked for Jerry Mabie of Delavan.

In 1886 he took his own show on the road, making Evansville his headquarters. About this time he bought Big Charlie, the elephant, from the Ringling Brothers. Big Charlie was reputed to have outweighed the famous Jumbo. Under the dexterous training of Hall's

daughter, Mabel, he became tractable and proved a good invest-
ment for many years. In later years he became more and more unmanageable and had to be killed.

Hall was the first circus owner to take his show out of the country.
Later he chartered the schooner *Emma Fox* and carried his circus
to the West Indies and South America. He showed in the Bahamas,
Trinidad, and back to the mainland, having stands in many of the
cities in the Amazon region. The outbreak of the Spanish-American
War found him showing in old Mexico.

Among the performers whose talents contributed to making "Popcorn George" Hall's name known in circus history was Lou, his wife,
known professionally as Zula Zangara, a snake charmer, who was
especially adept in training "cats." She was known to have trained
many "outlaws." On one occasion Mrs. Hall took her husband's circus
to the West Indies alone and carried on for some time before the
Colonel joined her. Hall's daughter, Mabel, won fame as the only
woman elephant trainer; she also rode "high school," or trained,
horses.

Dolores Vallecita, Spanish lady, trained six leopards to do the
following acts for Hall: the rolling globe, the seesaw, the electric
wheel, pyramids and pictures, ending the act by the leopards' playing chimes as she played the piano.

One of Hall's biggest attractions was Captain Bates and his wife.
Captain was eight feet tall and weighed 550 pounds. Mrs. Bates was
eight feet two inches tall and weighed 480 pounds. They were the
tallest married couple ever on exhibition.

"Popcorn George" was the last of the old showmen. He taught all
his children to be circus performers and managers, and for three
generations there was a Hall circus to set up its big top and entertain the multitude of people who each summer succumbed to the
lure of the sawdust ring.

chapter 8

BURIED TREASURE TALES

O<small>NE</small> Sunday afternoon we went out to Gotham to investigate a treasure tale: the famous yarn of Bogus Bluff. Along the Wisconsin River, between Gotham and Muscoda, on the river's right-hand bank, there rises a very high bluff. On its lower slope it is covered with brush and small trees, but near the top a wall of stone rises for twenty or thirty feet, and in this stone, if you know just where to look for it, is the opening of a cave—not a very large cave, it would appear from the outside, but a cave which, nevertheless, is one of the famous outlaw hangouts of Wisconsin.

We had with us several hundred feet of strong cord which we planned to use to guide us back to the opening after we had explored inside; we had been told that the cave, within, was extensive, with many passages and ramifications. We were, of course, not the first to explore Bogus Bluff. Probably a thousand other adventurers had been there before us, but there was a lot of mystery for us in the visit anyway, despite the many initials that were carved into the rock. For we were on the trail of a treasure story that involved a band of bold counterfeiters who performed here their desperate trade in the 1870's and who were finally captured by a brave detective who posed as a local farmer.

We had heard the legend of buried money in the cave—a lot of money, probably counterfeit, but money nevertheless. We were out

233

to see for ourselves the setting of crime, and perhaps, just perhaps, we might stumble onto something that the many other previous explorers had missed. So, with a couple of flashlights and with our cord trailing out behind us, the outside end fastened to a stout tree, we entered the cave.

The tunnels of the cave are not too large. We bent double, then suddenly we were on hands and knees. We shone our lights around the low walls and kept going. We had heard that the money was buried in a large inner chamber, and it was for this chamber we were looking. Finally, after our cord was about played out and our elbows and knees were in worse condition, we did enter a larger place in the cave, a sort of chamber high enough to stand in and quite wide enough to bury some money in, if anybody wanted to do that with money.

We stood silent, flashing our lights, and I began to shuffle around in the dirt of the floor, kicking gently at this or that, and my right toe encountered an object, quite buried, and the thought flickered through: Well! Maybe I have discovered something. I leaned down, my fingers uncovered the round metal object, and I lifted it and held it in my light. It had once been treasure, all right, but no longer. Once it had held a delightful amber fluid, and still legible on the side of it I could see: SCHLITZ.

But buried treasure, like empty beer cans, is likely to turn up anywhere, and is a fascinating subject in any region. Probably nothing clings like a buried treasure legend. Wisconsin hasn't had pirates who buried iron-bound chests loaded with pieces of eight on sandy beaches or lonely islands, but she has her share of treasure tales nevertheless.

Charles E. Brown, late curator of the Wisconsin Historical Society Museum, had a deep interest in these treasure stories and knew the locations of most of the supposed loot. We present some of Charles Brown's yarns as told to him by a number of persons.

THE SECRETED COIN

Bill Tompkins was an early settler in the vicinity of Portage. He owned a farm on the Madison to Portage road, now Highway 51, at a distance of about four miles south of the city. A roadside gas station now occupies a small part of it.

Tompkins was said to have brought with him from the east, when he came to this part of Wisconsin, a large sum of money, reputed to be about $50,000 in amount. This money he carefully secreted for safekeeping somewhere on his farm, no one but himself knowing just where he hid it. He made a good living for that time by farming, hunting, and fishing.

After his death, some years later, a search was made for his hidden wealth, which could not be found. His family sold the farm afterward and moved to Portage or elsewhere. Some years later, a daughter found among her father's belongings a rudely drawn map which was believed to give the location of the secreted gold. In her determination to retrieve his hoard she went to the farm owner and generously offered to give him a certain part of the money if he would permit excavation for its recovery. This the farmer refused to do. If the gold was buried on his farm he proposed to regain it for himself and not to surrender even a part of it to anyone.

He dug everywhere, in every likely spot. He did find, it was reported, a few coins placed in tin cans, while he was digging postholes, but he never did happen upon the main cache of gold. Of course he was much disappointed. In later years other gold hunters also dug for the hoard but also with no result. The money remains lost.

Presumably the original owners' descendants retained the map. Now, after years, it is reported that a granddaughter of Tompkins is endeavoring to purchase the old farm, perhaps with the plan of again attempting the recovery of Bill Tompkins' well-hidden gold.

THE INDIAN TREASURE CACHE AT MILWAUKEE

Peter Sahpenais, Potawatomi Indian, of Carter, Wisconsin told this story:

This story was told by my grandmother where they was living in Milwaukee River about 1833 or 1834 and from that time they move to Canada and was there for few years and came back to Michigan and stayed there ever since. But one thing I like to find out. There is hidden treasure there my grandmother told me her father and mother work very hard all night digging a pit and was walled with thick birch bark which they had for roofing and was three layers and five or six brass kettles, three kettles upright and three kettles upside down to cover the bottom ones. It was a large kettle again medium size and small one inside this kettle contains necklaces and earrings and silver and gold and some medicine too. But the money was tied in a buckskin and put away about 1834, they had payment about in 1833. This was the last payment from the government and there wasn't any stores at that time. So they didn't spend any of the money they have been keeping it now you can find out about it. There was one white man name was Juneau who had some trading he trade some powder and lead. It is a second bend of river up stream from where Juneau house was you can almost tell how far this would be. She said in early mornings they could hear Juneau chopping wood as far as sound of echo could go that how far up river where there had money.

But I couldn't tell just how tall my great grandfather was but to say about six feet or more. This money is been there since if nobody didn't digged out. There was many houses or village when they come back and they feared that they might fight with them so they left the money there.

SILVER MOUND

Silver Mound, a V-shaped mound or ridge near Alma Center, in Jackson County, Wisconsin, has been quarried by the Indians, perhaps for centuries, to obtain material for the manufacture of stone implements useful in their domestic life, in hunting, fishing, and warfare. The material obtained here is quartzite, a metamorphosed sandstone, largely of a sugary white and whitish color. This hard and durable rock the natives here roughed out with stone hammers into leaf-shaped forms of various sizes. These blanks they bore away to their villages and there fashioned the material into spades, hoes, celts, knives, scrapers, and projectile points.

The entire top of the Mound is scarred with shallow pits which the Indians dug and quarried to get a quartzite of a desired quality.

On the Mound and in the fields below are workshop sites where the quartzite blocks were dressed down into desired shapes.

There is a story that in about the year 1697 the French trader Pierre Charles LeSueur visited this region and from the top of another mound viewed through a spyglass the Indians quarrying and bearing away rock in bags from this Silver Mound. This rock, because of the care they devoted to selecting pieces for their bags, he naturally supposed to be precious metal, probably silver ore. They were hostile Indians of a tribe from beyond the Mississippi. He did not wish to encounter them.

This location he marked on a map of the region. In 1698 LeSueur returned to France and there obtained permission from the government to undertake mining operations at the Mound. In 1700 he returned to Louisiana in America. He brought with him a party of miners. With these he traveled up the Mississippi in a large vessel. With smaller boats he went up the Trempealeau River and then proceeded overland to the Mound. Here his miners sank a shaft and did other prospecting. They were disappointed in finding no silver. When the party left they cached their mining tools and some of their other equipment at the Mound.

LeSueur died after his return to Louisiana colony. Later his map, or a copy or it, was obtained by others from a very old French recluse at St. Louis, and another party was organized there and began mining at Silver Mound. Their efforts were also in vain. They found no silver but they did discover the cache of spades, picks, and sledges, presumably the very implements left behind nearly half a century before by LeSueur. They were badly rusted.

The belief that Silver Mound contains veins of silver has persisted, and parties of white men have continued to dig at the Mound for the elusive metal since that date. Other men and parties have mined and dug there in 1856, 1872, 1873, and 1895. Samples of the rock were sent to England and elsewhere to be assayed, but no trace of silver was found in any of these specimens. The mine is a "lost" mine.

The Indians say that there is silver in Silver Mound, and that their great-grandfathers obtained the metal there. But a great spirit, Waucondah, guards the treasure and no white man will ever find it.

LOST TREASURE YARNS

In about the year 1829 or 1830, a small steamboat was puffing up the Wisconsin River, on its way to the U. S. frontier Fort Winnebago at Portage. In its cargo were several chests of coin intended for use in paying the wages of the soldiers stationed there, and for other uses. When this ship reached the present vicinity of Lone Rock, it struck a snag in the river bed. Water poured into the hole thus made in its bottom, and the steamboat began to sink. The coin chests were therefore removed and conveyed to the river bank. Above this east bank of the river there rises a high bluff with a steep slope down to the river bank. Here the coin chests were placed in a pit dug in the top of the bank for this purpose. The Indians of the surrounding region were at this time rather unfriendly, or hostile, to the whites. It was hoped to thus save the rather heavy chests from them until they could be recov ered and taken to the fort.

The ship soon sank to the bottom of the river and its crew was left to make the journey to the fort on foot. It is not known whether or not they were killed by the Indians on their way. Nor is it known whether the coin chests were ever recovered and taken to their destination.

This story was told to me by a Mr. Gael Moore of Lone Rock in about the year 1906. We crossed the river to the site of the early disaster. There on the bank we saw quite a line of pits which a credulous treasure hunter or hunters had dug in an attempt to locate the mythical treasure chests left there so long ago.

THE LOST PAYMASTERS CHEST

In about the year 1828 some soldiers were conveying across country, presumably from old Fort Dearborn at Chicago, a chest of coin intended for the U. S. Army paymaster at Fort Crawford at Prairie du Chien. The chest was not light, and its guard was small in numbers. They had been on the trail for several days. They knew that a war party of Indians were following them with the intention of attacking them, should a favorable opportunity to do so occur.

It was just at the beginning of winter. When they reached Lake Mendota, at the present site of Madison, they found its surface already frozen. They walked out on this ice, and when they reached its middle they heard the war cries of a large party of Indians, who in their pursuit of the little company had already reached the bank which they had recently left behind. There was a hole in the ice nearby, and in order to save their own scalps from the savages, the two soldiers who were carrying the coin chest, which was hindering their rapid flight, now dropped it through this opening. Thus relieved from their burden, the soldiers fled rapidly to the western shore and succeeded in making good their escape. Needless to say that this mythical coin chest has never been recovered.

Note that a similar story is told about Lake Poygan, and perhaps about some other southern Wisconsin lakes.

TREASURE CAVE

Sometime in the twenties of the past century a keelboat was coming down the Wisconsin River from Fort Winnebago at the portage. On this primitive craft was a chest of coin and other valuables to be delivered at Fort Crawford at Prairie du Chien.

When the boat neared the mouth of the Wisconsin, after an uneventful journey, it was learned that a gathering of hostile Indians, Winnebago or Sioux, was in the vicinity of the Fort. As the chest could not be delievered without great danger and probable loss, the captain decided to provide for the safety of its contents by burying it.

The place selected for its disposal was beneath the floor of a cave, since known as "Treasure Cave," located up near the top of the high river bluff in present Dewey State Park. This accomplished, the keelboat proceeded on its way to the Mississippi. It luckily escaped Indian attack.

Later in that year or the following year, when an attempt was made to recover the iron-bound treasure chest, it was found that a large landslide of rock and soil had taken place, completely covering the entrance to the cave. To attempt its removal with only a few tools and men would have been a very difficult undertaking, and the treasure was allowed to remain securely hidden. Then came the years of Indian unrest leading up to the Black Hawk War, and nothing could be done to retrieve it.

In recent years men have dug for the chest in the cave floor and on the bluff slope, but with no result.

TABLE MOUND

Table Mound is located north of the highway, about midway between the Dane County villages of Black Earth and Cross Plains. This high, flat-topped Mound, one of the highest in southern Wisconsin, is a favorite picnic place of the region in which it is situated.

A legend of this Mound, which appears to go back to early days of settlement of this region, states that a band of marauding Indians who had plundered some white settlement or trading post of its coin and other treasures, being pursued by soldiery or irate whites, buried it in some place that they thought secure, on the Mound top.

During the passing years various persons, eager to possess this treasure, have searched everywhere on the Mound for it, but it has not been found. Test holes have been dug for it in various likely places on the Mound. Indians visiting the region have also been questioned but have not divulged its location. This legend, which has no foundation in fact, so far as can be discovered, will probably pass on to coming generations of farmers and townspeople in this region. There are said to be other versions of this "lost treasure" yarn.

THE OLD SILVER MINE

A clairvoyant living at Eau Claire once claimed to have been informed by her Indian guide, Big Heart, that at a certain place four miles south of the city a rich silver deposit was located. This was in the seventies. Bill Pond, a logging contractor, had faith in her prophecy. He went to the place indicated and dug a shaft or pit down through the soil and into the sandstone rock beneath. No silver-bearing rock was found. The silver mine was a sore disappointment. One man did afterwards show a bead of silver. This he claimed to have been assayed from the rock disturbed in this profitless digging.

This place, still known as "the Old Silver Mine," is located at the base of a sandstone ridge across the Chippewa River from the once thriving lumbering settlement of Porters Mills. This town is no longer in existence. For years "the Old Silver Mine" locality was a favorite picnic ground of Eau Claire people. There was then there a fine grove of oak trees and other attractive surroundings. Some of the trees have since been cut down. Because of the mythical mine the locality is one of romance and mystery.

THE LOST MINE

Jan Trewitt, a Cornishman, lived in a shack in one of the little valleys or "hollers" in the Platte River country, not so very far from Platteville, in southwestern Wisconsin. He there did a bit of farming and worked a little at lead mining. Jan, when not otherwise engaged, was always roaming about in the wild hills searching, it was thought, for lead prospects. Once, after such an expedition, he returned with a bag of lead ore. This he somewhere disposed of to his advantage. Soon thereafter he brought in a second bag. This sold, he disappeared in the hills again. His goings and comings were very mysterious. Sometimes he would remain away from his shack for a number of days or perhaps a week. He had money and he had never had any before. He seemed to be getting more and more prosperous.

Jan was very secretive about his wanderings. He would tell no one where he got his mineral. Some of his neighbors made attempts to track him to his "mine," but Jan was wily and shook them off in the brush, or led them on wild goose chases. All efforts to discover the source of his wealth failed. Some of his neighbors began to be suspicious of his sudden prosperity. Soon it was talked about that Jan had entered into a secret compact with the Evil One. He was trading his soul and body to that demon for worldly gain. This, Jan, when questioned, did not deny. Lights were sometimes seen in his cabin late at night. It seemed certain, then, that Jan was receiving a visit from his master, the Devil.

It was during this year that Jan once left again on one of his secret rambles. After the passing of several weeks he failed to return. He never did return. He was never again seen or heard of. Careful and continued search was made for his "mine," which everyone surmised must be fabulously rich, but it was never found.

THE POT OF GOLD AT CLARNO

The following tale of lost treasure was related to me by E. G. Gloege of Monroe. It is known to others.

Years ago there resided at Clarno, a town near the southern boundary of Green County, on a farm, an old man who was reputed to possess a large sum of money. He lived a very frugal life, spending very little money at any time, and never telling anyone where he kept his hoarded wealth.

Within a few years this old man died. After his death his relatives and friends searched every part of the premises for the secreted money but could find no trace of it. It had been very carefully hidden. The old house, the barn, and other structures on the grounds were examined, and the land surrounding the place dug over, but no discoveries were made.

The farm was sold to others. Some years passed by and the matter of the "lost treasure" was quite generally forgotten. At about this time, according to the story, there appeared at a bank in a neighboring town, presumably in Illinois, a stranger who presented to the banker a gold coin of which he wished to know the value. It was a curious foreign piece. The banker recognized it as a great numismatic rarity. He asked its owner how he had come into the possession of the coin, and wished to know if he had any more. The stranger stated that he had found a lot of similar coins and was told to bring them in to the banker for examination.

Within a few days he returned bringing with him a bag containing, it was said, a large number of gold coins. These represented a very large sum of money. The banker convinced the owner that under a government law of treasure trove these must be left with him until the matter of their finding could be fully investigated and their ownership proved. This the finder consented to do. When he returned, some time later, to see the banker, the bank was found to be closed. The banker had quietly disappeared and had taken with him in his flight the fortune in gold coins.

It was later learned that the finder had found the gold in an old metal can at the bottom of a dry, unused well on his farm. Thus the hoarded wealth of the former owner of the place had been found after years, and only to disappear again. Just how large a sum of money was represented by the gold coins found in this can, and how the original owner obtained these rare and curious foreign pieces, will probably always remain a neighborhood mystery.

COON ROCK CAVE

This cave is located about four and a half miles west of Arena in Iowa County, on the farm of George Hodgson. It is high up in a bluff. Its entrance is about nine feet high and six feet wide. Its narrow passage is barely high enough and wide enough to crawl through comfortably on one's hands and knees. The floor is sticky clay. The passage is of quite uniform width with no rooms of any size.

Coon Rock is a promontory that juts out to the East from the regular line of bluffs on the south side of the Wisconsin River. Two legends have grown up around Coon Rock cave. One concerns itself with the kidnapping of a ten-year-old girl. She was alleged to have been held captive in this cave for a number of months.

A second legend claims that in the days when the Wisconsin River was still used as an important medium of travel, a government shipment of gold was taken by a band of daring river pirates, chucked into a crevice in Coon Rock cave, and covered with red clay. This legend has caused a wide search for treasure. Digging over wide areas in this part of the bluff to discover the closed passage is evident.

THE ST. CROIX LOST TREASURE

John J. Johnson of Nashota told this story:

I was up in St. Croix County, Wisconsin, one summer, and got well acquainted with an old man by the name of Hulbert. He had a small log cabin and forty acres of land, a wife and two children. He was very tight and lived almost like a hermit. He used to draw water with his oxen about a mile the year round because he was too tight to dig a well forty feet deep. The neighbors said he had plenty of money hid in the woods. Even his wife didn't know where he had it hid. It may still be buried there.

THE BOOT TREASURE

About five miles northeast of Nashota there was a farm that changed hands several times. In an early day on this farm there was a shallow pond that dried up in recent years. A few years ago the farmer decided to plow it up. There were some large willows near the edge which he had to dig out, and in doing so he found an old boot almost decayed under one of them. In it was a hundred dollars in gold coin.

This man took them to one of the banks in Milwaukee and left them until he could decide what to do with them. The only explanation that was ever made for the money was that there was a man who worked for one of the nearby farmers and who enlisted in the Civil War about 1862. They thought he might have put it there intending to get it when he returned. But he never came back.

THE FINCH BURIED TREASURE

There are many wild-eyed tales of buried treasure connected with the famous outlaw family known as "the Fighting Finches," members of which lived in the country around Lake Mills and Jefferson. It seems unlikely that this gang actually had any great wealth, however. The outlaws were never known to have much money at hand, and they were perhaps too uneducated to appreciate the value of other kinds of likely prizes. They were horse thieves and highwaymen, but it is probably unlikely that any of their victims contributed enough to warrant burying the loot.

Finch caches of hidden treasure were supposed to exist near Lake Mills, Fort Atkinson, and on the northwest shore of Lake Koshkonong. In 1882, a farmer near Lake Mills discovered a jar containing money. The dates on some of the coins coincided with the date during which time the Finches had been at the height of their power, and so the money, from the 1830's, was believed to have come from a Finch cache.

chapter 9

PRACTICAL JOKERS, HOAXERS, CHARACTERS,
AND TRICK PLAYERS

The greatest trickster of them all was Gene Shepard of Rhinelander, Wisconsin. He made his name immortal as the inventor of the "Hodag," that fierce and mythical woodland beast, and Rhinelander to this day is known as "the Hodag City."

The "Hodag" was only one of hundreds of Shepard pranks which he performed at every opportunity for nearly forty years in the Rhinelander area. He was a master cartoonist and decorated his personal letters to friends with drawings of Paul Bunyan's lumber camp, which Gene claimed was "on the Onion River about forty miles west of Rhinelander."

Gene Shepard was also sought after as a timber cruiser or "land-looker." Matt Stapleton, old-timer of the north woods country, said, "Shepard came to Oneida County before 1889. He had made new maps of Northern Wisconsin and Oneida County and had given names to most of the lakes in the region. Tim Lennon, another great landlooker, had teamed up with Shepard and more money was paid to them for their estimates of pine timber than to any other two men in the state. I soon found that these two men were well posted on meanders of lakes and rivers and knew all the section corners and could be depended upon. We soon became fast friends. Everyone knew Shepard the land man. He often called upon me to go over tracts of timber with him, and we often went down to the U. S. land office at Wausau."

MATT STAPLETON'S ACCOUNT OF THE POODLE DOG

I will never forget one trip that we made together. We sat in the middle of the passenger car, I occupying the aisle side of the seat. Those were the days when the poodle dog first became popular. Every woman, and especially the ladies up around Hurley, had one of these creatures for a pet.

There was one of these ladies in our coach. She was a beautiful woman and was traveling south with her poodle. She was well-dressed, wore a wide-brimmed red hat, and was an elegant stepper.

It was a warm day and the dog was very thirsty. Her seat was at the front of the car. In those days there was an ice-water tank at the rear of every car and she made a few trips to the rear with a silver cup to get water for the poodle. As she passed on one of these little journeys, Shepard kicked our seat and barked like a dog. He called to me then to keep that dog of mine quiet or he would call the conductor. Of course the car was in an uproar.

Then he whispered to me that the next time she went by I should pinch one of her legs. He would bark very loud as I did so and she would think that my dog had bit her. This we thought a good joke.

The lady soon returned for more water. Then Shepard nudged me to get into action. So, just as she passed me I gave her near leg a terrible pinch. Then I waited for Shepard to bark, but he never made a noise of any kind. The lady turned quickly around, greatly surprised, of course, and slapped my face. Shepard made matters worse for me. When she screamed he called out that a low-down lumberjack like myself ought to be thrown off the train for pinching the leg of a "nice lady" in a car full of nice people. I shrunk to small size then and tried to get under the seat, while the passengers roared with laughter. Of course the Hurley lady became my bitter enemy for the rest of that ride.

There are some other versions of the same yarn that are worth telling. Mrs. Isabel Ebert of Tomahawk Lake says that she heard other versions in Madison. She relates: "Shepard was going down to the city—to Oshkosh or Milwaukee. He was sitting next to the window and somebody else was with him—one story was it was a man who wanted to buy some timber and Gene was taking him around. Another is that it was just some friend, and the third story is that it was Archie Sievwright. And that woman—one story is that she was a kind of foreign-looking woman. She came in carrying a baby and sat down opposite Gene. She had her leg kind of stuck out in the aisle and Gene said to the fellow sitting beside him, 'You reach down and pinch her leg and I will bark like a dog.' So this fellow pinched but Gene didn't bark. The conductor almost put them off the train. The man who had pinched had to act like he was crazy the rest of the way.

"There is one more version I heard," said Mrs. Ebert. "As they got near Oshkosh a foreign-looking family got on. They were apparently going to a big picnic or something in Oshkosh. The father was a great big man. The daughter sat down opposite Gene. The father had a big picnic basket. When Gene's companion pinched the girl the father was going to beat up the fellow who did the pinching. The conductor came and Gene said, 'Never mind, I am taking him to the insane asylum at Oshkosh.'"

Lloyd Taylor of Rhinelander related a version he heard from his father, Arthur Taylor: "The tale involved Shepard, who was sitting on the window side of the train, and this man, whoever he was, who knew Shepard's ability to bark like to dog. A woman was sitting across the aisle. Gene said, 'You reach over and grab her and I will bark like a dog.' The woman was apparently a large type of woman, a peasant type, and as I heard the story the stocking that was exposed was striped with the stripes going horizontally. Whoever it was that was with Gene, he made a good grab, and Gene sat looking out the window when this woman turned around. She had a large, family-size umbrella and started beating hell out of this man. Gene said, 'Oh, you mustn't do that. He's crazy. I'm taking him to the asylum at Oshkosh.'"

SPENCE BROWN'S POODLE DOG YARN

You've heard the one about Shep (Gene Shepard). He was going to Wausau to file on some land, and there was somebody on the train

248 WISCONSIN LORE

with him that was going to file on the same piece of land. So he made an agreement with the fellow.

There was a woman with a baby in her arms who had been bothering them quite a lot by walking back and forth in the car. Shep could bark like a dog. Shep said to the fellow, "Next time she passes you, you pinch her and I'll bark," and so when the girl came by again, the fellow nudged Shep and reached out and pinched the girl. But Shep didn't bark. When they got to Antigo this girl had this fellow arrested and had him taken off the train.

So Shep got into Wausau and filed on the land ahead of this fellow.

ALLEN BROWN'S POODLE DOG STORY

The one I got was, Shep and this fellow had been looking over the same timber. They had to transfer at Eland to get to the land office at Wausau. Shep sent a telegram to the sheriff describing the man and saying he would be setting with him. When the time came the sheriff got aboard the car and said to this fellow, "You answer the description and I'm holding you." And Shep went on and filed on and entered this timber land.

RONALD REARDON'S POODLE DOG VERSION

Well, Shep just boarded this train and he sat with this salesman in the seat. And Shep was on the inside and the salesman came and sat down with him and in the seat in front of them was this teacher. The salesman knew a little about Shep evidently, but not very much, so Shep fixed it up for this salesman. He said, "You reach over and pinch her leg there and I'll bark like a dog." So the salesman reached over and pinched her leg but Shep didn't bark. That's the story as I've heard it told in the store many times. No one was trying to embellish it.

FRITZ STERLING'S POODLE DOG ACCOUNT

Well, Shep he pulled a good one on a fellow by the name of Ben Sweet. He was a Milwaukee man with money who was always investing in timber or looking for investments. And he used to get Shep to go with him to look over a piece of timber and they were on a train one day ... you got to remember that this Ben Sweet was a gullible individual. They sat in a seat in one of the old cars and Shep sat next to the window and Sweet sat next to the aisle. One seat across from them and just ahead were a couple of big, chunky—I think Norwegian—girls. One of them sat with her leg outside in the aisle—like that—with her dress pulled up a little bit. Shep could bark like a hound. He says, "Ben," he says, "you reach over there and grab her by the leg good and tight and I'll bark like a hound and we'll scare the stuffings out of them." So Sweet reached over and grabbed the girl by the leg, and Shep just sat there by the window and didn't make a sound. They both had to leave that car.

MATT STAPLETON TELLS ABOUT THE WILD KENTUCKIAN

Once Shepard and I reached Gagen Junction too late to get our train. We had been out in the snow all day and were cold. We had to wait there until 2 A.M. to get a train to Rhinelander. We went to a real roughhouse saloon, where many were drinking, to warm up. Among those in this joint was a rather wild and rough-looking Kentucky trapper and hunter. He was drinking hard and when he got stewed he told everybody that he was the sole survivor of a bloody Kentucky feud, that he was not afraid of "hell or hot water," and loved whiskey and a good fight. He had a fine gun and a lantern. He showed three notches on his rifle stock which represented as many men, whom he had killed in cold blood. He was just spoiling for a fight at the time. Of course none of the lumberjacks present wanted any trouble with a tough customer like him.

Shepard and I sat back in a dark corner. We were afraid also, but Gene said the Kentuck had a nice lantern, and I said he had a good gun. Gene said the man was going to Crandon and would leave before we did. "When the time comes," Gene said, "you must have a fit and I will call on that brave Kentuck man to help hold you. Then you must bite and scratch."

Soon, then, I slid down on the floor and began to roll around and make wild sounds. Shepard had moved over and was talking to the wild Kentuckian. He said to him as I fell, "Come over and help me quick. That fellow is having a fit. He was bitten by a mad dog last summer." When the Kentuck got to me I got a good hold on his legs.

Shepard, who was doing his best to help also, jerked him down and I started barking and biting him. Shepard held Kentuck's arms tight and tried to drag him away from me. Everyone in the place was wild as Shepard kept telling the Kentuck I had been bitten by a mad dog. But we had the wild man down, and although he squirmed and yelled, he was helpless. The crowd was trying to hold me. Shepard got a pail of water and dashed it over the Kentuckian. Then I fainted and let him go. He got away with remarkable speed, and I guess he is running yet. We never saw him again. When we left there was no one to claim the lantern or gun, and we were obliged to take them with us for safekeeping.

THE LORD WILL PROVIDE

Gene Shepard was once on a cruising job with a friend, at Trout Lake, and it came noontime. The friend asked what they would do for lunch. Shepard was calm and solemnly said, "The Lord will provide."

Presently a picnic party came in sight in a boat. Shepard plunged into the water up to his armpits, crying pitifully, "We're lost! We haven't eaten anything for three days!" The picnickers in the boat offered some of their lunch but were a little surprised when Shepard waded out and took the whole basket of lunch, then waded back ashore to share the victuals with his friend.

ENTERTAINING THE LADIES

Curious ladies, especially schoolteachers, visiting Gene at his home in what is now called "The Pines," would see him munching a confection from a small glass jar. "By the way," Gene would say, "do you ladies like maple sugar?" They would indeed. Gene would then shove toward them a duplicate jar of the pulverized sugar—but this jar contained strained sand.

Then the ladies would be asked whether they'd care to see the basement exhibits in Shepard's den. Of course they would. Gene would indicate the steps going down to the den. Just as his visitors reached the bottom, he would emit the most ungodly, spine-tingling screech, and at the same moment turn off the lights.

Gene could imitate a dogfight to perfection and would do so suddenly in a crowded dining room. The manager would have to explain to the terrified guests, especially the ladies.

The ladies soon learned that, while Shepard was an entertaining fellow, they had better watch out for themselves. Mrs. Isabel Ebert said: "I knew Gene Shepard after the fall of 1908. There was a big turnover in the teaching force at Rhinelander that year, and I was one of the new teachers. One of the first Saturdays in September, Gene Shepard invited two teachers from the grade school to go driving—he was going to show them the town. He called for them in a light, two-seated open carriage drawn by a team of small black horses. When we got back to our rooms that afternoon we found those two teachers in pretty bad shape. Gene had taken them along Thayer Street to show them the sawmills. When he approached the railroad tracks he dropped the reins over the edge and gave his wild yell, and the horses tore right down the tracks. The wheels on the right side went over the open rails. Miss Lenehan was thrown over the side of the carriage and the wheels passed over her. She was very bruised. We heard a great deal about Gene Shepard after that."

Lloyd Taylor said: "One story I think is interesting is a little different than the usual Shepard story. Gene Shepard was very helpful in many colorful activities of the county fair. For example, when they would take a display from Oneida County down to the state fair at Milwaukee. The years were probably 1912 and 1915 or sometime in there. They were fixing up a booth at the State Fair featuring the agriculture of Oneida County, and one of the colorful things they had was everbearing strawberries which were apparently grown in a wooden bucket of some kind, and here I have to rely on memory of the story. A woman who I remember as a Mrs. Frazier represented either the *Milwaukee Sentinel* or the *Wisconsin State Journal*. Apparently her family were the publishers of the paper. She was interested in this display of everbearing strawberries. Mr. Shepard was busy doing the artwork and writing the sign cards on various displays, and my father was explaining these everbearing strawberries to this woman. She was quite amazed at such a thing as 'everbearing strawberries.' She rather questioned father's explanation. She said, 'Look, Mr. Taylor, if I find this booth is bringing out any misinformation I certainly will write you up in a very unfavorable manner.' That was too much for Gene Shepard, and so father said, 'Mrs. Frazier, I think this gentleman here can tell you more about these everbearing strawberries.' She turned to Gene Shepard, and he looked at her very innocent, and he said, 'Mrs. Frazier, I have something here far more interesting than the everbearing strawberries.' So he took her to a display of very peculiar and ill-shaped potatoes which they had brought down for this specific purpose because they were unusual-looking. He said, 'Now these are wild potatoes—these potatoes have been growing out in the woods in an old lumber camp of Paul Bunyan that I just found last summer.' He said they were probably thrown out by the cook and they grew wild, and he said this is the way they grow wild. And he said, 'Mrs. Frazier, there is a very peculiar thing about these potatoes. They are excellent eating, but you must peel them very very carefully. If the least bit of peeling is eaten, it is a drug—it will make you do the craziest things.' He said, 'Mrs. Frazier, you would climb a telephone post and you would come down the telephone post head first, and you would look like the very dickens doing that.'"

THE PERFUMED MOSS

Then, where ladies were concerned, there was the yarn about Gene Shepard and the perfumed moss. Ronald Reardon, druggist of Rhinelander and close personal friend of Gene Shepard in the old days, said that Gene had the drugstore keep a particular brand of perfume on hand called Dactylis—a coined name, Reardon said, for a brand of perfume:

It didn't smell like lily-of-the-valley or arbutus or violets or anything. You see, it had a peculiar odor of its own. But when Gene wanted to pull that on anybody he'd just go out somewhere and find some moss, and then he had his atomizer and he'd spray that moss good with Dactylis. Then maybe there'd be a group of women in town—women fell for that perfumed moss best—a woman's club, or a garden club or something, or a group of schoolteachers. Gene he'd take them into the woods by a devious route, and after a while they'd come on this patch of moss that Gene had sprayed. Gene would talk a while about this particular species of moss, and then he'd invite the ladies to get down and smell it. I told you that

Dactylis had a peculiar odor. Well these ladies would begin to exclaim, and then they'd dig up clumps of that moss to take home.

Gene was always up to something. He built a boat, you know, a big one, about forty feet long, with staterooms on the deck. And he was going to invite all the old maid schoolteachers around here to take a ride with him down the Wisconsin River and into the Mississippi and so on down to New Orleans.

He had this boat fitted out with a mahogany finish, a big three-cylinder gas engine. She had a rear paddle wheel. Well, after Gene got it all done and wanted to move it to the Mississippi River he found out it was too big to go under the bridges, so they had to get rid of it and they loaded it on one of those gondolas on the North-western and they pulled it up beside the old pump station. They put the boat in the water there and we took a ride on it. I'll always remember that paddle wheel. It would go right over the booms, of course. They would go flying up in the air behind.

I suppose that boat cost Gene about thirty thousand dollars. He had special silver made for the table, and she had a silver bell. He wanted those old-maid schoolteachers to have a good time. Well, the boat never moved away from Rhinelander. It just rotted to pieces, little by little. Finally somebody got the bell and they preserved that. In fact the Antigo and Rhinelander football teams play for that bell every year. Last I remember of the boat it was just a few staves sticking up out of the water.

Shepard had plans for a unique sawmill on his place, "manned entirely by women." He was also planning to have the body of one Helen Hunt disinterred from Iowa soil and buried near the mill. Then, should anyone lose anything, it would be simple and convenient to "go to Helen Hunt for it."

GENE AND JUDGE LANDIS

While cruising another time near Trout Lake, Shepard saw a new boat tied up by the shore. He calmly appropriated it, rowed up the lake, where he finished his business, then returned the boat to its original anchorage and tied it up. The boat's irate owner came charging up to Shep. He was obviously a city feller, with ice-cream pants. "Listen here. I want you to know that that boat is mine. I paid for it, and it's mine." Shep, who was a hulking fellow with a barrel chest, clutched the city feller by the lapel and growled, "See here, young man. There's an unwritten law in these parts that you don't seem to know about. And the law is that we can take anything, just so long as we return it. We always return what we take—that's the unwritten law. See, your boat's right back where it was."

The city man, who turned out to be Judge Kenesaw Mountain Landis, assented to the forest law and became Gene's close friend.

GENE'S OWL HOOT HOAX

Gene was walking down a woods road one evening with a couple of young men from the East, who were camping with him. Passing among some tall trees, the group heard an owl in the top branches set up a great hooting.

"What's that?" cried the young men.

"My God!" exclaimed Gene. "It's wolves! Wolves are upon us! You fellows run for your lives. I have heart disease. I can't run. But never mind me. Run! Save your own lives!"

So the two young men dashed off down the road as though the Devil were after them.

Later they returned to camp with ax and guns to save Gene. Gene was sitting on a stump. He explained, in elaborate detail, how he had saved his life by climbing a tree, and how he had come within inches of suffering a horrible fate from the bloodthirsty pack.

BEARS LOVE GREEN CORN

Did you hear about the bear? The way Shepard could lead up to those things. On this bear thing, now we didn't know what he had in his mind at all. We were going down the river and he'd keep seeing bears running up the bank. Well nobody else saw them except Shep, but he finally got them all imagining that they could see the bears too. So then when we camped this night, why then he pulled this here deal. We had this green corn in the tent and two tenderfeet along. So he put this big rock up behind the tent and tied a rope on it and put a lot of dry brush around it and in the night pulled the rock down. "Scram," he said, "here comes that bear." Then he told these fellows to get that green corn in the tent because the bear was after that. So they ran out and grabbed all that green corn and hauled it into the tent, and, of course, I was sleeping with Shep in another tent. But Beaver (Crosby) was in with the tenderfeet, so they pulled that green corn all inside the tent and Shep gave the rope a pull again and it got closer to the tent, you know, and he says, "Get that green corn out of the tent. He'll be right in the tent there after it." Well, you should have seen that green corn fly. But he always had something like that.

Told by Ronald Reardon

WILD POTATOES

Once it was County Fair time up in Rhinelander.

This year Gene had a lot of unusually small potatoes from his farm. He knew they were practically worthless, but he brought 'em in to the Fair and put 'em on display, anyhow. Folks gathered around to ask what they were.

"Wild potatoes," said Gene with a straight face. "Yessir, *wild* potatoes. Grow only in a little woodlot on my place. Their flavor's delicious. No ordinary potato can touch 'em!"

Well, you can guess what happened: Gene sold all his "wild" potatoes that day in record time. Got a good price for 'em, too.

Gene Shepard was a character the like of whom will never be seen again in Wisconsin. He was the absolute epitome of north-woods humor, free-spending, wide ranging. Many years have passed since the lumber industry in Wisconsin reached its climax, yet the Gene Shepard influence, the Paul Bunyan influence, is still strong.

In 1897 the north country boiled with excitement over the capture of a strange beast near Rhinelander, Wisconsin. The story was that Gene Shepard, a timber cruiser, had corralled the grotesque man-killer—a cross between a dinosauer and a bulldog.

For the full yarn of how Gene performed the capture we quote the account of Luke Sylvester Kearney, better known as "Lake Shore" Kearney, who personally wrote up the famous event in a delightful small book called *The Hodag*.

THE HODAG'S CAPTURE

It happened just at twilight. Eugene Shepard, a naturalist of the north woods, was taking his customary quiet stroll into the forest, striding down a favorite trail, breathing the fragrance of the tall pines and hemlocks. Suddenly, he became aware of an unusual odor. Stopped short by the stench, he searched through the depths of the foliage until he discovered a strange creature, so unlike anything he had ever seen before that it was beyond description. Though a student of woodlore and of both prehistoric and other wild animals, Mr. Shepard could not classify the monstrosity, which gazed at him with glowing green eyes, sniffling from flaming nostrils.

The animal's back resembled that of a dinosaur, and his tail, which extended to an enormous length, had a spearlike end. Sharp spines, one and a half feet apart, lined the spinal column. The legs were short and massive, and the claws were thick and curved, denoting great strength. The broad, furrowed forehead was covered with coarse, shaggy hair and bore two large horns. From the broad, muscular mouth, sharp, glistening white teeth protruded.

This strange animal of the woods had an alert look, and the swish of his tail made the earth tremble. When he exhaled, an obnoxious odor penetrated the atmosphere for some distance. Mr. Shepard was trembling and speechless as he gazed on this horror of the forest. The great naturalist, who had conquered all before, was at his wits' end. Not a man to be overwhelmed by long odds, he began to form a plan by which he might capture this animal. And so, still shaken by what he had seen, he hastened to the nearby village to disclose his startling information to the Ancient Order of the Reveeting Society.

In the ancient tent of this mysterious order of the Reveeting Society, behind the closed flap, he related his experience to those great, world-renowned men, selected from the farthest corners of the earth, men of great courage and chivalry. They were men who in the rough-and-tumble fight with a bear would toss their guns into the brush, stick their bowie knives into a nearby tree, and take on the big bruin with bare hands. This was the type of men he selected to help him capture this formidable nondescript.

How to capture the Hodag was a real man-sized job, and none realized it more fully than the heroic Mr. Shepard. He ordered a crew of men to dig a large pit, several miles from the point where he had first sighted the animal. This huge excavation, which was fifty feet in diameter and thirty feet deep, was covered with poles thrown across the opening. The trap was then carefully hidden by limbs and grass, laid carefully across the poles.

Well pleased with his strategy, Mr. Shepard selected a man from the north woods to help with this daring adventure. This young man, fleet afoot and a noted ski-jumper, with many honors and medals, was considered to be the person most capable of engaging in the exploit. (By request, his name is not mentioned because modesty as well as bravery was one of his outstanding characteristics.)

Because the Hodag relished beef on the hoof more than any other food, a gentle ox was selected to bait the beast. The hero led the ox through the dense forest until he came in sight of the monster. Then came a growl so deep, loud, and sepulchral that it fairly shook the earth, causing a vibration so great that it started a great shower of leaves and limbs from the giant trees. The ox became frantic, but his brave leader steered him along the blazed trail with great speed. On they went, toward the pit, followed closely by the Hodag, bent upon capturing his prey! Though the beast's powerful legs were short, he covered the ground with unbelievable swiftness, tearing out trees and the heavy growth of underbrush and leaving in his wake great gashes in the earth. At intervals, one could hear an undescribable growl, and with each breath the monster emitted an odor that baffled description! Finally, only one hundred yards separated the great animal from his prey, then forty, and then twenty yards. At the crucial moment, one could hear the gnashing teeth of the pursuing beast coming together as he opened and closed his ugly jaws.

The leader directed the ox in such a manner that he avoided the pit, but the impetus of the great Hodag carried him forward over the mass of branches and grass, which covered the trap. In he crashed into the pit, emitting a terrible roar that could be heard for miles. Friendly hands led the hero away, and the ox, with tongue hanging from his mouth, was rewarded with a good bed and plenty to eat that night.

This, dear reader, is a true and authentic account of this holdover from prehistoric times, Wisconsin's ferocious Hodag.

Told by "Lake Shore" Kearney

Shepard took the Hodag on a circuit of county fairs for all to see. First at Wausau, then at Antigo, on and on, thrilling a gaping throng wherever it was displayed. Shudders and gasps were the standard reactions as viewers' eyes fell upon the brute cowering in a corner of the weakly lighted tent. And in the dimness, the animal's groans, blinking eyes, flame-snorting nostrils, seemed as real as anything the thrill-seeking men, women, and children ever cared to see and hear.

Yes, the Hodag was indeed a find! It was "box-office" in a way that publicity men dream about but seldom see! Shepard must have relished the expressions that crossed the faces of the gullible when he said, "It will eat nothing but white bulldogs, and then only on Sundays!" But when, finally, staid, serious-minded writers, scientists, and museum representatives came West to study this startling specimen from out of the dead past, Gene Shepard's fun was over. He had to bring his creature out into the open!

The Hodag was no more. It was now explained to a public which "likes to be fooled" that the fierce animal was the creation of a clever woodcarver and Shepard. A well-shaped wooden body covered with oxhides and embellished with spines that were bull's horns, bear's claw eyebrows and other such things—and the rest was easy.

Several years afterwards, the Hodag met its fate, "burning to death" in a fire at Ballard Lake where Shepard had built a summer resort. Otherwise the notorious beast might still be thrilling the public today.

The Hodag was just one of Gene Shepard's famous hoaxes but there is no doubt it was his greatest achievement.

MORE ON THE HODAG

S. B. Gary of Rhinelander says that the Hodag was captured on February 30, on Section 37 (there are only thirty-six sections in a

Township), and reported that the acre of ground upon which Hodag was discovered would shortly be moved within the city limits. When the Hodag was not visible, Shepard announced that it was fifteen hundred feet underground, and was expected out any day. An interested visitor would wait around for him to emerge.

JOHN REMO TELLS ABOUT SHEPARD'S FUNERAL

His funeral now, when it come time for his funeral. I used to go down there quite often and I knew him well. But that funeral business, Shepard belonged to the Masons here, but Kolden, you remember Kolden, Kolden and I were sent down to stay with the corpse. Oscar Kolden. So we were downright ready to represent the Masonic Lodge and to be there with Shepard, you know. So sure enough, by gol, the Missus, his second wife there, she came out with the pillows and it happens there was a bed out in the front room and she began to make the bed and I says to Mrs. Shepard, "You're not making that for us." "Yes," she says, "nobody can stay up here." She says, "If you're going to stay here you'll have to go to bed." And I says to Kolden, "Kolden, if we've got to go to bed, I'm going home to bed. There is no use going to bed here. We came here to represent the Lodge and we are supposed to stay with the corpse."

"No," she says, "you can't stay here."

"All right," I says. And Kolden says, "All right," so we left.

And did you know that that night, and others can tell you the same, it was the worst storm that we ever had. They had shoveled out the snow but you know everything was filled right up and the next morning when they come after the corpse, by gol, you know, the hearse come in one way, and everybody come in from the back and there they were so they had to unhitch the horses and dig out so the horses could get back, and they finally turned the hearse around so it could get Shepard. That was the worst storm that ever I knew of and there they were blocked up. And when we got out to the cemetery we walked.

Alec McRae was to read the Bible. Every once in a while it would snow. Anyhow, I had this umbrella, I opened it up and held it over, and every once in a while great big flakes that big would come down on the Bible, you know, and Alec kept a-reading it, and a gush of wind, a kind of a twister, came and it just grabbed the umbrella and me too, and I hung right on to it and I wouldn't let go of it and, gol, you know, and finally it raised me up and dropped me down again, but you know, the handle come off and there I was, and up went the umbrella and every eye was on there watching that umbrella go. John Remo had the handle.

And you know we fooled around until past—you've been to a Masonic funeral, they used to put a sprig of myrtle, well, the whole coffin was full. Hildebrand had just got a new outfit that lets the coffin down into the grave and so he was busy around there getting that. That was something new. The body went down when they pressed the button, and you know he got around there and it wouldn't go down. It went down about a foot and then it stopped. Hildebrand went around trying to do it and the grave caved in on the side there and in fell Hildebrand. I could hear Shepard a-laugh in there. Hildebrand come pretty near getting clear in. Somebody got ahold of him and pulled him out. And did you know, everybody was snickering and laughing. Well, while they were doing that, you know, what with flowers and everything after this, it seems another kind of a twister come and blew every flower away. There wasn't a flower left on that grave. Did you ever hear that?

TALES OF OLD SHERIDAN

Harland Hays of Gays Mills told us about Old Sheridan, who rivaled Gene Shepard as a great trickster:

Old Sheridan was a Kickapoogian; he lived, worked, played, and died in the Kickapoo Valley in southwestern Wisconsin years ago, yet he lives on in legend.

My earliest recollections, going back some sixty years, are of my parents, grandparents, uncles, aunts, and neighbors, as they gathered at not infrequent occasions, telling stories of the things Old Sheridan said or did. In those early days folks could gather and entertain each other. In fact they had to, for how else could they be entertained? At that time there were no television sets, no radios, no movies, no phonographs, not even party line telephones.

As a child, Old Sheridan was just a fellow in a story, like Robin Hood, Rip Van Winkle, or David, the little boy who killed the giant.

Therefore I was surprised in later years when I met an older man, Bert Hanks by name, who told me that Old Sheridan had been a real person. Bert, with his parents, had lived neighbor to Philip Sheridan, who in his declining years was always referred to as Old Sheridan. Bert said that Sheridan was a tall, powerfully built Irishman with a very homely face. He added that one day someone risked his life by asking Sheridan what made him so homely. The reply was, "Well, I'll tell ye. It's through no fault of me own. The lady looking after me mother at me birth wrapped me up and laid me with me face too close to the fire, and me face warped."

Sensing that I still reserved doubts about his story, Bert concluded, "I tell you he was our neighbor, and he died a good many years ago when I was a small boy. He was laid to rest in the St. Phillips Cemetery, about eight miles east of Gays Mills on Highway 171, and he was a marker with his name on it." Later as I passed the cemetery, I stopped to look. Yes, it is there.

James Cullen, Crawford County Judge, likes to tell a story of Old Sheridan which goes like this: It seems that Sheridan had a very coarse, wirelike beard, which he shaved occasionally with a straight razor. When the razor did not cut to suit him, he would stroke it a few times, back and forth on the grindstone. Pulling the razor across his face with a sound as if someone were scraping a hog, Sheridan would be pleased and shout, "Now listen to her roar!"

FILL UP ME JUG

One evening Old Sheridan entered a Bell Center Saloon carrying a gallon jug which was half full of water. Going up to the bartender, he ordered, "Fill up me jug with alcohol. My supply is gettin' sorta low." The bartender complied and handed the jug, filled to capacity, back to Sheridan. Whereupon the latter demanded, "Charge it."

"Can't do it," said the saloon man. "It's strictly cash."

"All right," growled Sheridan, "I ain't got no money and I ain't got no credit. Take back your half gallon." The bartender poured back a half gallon and Sheridan went happily on his way with a half gallon of 50 per cent alcohol.

FREE LABOR

Old Sheridan was once engaged by a neighbor to dig a well on a property to which the employer expected to move as soon as the well was completed and water was available. By noon Sheridan had the hole dug to such a depth that his head was below the surface. He had, however, provided himself with a ladder which he ascended and went through the woods to his home nearby where he ate his dinner. Returning to his job he found the soil had caved into the freshly dug hole, nearly filling it. Taking off his hat and vest which he always wore when not working, he laid them beside the hole and returned into the woods.

Presently a neighbor came along, saw the hat and vest and the earth-filled hole. He hurried away but soon returned with some men and boys equipped with shovels. Quickly the earth was removed and the kindly neighbors were relieved, but mystified, to find no crushed and mangled Sheridan at the bottom. At this moment Sheridan came back out of the woods, thanked the men very cordially and explained that he had gone back to the house to attend to some forgotten chore and "the well must have caved in."

A WHOPPER

Years ago, before soil conservation or rural electrification were even imagined and there were no telephone lines, in this part of the Kickapoo Valley at least, a couple of hardy descendants of the Pilgrim Fathers, or some other European Fathers, were working one forenoon in a valley field when down the hill road came Old Sheridan on a horse, going at a pretty fast gait.

One of the men called out, "Hey, Sheridan, stop a moment and tell us a big lie." Sheridan slowed up a trifle and shouted in reply, "Can't, ain't got time. Uncle Billy Evans is dying and I'm goin' for the doctor. Giddap." And down the road he went in a cloud of dust.

"Well," said one of the men, "too bad about Uncle Billy. Old Sheridan is always on the job to help anyone in trouble and that's a fact. I guess we had better go up. Maybe we can do something to help." So up the hill they climbed. When they reached the Evans home and found Uncle Billy busily working in his field, they realized they had received that for which they had asked—a big lie.

BUYING A BED

Once, so one story went, Sheridan traveled over the hills with his team and wagon to the Mississippi River Valley. Late in the evening when it became dark and the kerosene lamps and candles had been lighted in the houses, Sheridan drove into the little town of Lynxville. When he came in front of the Lynxville Hotel he stopped, tied his team to a convenient hitching rail and entered the lobby. The landlord was behind his desk. Sheridan approached him and announced, "I'd like to get a bed."

"Well," was the businesslike reply, "I have a single bed in a small room or a double bed in a large room."

"How much for the single bed?" asked Sheridan.

"Seventy-five cents, cash. Do you want it?"

"Can I see it before I make up me mind?"

"Sure, follow me," and the landlord started up the stairs followed by Sheridan, who after thoroughly inspecting the bed said, "I'll take it. Here's your seventy-five cents."

With a "Thank you. Good night," the landlord went back downstairs to his desk in the lobby. Fifteen minutes later down the stairs came Sheridan, carrying and dragging the pieces of the bed with him.

"What's going on here?" demanded the landlord.

"I'm just taking me bed out to the wagon," replied Sheridan.

"Your bed, did you say?" roared the landlord. "That isn't your bed. What do you think you are trying to get away with?"

Without slowing his progress, Sheridan replied pleasantly, "Sure and it's me bed. I asked you how much for the bed and you said seventy-five cents and I gave you seventy-five cents. A bargain's a bargain." And while the landlord stood speechless Old Sheridan, with the bed, disappeared into the night.

A GOOD COW

Sherman Miller and William Kelly were neighbors, separated by a four-hundred-foot, forest-covered hill. Each had selected a homesite near a spring of clear, cold water gushing out between layers of rock at the base of the hill. They met one day in Kickapoo. "Where you headed?" asked Sherm.

"I'm looking for a good milk cow," replied William. "Mine are all dry and won't freshen for a couple months or so. Need milk for the kids, and a little butter, you know."

"Got track of one yet?" inquired Sherm.

"Old man Winchell was telling me that Phil Sheridan might have one. I'm driving over the hill to see him," replied William.

"Sheridan does have some good cows, all right, but you want to be on the lookout if you deal with him. He's pretty tricky, folks say," advised Sherm.

"He won't trick me," said William confidently. "I'm a pretty good judge of cows. They say that Sheridan won't tell you an out and out lie, so I'll watch him for any tricks. Well, I got to get along. Take care of yourself. Giddap."

Phil Sheridan was home when William arrived at the Sheridan homestead in midafternoon. He had just driven up by the barn and was unhitching his horse from the double-shovel cultivator. For a long time the two men talked of the weather, local gossip, and every topic concerning farming, except cows. Finally, not receiving an opening from Sheridan, William asked casually, "How many cows are you milking, Sheridan?"

"I'm milking four right now. Got a couple to freshen sometime next month. Then I have three heifers coming in late in the fall," replied Sheridan and then asked, "Would you like to see them? They are in the lot behind the barn."

"I might look at them," said William warily.

Sheridan went to the nearby corn crib and returned with a pail full of nubbins. The two men went around the barn. The cows came toward them when they saw the pail of nubbins, and heard Sheridan call, "Co Boss, Co Boss." He bribed three of the cows to come to the fence by holding the small ears of corn out to them. He told William about how gentle they were, and that each gave a big mess of milk. William kept looking at the cow standing back while Sheridan continued talking the good points of the three close by.

"I like the looks of that other one," said William. "Can you get her over here so I can see her good?"

"Sure I can," replied Sheridan amiably. "Come Daisy, you can have some corn too." As Daisy reached through the fence for the nubbins, William appraised her critically, noting her smooth, well-rounded udder, her ample capacity for food, her broad muzzle and wide, dished forehead. He was, as he had said, a good judge of cows, and all these points pleased him. He asked, "Do you want to sell her?"

"Well, I don't. She gives a twelve-quart pail full of milk night and morning. You can have any one of the other three for fifteen dollars. Anyway, I don't think you would like Daisy. Sometimes she kicks with one of her four feet. I'd have to have more than fifteen dollars for Daisy, though."

"Twelve quarts night and morning, and her only fault is that she kicks with one of her forefeet. I might consider giving you twenty dollars for her," bargained William.

"The price for Daisy is twenty-five dollars," said Sheridan with finality.

"Will you guarantee her to be like you said?" countered William.

"Mr. Kelly," said Sheridan solemnly, "if you buy Daisy and she ever kicks you with any except one of her four feet you can have her for nothing. I'll pay you back the twenty-five dollars, and here's my hand on it."

Kelly said, "I'll take her. Here's your money, but you'll have to throw in a rope and help me tie her behind the wagon." They shook hands and the deal was consummated.

A few days later Kelly saw Sheridan and said, "Sheridan, according to our agreement you owe me twenty-five dollars."

"How's that?" asked Sheridan innocently.

"You agreed that if that cow ever kicked me with any but one of her forefeet, you would give me back my twenty-five dollars and I could keep the cow," stated Kelly.

"Yes, that was the agreement. Why do you say I owe you twenty-five dollars?" countered Sheridan.

"Why do I say you owe me twenty-five dollars? I'll tell you why you owe me twenty-five dollars, Phil Sheridan," exploded Kelly.

"That darned critter kicked me halfway across the barn with her hind foot."

"Well, her hind foot is one of her four feet, isn't it?" contended Sheridan, and added, "She has only four feet, and the foot she kicked you with was one of them, wasn't it?"

"By the Jumpin' Moses, Sheridan, you tricked me. I might have known I'd be tricked. If I ever deal with you again I'll have it in writing. Then I'll know how you spell your words," said Kelly.

WISCONSIN A MECCA FOR PRACTICAL JOKERS

Nowadays the prankster and practical joker has fallen out of favor. Occasionally someone perpetrates a mild prank on someone else but nobody really laughs. We even seem to have forgotten how humorous the practical joke can be, and we remember only its painful aspects, which may, indeed, be extensive.

This was definitely not the situation in Wisconsin's earlier days. Of all local entertainment, deceiving for amusement was probably the most popular. It was so in every new territory or state or community in the nation where human energy was high; the sky the limit so long as a man had the guts to stay and fight and lift himself up by his boot tops, and where any entertainment mostly had to be manufactured right on the home front. "There is no country, perhaps, in which the habit of deceiving for amusement, or what is termed hoaxing, is so common," wrote the celebrated English author, Captain Frederick Marryat, in his *Diary in America*. Everyone was a joker or jokist—made victims of others, or was himself victimized. Humor and fun were standard coin.

Professor Jonathan Curvin in his study of humor in Frontier Wisconsin,* states that trickster-humorists basked in a climate of smiling indulgence. Their outrageous inventions were accorded a kind of praise reserved in more sophisticated times for the deftest epigrams. The old folks and the wide-awake younger ones too developed an extensive prank-playing repertoire. They temporarily stole horses, cows, fowls, carriages, and everything else come-at-able; they sent out bogus wedding cards, frightened excitable individuals by arrest-

* *Early Wisconsin through the Comic Looking Glass,* Wisconsin Idea Theatre, 1945.

ing them on bogus charges for various crimes; sent the doctors posthaste where they were not wanted; caused prominent men to be
sued for fake bills of indebtedness; used young ladies' names to
invite Tom, Dick, and Harry to call; charged losses by theft upon
innocent but nervous parties, and kept the vicinity in an uproar
generally.

"Usually," the Professor continues, "the mischief-makers intended
no harm. Practical joking was regarded as legitimate entertainment,
a substitute for the more urbane recreations of older communities.
Even its roughest specimens were condoned."

It was thought to be wonderfully inventive when in the 1850's
Bill Buster, a lake boat employee of the Green Bay region, dug up
the body of an unknown sailor washed ashore and buried at Eagle
Harbor, cut up the corpse and packed it in a barrel, well salted and
labeled "pork." Then Bill sent the barrel to a prominent citizen of
Green Bay. Or, when a particularly moral member of the Wisconsin
Territorial Legislature drew from his pocket a handkerchief in
church, thereby causing the greasy playing cards which a wit had
planted to fly about in all directions, practical joking enjoyed a
triumphant moment.

The difference between practical jokes and hoaxes is purely one
of degree. Practical jokes are nearly always pranks designed to show
up the individual. Hoaxes are more deliberate, ambitious. They are
carefully fabricated untruths made to masquerade as truth, played
for greater stakes before a larger audience. While the practical jokes
were far more plentiful, hoaxes, too, were far from unknown in
Wisconsin.

The ghoulish story of Micky O'Brien's wake, which stems from
the files of the Richland Center *Democrat*, illustrates how the plot
of a practical joke may survive or recur. It is recalled that in the
1850's the ubiquitous "Shanghai" Chandler, then editor of the Portage *Independent*, had once crawled into the printing office vault for
a midday nap and had awakened in terror to discover at his feet
an imposing tombstone, on which was chiseled "Sacred to the
Memory of Julius C. Chandler," the work of his playful compositors.

Chandler's reactions were most satisfactory, according to an eye-
witness: "He wildly rolled his eyes in their sockets; his cheeks

blanched with fright, and he lay perfectly motionless as though it were sacrilegious to disturb the repose of the departed by moving, and more particularly as he was the supposed departed himself. He was respecting the solemnity of the occasion."

When Micky O'Brien died his friends gave him a grand wake. Dinny O'Toole played his bagpipe, the better to cheer Micky on his way. Jimmy McLaughlin danced a clog or two. Somebody recited a poem. And to assuage the pangs of parting with their comrade all had recourse to the friendly demijohn.

Tommy McCoy, his friends soon discovered, had taken a drop too much and had been rendered unconscious. Seeing Tommy thus impelled the other mourners to cunning action. In a moment Micky was out of his coffin and Tommy was in it.

After Tommy had aroused from his befuddled state he saw his friends filing past his awful bed, each one expressing appropriate but unwelcome sentiments. "Let me out!" shrieked Tommy. "I'm not dead!"

"Indeed, Tommy, but you are dead," was the answer. "Dead as a salt mackeral, and buried you'll be this very day."

At last Tommy gave a mighty heave. He was out of the coffin and out of the room and out of the house almost before the laughter had begun.

HOW TO FIX A SMOKING CHIMNEY

Yesterday, as a citizen was helping a tinsmith to elevate a smoke jack to the roof of an addition on the windy side of the house preparatory to hoisting it atop of a smoking chimney, an old man with a ragged bundle came along, halted and soon became interested. "That chimbley smokes, don't it?" he finally inquired.

"It's the worst one in town," replied the citizen.

"And you want to stop the nuisance, eh?"

"Yes, I do."

"And you think the smoke jack'll do it, do you?"

"I hope so."

"Well now, I kin stop that smoking in ten minutes and I won't hurt the chimbley or put up any smoke jacks," continued the old man as he laid down his bundle.

"If you do it, I'll give you five dollars," rejoined the citizen, who disliked the idea of disfiguring the chimney with a chimney jack.

"Kin I have the kitchen for five minutes?" asked the man.

The wife was instructed to vacate and the old man took possession. Removing the top of the stove, he poured in enough water to put out every spark of fire. Then, going out, he called to our citizen on the roof, "Has she stopped?"

"Well, I don't see any smoke at all. What have you done?"

While he was coming down the ladder the old man made off, eating a pie he had taken from the oven. The last half he had to bolt down on the run, but at no time in the race did the citizen, his wife, or the tinsmith get within twenty rods of him.

A FAIR TRADE

One day a stranger in an Evansville Tavern ordered a pound of crackers. When they were set down before him he asked if he might change the crackers for a glass of whiskey. The tavern keeper obliged. After drinking his whiskey the stranger started for the door. Without paying, of course.

"Here sir," called the proprietor, "you owe me for that whiskey."

"Oh no," rejoined the stranger. "You agreed, didn't you, to change those crackers for that whiskey?"

"Well yes, but—"

"And you have the crackers. Fair trade. Good day!"

TRICKSTER FROM SAUK COUNTY

One autumn morning in 1856, as Mr. W, banker and man of substance, issued forth from his home in Beaver Dam and braced himself for labor in the local financial vineyard, his sharp eyes detected in a nearby thicket a temptingly fat envelope bound in red tape. This envelope, Mr. W found upon closer inspection, bore a Cincinnati address and an unfamiliar name, from which fact he naturally concluded that it had been accidentally dropped on his premises by some transient stranger to the town. Exercising a somewhat dubious right, Mr. W lost no time exploring the contents. What he found made him dismiss any notion of going to the bank that day.

Mr. W had blundered upon treasures of unimaginable richness.

The letter he held in his by now trembling hand was in effect the last will and testament of a scoundrel. Writing from England to a dear friend in the Ohio city, this rascal confessed that he was the last remaining member of a band of river pirates who years before had infested the Mississippi. He was now in the twilight of his life, he wrote, and ready to give over his great secret. On a day long passed, the letter continued (with convincing illiteracy), his gang had found it expedient to bury a hoard of silver and gold coins at a point well inland from the upper eastern shore of the river. Thousands of dollars were in the cache, which was positively still intact. His friend might recover the swag, and live the remainder of his life in the lap of luxury, if he would but follow the directions on the accompanying map.

Mr. W next examined the map, scrawled on weathered parchment. It was beautifully explicit. It indicated that the treasure lay at a certain point on the shore of the Baraboo River upon an elevated piece of ground, such and such a distance from the rapids, between certain carefully described oak trees. It was in an iron pot, the location of which was marked by a charred stick planted in the ground above it.

Mr. W felt his heart pound with excitement. He could scarcely wait to lay hands on the booty. But caution warned him that he first had best make sure he was not being taken in by some frivolous joker. However, when he found on the local hotel register the name of the Cincinnati stranger, he laid his suspicions to rest. As inconspicuously as possible, he hitched up his buggy and started out toward his pot of gold.

The pirate's map directed him toward Reedsburg. En route he met an old friend from that village, Judge X. The men chatted together on the road. Perhaps the judge asked some awkward questions, or it may be that Mr. W could no longer contain himself, and so let the cat out of the bag. In any event, the judge, satisfied that the letter and the map were beyond doubt authentic, swore to keep the secret, offered to assist Mr. W, and, of course, agreed to share in the plunder.

A few hours of industrious map-reading and unobtrusive measuring of distances were sufficient to bring the gentlemen to the general location of the buried treasure. It lay somewhere, they were sure, in the shabby village block just north of the Congregational Church in Reedsburg. Who owned the property? A prominent citizen, Mr. Gay Sperry. And would Mr. Sperry sell the block to His Honor and the banker from Beaver Dam? Yes, but for a fantastic price. Mr. Sperry had reason to believe that his land was worth more than he had ever suspected. Just the day before, he said, a stranger from Cincinnati had offered him out of the blue a cool two thousand dollars! Mr. Sperry had then instinctively demanded an even higher price, but the stranger had been unwilling to do business and had gone off in a very bad temper.

But Mr. W and Judge X were made of sterner stuff. They accepted exorbitant terms without turning a hair; and they seemed strangely elated when the deal had been closed and they could take possession.

That night, while all of Reedsburg slept, Mr. W and his partner crept out to their site of riches. They had no trouble finding the charred stick; it was in exactly the spot the map had indicated it would be. And so, laying aside the coffee sacks they expected presently to fill with precious coins, the two men fell to with pick and shovel.

Mr. W and Judge X, unfortunately, found no gold or silver that autumn night in 1856. Not until morning did the awful truth flash upon their minds. Then they knew, somehow, that the stranger from Cincinnati and the English buccaneer were one and the same man. And that the man was L. Gay Sperry, of Reedsburg.

THE GREAT INDIAN SCARE

The great Indian scare of 1862 was a hoax started by rumors, practiced on a grand scale, and involving many persons, in fact, practically the entire population of Washington and Milwaukee counties.

Just who started it isn't exactly known, but in the autumn of 1862, Wisconsin counties along the lake shore from Racine to Manitowoc were convulsed by news of the massacre of Minnesota settlers by Siouan Indians. Migrating parties had returned with reports of unleashed savage hordes, rampant in slaughter.

These tales were repeated, mulled over, and exaggerated in minds already jittery from rumors that Southern rebel troops had broken through Union Army lines, and were marching upon Wisconsin. Remember, things weren't going too well for the Northern armies at the beginning of the Civil War. With this element of suspense weighted to the unrest of the day, the time was ripe for the reign of unreason that was to follow.

Milwaukee was fair game in September, 1862, for the last, largest, and most absurd of the Indian scares. Thursday the fourth was a dry, hot, dusty, and hazy day. A trace of bluish smoke was in the air from burning grass fields, but this autumnal tranquillity was soon to be rudely shattered.

Somebody somewhere in the region north of Milwaukee set on foot a report that Indian raiders were on the warpath. The story spread like wildfire through all the lake-shore country. Jumpy Milwaukeeans now began to interpret the innocent smoke of burning fallows as coming from towns put to the torch by rampaging redskins.

Toward nightfall their fears seemed to be confirmed by the arrival of scores of teams driven at breakneck speed, drawing wagons loaded with men, women, and children.

Vehicles rattled in from all directions laden to overflowing with frightened people seeking the safety of the city. All night crowds of people continued pouring into the city, their anxiety spreading terror throughout Milwaukee. Streets began to be blocked with oxcarts, wagons, and buggies, many loaded with household goods. All the main approaches to the city were crowded with fearful fugitives approaching in vehicles or on foot. Each train arriving from the north or west brought frightened passengers who had deserted their homes, all feverishly intent on safety, and many without means to pay their fare.

Outside the city of Milwaukee two halfbreed Indians gathering roots and herbs for Dr. E. B. Solcott were alarmed by the steady rush of vehicles and ran toward the road, axes and knives in hand, to beg a ride. Imagine the effect they made! Here were real Indians, armed with knife and axe! The terrified palefaces, far from giving them a lift, whipped their foaming steeds into even greater frenzy to escape them.

One distraught farmer hitched his team in wild haste to take his children to safety in Milwaukee, but by mistake snatched up some neighbor children and left his own astonished offspring standing pop-eyed by the road.

Another farmer filled his wagon with choice pigs and left his poor wife to fend for herself. Perhaps he reasoned it would be cheaper to get another wife than to buy a new supply of porkers.

The country north of Milwaukee was truly in a state of terror. On the morning of the fifth, the chairman of the Town of Richfield dispatched the following telegram to Governor Salomon: PLEASE SEND US TROOPS AND ARMS BY FIRST TRAIN. INDIANS ARE WITHIN FIVE MILES OF HERE, MURDERING AND BURNING EVERYTHING THEY COME ACROSS. THEY BURNED CEDARBURG LAST NIGHT.

As Governor Salomon was in Milwaukee at the time, the dispatch was forwarded to him from Madison. The Governor telegraphed to Washington County without delay, and eight thousand cartridges were hurried off by the first train. Nor did the Governor stop at this. He ordered Captain Lehmann of Milwaukee to proceed at once with his company of well-trained militiamen and protect the people of Washington County. As was his duty, Captain Lehmann obeyed. Under orders to shoot any redskin on sight, Captain Lehmann's men combed the countryside for hours without flushing a single Indian, and then marched, rather sheepishly, back to Milwaukee.

The local press began to see the ridiculous side of the whole situation and twitted the militia unmercifully. One writer, A. C. Wheeler of the *Sentinel*, so infuriated Captain Lehmann with his jibes and lampooning that he drew his troops up before the newspaper office, went in, and gave Wheeler a sound drubbing with the back of his sword scabbard.

The satirical stories continued, and Lehmann was intent upon returning to repeat his action upon the editor, but scouts informed him that the newspaper staff was waiting for him atop the *Sentinel* building, fortified by a pile of bricks, so the Captain wisely beat a retreat.

Meanwhile many of the communities to the north and west of Milwaukee were alarmed. The citizens of Merton stampeded in a body, leaving a deserted village in their wake. The number of wagons heading for Milwaukee that passed through Wauwatosa during the day and night of the fifth was said to be not fewer than four hundred.

When inhabitants of isolated farms witnessed the spectacle of highways near their dwellings cluttered with vehicles of every description carrying terrified passengers and household goods, and were tremblingly informed that four thousand bloodthirsty, rampageous Indians were not far behind, they too gave way impulsively to unreasoning panic and joined in the rush for safety.

Farmers without muskets or pistols snatched scythes, sickles, corn-cutters, carving knives, pitchforks, and crowbars to serve as weapons of defense.

Milwaukeeans having relatives in Waukesha had been worried by reports that the town was sacked. They were reassured by the arrival of a company of volunteers with arms and ammunition who had hurried in from Waukesha to aid in repelling the savages said to be attacking Milwaukee! Hotels and boarding houses throughout the city of Milwaukee were soon overcrowded. Scores of tired and timorous strangers arriving late at night had to sleep on lawns.

When scouts who had made an extensive search to the north of Milwaukee returned with assurances that all was peaceful, Milwaukeeans were readily convinced of the truth. But the panic in some rural regions lasted for days.

When the scare died down, the crowds of outlanders in the city began to feel a bit foolish, and many insisted they had just come into town for a few groceries or a new harness strap. It was a harder thing to explain why they had come with guns!

For what occurred in West Bend, in Washington County, we must rely on the story told by the editor of the old *West Bend Post.* Vague reports that Indians at Horicon were on the warpath filtered in to West Bend to cause some uneasiness, but when the Milwaukee evening papers confirmed the news of Indian hostilities, West Bend also joined in the prevailing panic.

What "capped the climax," according to the editor of the *Post,* was information brought by a messenger who came to the village late that evening from ten miles west on the Decorah Road, saying that a score of Indians was about to swoop down upon West Bend.

This spelled a night of terror for the villagers. The wild firing of guns and the roll of drums drove people out of their beds. "Children were bawling and men and women were seen running in all directions. Speeches were made advising the men to stand by their homes and their families till the bitter end. Picket guards were immediately formed, armed with rifles, shotguns, pistols, pitchforks, and whatever could be got hold of." Old muskets and pistols were taken to the village gunsmith who was kept busy all night repairing them. Women packed their silverware and valuables.

One woman living half a mile out in the country, who had been bedridden for over a year, was hastily dumped into a wheelbarrow and pushed to the village for safety.

Every half hour mounted men rode out to the pickets to see if anything had turned up. At Barton, a mile north of West Bend, a man stood picket all night armed with an ax and with nothing on but a nightshirt, as he dared not leave his post long enough to put on more clothes.

The people of the town of Farmington, in Washington County, appear to have remained more level-headed in the scare than some of their neighbors. The Farmington citizens learned of the danger from a man who was a sort of self-appointed Paul Revere. Only instead of riding from village to village on a horse, as did Paul, this Farmington fellow came wheeling along at a crazy speed, riding a vehicle with only the front wheels left on it.

The Farmington folk hid their valuables in a dugout on the Riley farm, and the whole neighborhood, men, women, and children, assembled to await what was coming. They decided to die together if that had to be. But when no Indians showed up after a night of waiting, they returned to their farms.

A vivid account of the scare at Port Washington, in Ozaukee County, was given by George W. Foster, schoolteacher, editor, and lawyer. I herewith present Foster's story in his own words:

"Means of repelling the attack in Milwaukee were seriously discussed. Saloon-keepers resorted to the protective measure of rolling kegs of whiskey out onto the pavement, with the idea that the redskins' love for firewater would cause them to forget their rage for slaughter, and that while they were transferring the contents of the kegs into their stomachs the white women and children would have opportunity to secrete themselves, while the men of the community, after the Indians had reached a state of drunkenness, would find it easier to defeat them than if they were sober."

Mr. Foster's account concludes with the remark that Sheriff Jacob Bossler sent his wife to Milwaukee for the purpose of warning the metropolis of the impending danger, and that the plucky little woman performed her mission without flinching.

The flurry of 1862 was the greatest and last of the Indian scares in the vicinity of Milwaukee. Straggling redmen made occasional appearances on the streets of Milwaukee long after the Civil War. Groups of them camped on the grounds of James Kneeland, between Tenth and Eleventh Streets, south of Grand Avenue, as late as 1876.

Told by Dr. Herbert W. Kuhum, in *Badger Folklore*.

THE PETRIFIED CAPTAIN D'ARTAGAN

All hoaxes are trifling when stacked up against "The case of the Wisconsin Mummy."

That remarkable gold brick was fashioned one January afternoon in 1926 in Ladysmith, Wisconsin. A hard-working reporter sat in the office of the *Rusk County Journal*, trying to figure out an angle for his feature story, due next day. He produced a story each week and signed himself, "Rusk County Lyre," spelled, for some obscure reason, l-y-r-e.

At last an idea. Here is the story he wrote:

Recently a firm in Chippewa Falls acquired a tract of land near here. Monday morning two employees of the firm, Art Charpin and Walter Latsch of Owen, set about clearing the land for their company. They noticed a large basswood, and felled it. Even though it had a large hole some 30 ft. above the ground, it looked like good timber. Monday afternoon they struck their saws into the basswood at a point where they expected a cut would give them a 20-foot log and eliminate the portion affected by the large hole. All went well until half way through the log the saw struck a rock. Latsch and Charpin cursed, because they knew their saw would be dulled.

After some labor, the men turned the tree trunk over and began a cut on the other side. Before long the same difficulty was encountered, but by turning the trunk about, the cut was finally completed, and the log rolled away, revealing what threw the men into a bad fright. There, staring up at them, was the ashen face of a man. And there, encased in the living trunk of the tree, was the entire body of a man, fully clothed in coarse homespun and buckskins, which fell away when touched, and the head had been covered with long hair which had been tucked up under a coonskin cap. With the mummified body in the hollow tree was an old muzzle-loading flintlock rifle and a muzzle-loading pistol of fanciful design.

In a pocket of the man's clothes, which were like ashes, were found several decayed bits of paper and a few French gold coins, one of which bears the date 1664. The only clue to the man's identity was a scrap of official-looking paper, bearing the name, Pierre D'Artagan, and signed, Jacques Marquette.

At first the men's story was laughed at here, but finally it got to an official who, perceiving the state of "nerves," which the men displayed, decided there must be something to it. A party of four, including the writer, made a trip to the small clearing, and what we witnessed was ancient tragedy.

For all that it seems the height of incredulity, it is believed on good authority that here in Rusk County has been found the body of Cap. D'Artagan, who was lost from Marquette and Joliet's party on their trip down the Mississippi in 1673. The solution to the body being found in the basswood tree is advanced in the theory that D'Artagan, pursued by Indians, crawled into the hollow tree to hide and being unable to crawl out, died there. The peculiar action of the sap of the live basswood petrified the body and preserved it for the discovery by the Owen men.

The body will be brought to this city, where it will be shipped to the State University, and it is probable that if present suspicions are verified, it will be offered to France. D'Artagan was very close to Louis the Great.

This is the story that was published on January 21, 1926, on the front page of the *Rusk County Journal*, under a two-column head.

Within a couple of weeks other Wisconsin papers, the *Muscoda Progressive*, *The Courier* of Prairie du Chien—weeklies, and dailies, too, were copying what they recognized as a "darn good story," often adding learned accounts from the history books of the travels in the northwest of Joliet and Marquette, and the disappearance of Captain D'Artagan.

On February 20 the editor of the *Rusk County Journal* received this telegram: HAVE STORY OF PETRIFIED BODY. CAN YOU VERIFY? RUSH REPLY COLLECT. WHAT DISPOSITION BODY AND PICTURES AVAILABLE. RUSH TONIGHT. LIBERAL CHECK. EVANSVILLE COURIER.

The petrified man had reached Indiana: "Great Heavens!" gasped the editor. "They believe it!"

Yes, apparently "they" did believe it. Next day came another telegram: IS THERE ANYTHING TO STORY OF FINDING PETRIFIED BODY EARLY EXPLORER? IF NOT A HOAX, WE COULD USE IT. DULUTH HERALD.

The harassed editor immediately answered both inquiries, explaining there was nothing to the petrified man story, that it was really and truly a hoax.

No sooner had this been done, however, than there strode into the editor's office an irate village official bearing this letter: "To the Mayor, Ladysmith, Wis.: Recently, my attention has been called to an article in one of our local Nebraska papers in regard to which a petrified man was found in or near your city. For the benefit of our students, who have taken up this discussion in current events, will you inform me whether or not this story is credible? Dewey A. Grange, Albion, Nebraska."

Meanwhile, William Schrump in Portland, Oregon, read the story. A fine chance, thought he, to advertise his home town, Ladysmith. On the following Sunday the Portland *Oregonian* carried the story to West Coast readers.

Back in Ladysmith, the editor was having a rough time. Letters from all over the country piled up on his desk. They wanted stories. They wanted pictures. The wanted proof. The editor wanted *out*. His face grew pale and thin and wore a haunted look. He spent all his spare time answering letters.

By this time large numbers of visitors began arriving at the Historical Museum in Madison, asking to view the remains of the petrified man.

It was time to call a halt. So Joseph Schafer of the Historical Society wrote in the March issue of the Society's bulletin that the remains of the petrified man had not been received at the Museum, and that it was doubtful they ever would be. A scholarly dissertation accompanied this disappointing news:

> First, [wrote Mr. Schafer] how can a body of flesh be changed to stone or petrified except by the substitution of mineral matter for the decaying cells of the body? Second, what is there about the sap of the basswood tree that could possibly carry mineral matter to a decaying body in its hollow inside? Had the trunk of the tree imprisoning a human body been deeply enough buried in the earth to permit water-bearing mineral matter in solution to play upon it under certain conditions, no doubt petrification would be possible. But a body in a standing tree could not be reached at all by mineral impregnated water. Third, if the body of a man in a tree had been petrified, how would the integuments of his clothing escape the same fate.

This report brought sanity at last to the life of the Ladysmith editor, who published it in full, with this valedictory: "In this clear-cut analysis, the State Historical Society man proves that the petrified man could not have existed. That has always been somewhat our own opinion."

And so the petrified man was laid to rest. The mailbag of the *Rusk County Journal* returned almost to normal. And the strings of the Rusk County Lyre became muted and discreet.

THE MAN FROM NEW ENGLAND

The refined gentleman of advanced years who in 1850 took up temporary residence in the village of Monroe brought cheerful news. The farmers of the vicinity were not averse to turning an easy dollar when the opportunity offered itself, and those with large holdings of land were particularly hospitable to the newcomer, who gave his name as Mr. Hitchcock, late of Vermont.

Mr. Hitchcock amiably sketched his background. He represented, he said, the New England Agricultural Society. This organization, composed of thrifty Yankees, had managed to amass and deposit in the bank at Woodstock, Vermont, a considerable fortune; and, after having founded and endowed an eastern college, was prepared to buy up favorable tracts of land in Wisconsin. Hitchcock, delegated as purchaser, indicated that money was no object. "What," he asked, "have you got to offer?"

In no time at all Mr. Hitchcock became a remarkably popular man. The first gesture on his behalf was the establishment of a Green County Agricultural Society and his election as president for as long as he wished to remain in Monroe. He soon married an attractive local widow and was accorded a charivari, during which three goats were persuaded to appear at the window of the happy couple's bedchamber.

Every day groups of citizens would escort Mr. Hitchcock on tours to inspect their land, guarding him as jealously as they might a royal guest. Once, coming upon a brook at Spring Grove, they were pressed for a means of getting Mr. Hitchcock across to the opposite side without wetting his feet. One offered to fit his own boots over those of the favored gentleman, another volunteered to improvise a bridge with his coat. It remained for John Taylor, a land agent, hence accomplished in courtesy, to do the only really gallant thing— to lift Mr. Hitchcock up bodily and lug him across to safety.

To these and other niceties Hitchcock responded with gratitude and, more substantially, with fantastic purchases of land. He placed an order for the entire township of Clarno. He bought a thousand acres here, a stretch of timber there. He ventured out to buy yet more land in adjoining counties.

Finally Mr. Hitchcock announced that he had fulfilled his obligation to the New England Agricultural Society and that if his creditors of Green, Rock, and Dane Counties would kindly meet with him at Monroe, he would settle his contracts.

Nobody refused the invitation. On the appointed day a sizable crowd of farmers and land agents surrounded the beneficent Hitchcock, who was prepared with a sheaf of blank drafts to be used against his society's fund in Vermont. Rather surprisingly, he confessed that he was unable to write himself and so requested Mr. Dunwiddie, a local lawyer, to make out the drafts for him. It took Dunwiddie a full day to finish the job.

As it turned out, Dunwiddie need not have bothered. Mr. Hitchcock's drafts were presently discovered to be worthless. Mr. Hitchcock was never discovered at all. Leaving behind his bride, his hat and his coat, he quietly evaporated. The Monroe citizenry agreeably put him down as an eccentric.

They did not nurse any hard feelings, apparently, for at the next regular meeting of the Green County Agricultural Society, when it became necessary to choose a new president, it was decided to elect the man who had most generously served the ex-president, Hitchcock. Of the many prospective candidates, several had loaned horses to the eastern visitor, or had donated neighborly gifts, or had given extravagantly of their time and solicitude. Only John Taylor, however, had ever carried Mr. Hitchcock across the brook at Spring Grove. He won the election handily, and the members settled down to discuss various methods of transporting butter to market.

Told by J. W. Curvin

BOTKIN AND HIS BARABOO BLUFF

The year is 1847. Alexander Botkin, candidate for the territorial house of representatives in Madison, faced the good people of Baraboo and considered how most effectively to approach them. Botkin, who had come to Madison in 1841 as assistant secretary for the state under the territory, was convinced he could sway the voters in his direction, for he had learned a trick or two about campaigning.

He eyed his opponent from Marquette County from across the improvised stage. Campaigning together was an accepted practice, for it gave the voters a chance to make up their minds once and for all, with no room for doubt, as to which was the likeliest incumbent.

It so happened that it was Botkin's privilege to speak first. He began by complimenting the intelligence of the audience, then rhapsodized over the Baraboo valley. He pointed out its natural beauties, its marvelous advantages of water power, manufacturing privileges, and productive soil. This of course, was the build-up by which he hoped to win their votes.

Stepping forward on the platform, Botkin exclaimed, "One thing you especially need, and you are justly entitled to it; that is a good road over the bluffs. How can you procure it? How can that most desirable end be obtained? If, through your suffrance, I have the honor to represent you in the territorial council, send me your petition to organize a company for the purpose of macadamizing the highway over the bluffs. You don't desire to subject the inhabitants of Sauk Prairie to pay toll on the way to your mills, nor persons coming to transact business at the county seat. Hence, I shall endeavor to get an appropriation from the territorial treasury to macadamize that road."

Midst wild cheers, whistles, and clapping of hands, Botkin sat down. His opponent, bewildered and dismayed by Botkin's success, took the stand. He began to speak while casting about wildly for some point Botkin had overlooked. There didn't seem to be any so he ended, lamely, by making the same promises and said he, too, would see that they got a road over the bluff if elected.

A few days later the two candidates met again at Prairie du Sac on the other side of the bluff. Since Botkin had spoken first at Baraboo, it was his competitor's turn to open at Prairie du Sac.

Still smarting under the beating he'd taken at Baraboo, he decided he'd not only take the wind out of Botkin's sails, he'd steal the sails. Smiling benignly, he began by sympathizing with the citizens for being practically cut off from the beautiful valley of Baraboo by such miserable roads, and he promised right then and there to right the situation upon his election by putting through a bill in the legislature to macadamize the road over the bluffs.

Prairie du Sac, at that time, was still smarting under the blow of having lost the county seat to Baraboo. They hoped to get it back, and were opposed to anything that contributed to the advancement and welfare of the opposing city.

When it was Botkin's turn to speak, he stepped forth confidently, smiled at his opponent, turned to the audience, and said, "Fellow citizens, I am astonished at the diabolical proposition made by the gentleman. What is it that the promises? Why that you shall be taxed to build up a town in a barren, worthless, rocky, stonebound region, where there is no town, nor never ought to be one! When I look upon your beautiful, rich prairie, your magnificent river, the trade and business which must necessarily center here, I think with indignation of the proposition made by my opponent, that you should be taxed to help build up a competing town where neither God nor any sensible man ever intended there should be one."

Botkin carried both sides of the bluff to win the election.

GEORGE B. ELY'S LAW PRACTICE

Even though now and then the law might be crudely administered, and in spite of the sometime inelegant deportment of bench and bar, it should not be assumed that these early tribunals were held in disrespect. They symbolized justice for the people, and woe to the critic from outside who mistook the shadow for the substance.

George B. Ely appeared in Janesville during the 1850's to establish a law practice. He nailed up a glossy diploma from a New York law school, put out his shingle, and stood ready, as he put it, to "teach the backwoods some law." He incautiously remarked that the local court wanted dignity of procedure which only a George B. Ely could, by his example, supply.

Hearing of Ely's noble purpose, the legal fraternity of the town met in secret conclave. In due time Isaac Woodle paid a formal call on Mr. Ely and begged him to apply his superior talents to a crucial case.

Exhibiting documents meticulously drawn to the letter of the law, Woodle outlined the suit. William Wheeler was charged with stealing a dollar bill from William Hodson. Mr. Ely might gather from the small amount of money involved that the matter was a trivial one. Actually, said Woodle, momentous principles were at stake. An innocent man was being railroaded on a trumped-up charge. Woodle hinted darkly that ruthless schemers were in the background, plotting to ruin poor Wheeler. It was a case for a master defender, for a man not only versed in the finer subtleties of the law, but one who had vision, and a belief in the high dignity of his calling. No Janesville lawyer, alas, could possibly meet so strong a challenge, none, that is, except Mr. Ely. Would he take the case?

Mr. Ely would. "You flatter me," he said with a fatuous smile.

After nights of laborious research and preparation, Ely appeared at the trial impeccably dressed as the gentleman attorney. The courtroom was packed.

Solemnly the court read the charge. Wheeler pleaded "not guilty." The complaining witness, however, said that he could positively identify the stolen dollar bill.

"But how is it possible," said the alert Ely, "that out of all the millions of bills in existence, you are able to identify this single one?"

The judge, too, remonstrated with such a claim, and was met with a most unexpected rebuke.

"Shut up, you old fool!" shouted the witness.

From that moment Ely's worst fears about western jurisprudence were more than realized. The unruly crowd booed and shouted and stamped their feet. Witnesses quarreled with the judge, and insulted him in the most shocking fashion. The place was in a bedlam.

"Your Honor!" cried Ely, above the din. "Is there no way of stopping this mockery of justice?"

"Not in Janesville, young man," replied the judge sadly. "Not in Janesville."

Suddenly the door at the back of the courtroom was flung open. In marched a grotesque fellow, barefooted and dressed in cast-off garments. He carried over his shoulder a string of vile-smelling fish. Reaching the table where Mr. Ely had carefully arranged his legal papers, he tossed down his catch. Then, drawing from his pocket a pack of greasy cards, he leered at the court, and bellowed out an astonishing invitation, "Gather 'round, folks. I'll play anyone in the house for them bullheads!"

Up to this moment the judge had played his part with sober skill. Now he broke down completely. As he spluttered out his order for adjournment, and the helpless laughter shook his frame, it dawned upon Mr. Ely that he had been wasting his precious talents in a mock trial.

Mr. Ely lived it all down in time, and since he never mentioned it thereafter, it may be presumed that eventually he found a dignity in the jurisprudence of Janesville which had escaped his notice before.

Milwaukee Journal, October 28, 1928

JUDGE IRVIN

The Hon. David Irvin was the first United States District Judge who presided in Walworth County. He was a Virginia gentleman of the old school and kept the dignity of the law, while on the bench, as only such a gentleman could.

His Honor was a bachelor of somewhat eccentric habits. Having no family of his own he spent all his affections, generously, upon his horse, Pedro, and his dog, York. He was extremely fond of hunting and prided himself on being an unerring marksman. The judge never admitted that he had missed a shot. One day, when he was in bad luck, he fired into a flock of ducks several times, failing to bring down a single bird. At each futile discharge he would say, "It is astonishing the amount of lead those birds will carry."

The judge always hunted smaller game, such as prairie chickens, squirrels, pigeons, and quail, stating that the skill of a marksman was required to bring them down and have more than a handful of feathers left. Judge Irvin held court at the Post Office, which consisted of one room. The small log building had been built personally by Postmaster Rockwell. This single room was also used as the Register's and Clerk's office for Walworth County. After hearing a case the jurors were sent out under a burr oak tree to deliberate.

His Honor was a constant sufferer from neuralgic pains in his back and heard his cases in a half-reclining position, when pain was severe. His seat was constructed in the form of a lounge, with one end raised, into which clamps were set to hold an upright board, slanting back a little, against which he could recline. No attack of pain was so severe though, as to prevent his going on a hunt if he had set his heart on it. During the hunting season, it must be admitted, when the pleasures of Nimrod warred in his conscience with the duties of Solomon, his neuralgia served him well.

It was ever noted that on those perfect hunting days of Indian Summer, when the squirrels chattered outside the courthouse and the tantalizing October air tempted all right-thinking men to the fields and woods, the judge would be afflicted with his most excruciating attacks. Then his writhings and grimaces, expressive of intense agony, would move counsel in sore pity to recommend that court adjourn until the judge was in better health. Then, with just the right shade of heroic reluctance to postpone his duties for even a few hours, Irvin would finally comply.

Judge Irvin, according to a colleague, the Honorable George Hyer, loved to gossip of himself, his horse, and his dog, "and it was difficult to tell from his conversation which of the three he thought most of." Many a suitor in the Irvin court was to discover the love the judge bore his rangy sorrel, Pedro, and his pointer, York. So established was the unwritten protocol that none but the fledgling would risk a hearing there without first giving Judge Irvin a hearing on the ancestry and astonishing traits of his "thoroughbreds." With certainty and satisfaction his honor could trace every blooded horse or dog back to some famous stock in Virginia.

"Any man who wanted to gain a case in Irvin's court," declared Andrew Elmore, the genial "Sage of Mukwonago," "had only to go hunting with him and let him claim all the game that was killed, or pet his dog. During the hearing of one of my cases there was not time for a hunting expedition, but I fed that dog crackers and cheese until he followed me wherever I went. The case was decided in my favor, and after the decision, I thought the dog had followed me long enough. I turned around and gave him a kick. The yelps of the dog had hardly subsided when I heard the judge say, 'Mr. Clerk, this judgement is set aside and a new trial granted.' That kick cost me two hundred dollars."

During one of the sessions in Madison, the news of a local horse race, a rare entertainment at the time, caused a certain restiveness in the courtroom. The lawyers at the bar, the members of the jury, as well as the spectators, all were anxious to have proceedings suspended so that they could make for the racecourse. But Irvin stubbornly refused to adjourn, not because he could not bear to see justice delayed, but because to his way of thinking the horses scheduled to run were imposters of such doubtful lineage they deserved to be ignored. To everyone else, however, a horse race was a horse race. So a few ingenious minds set about to force an adjournment.

York, the nonpareil, never absent from his master's fond sight, was a fixture in the courtroom wherever Judge Irvin was presiding. He occupied a favored place on the floor. In one of the rare intervals when the judge was not gazing soulfully at him, York was adroitly whisked out of the room and secreted in the tavern next door.

The scheme worked perfectly. As expected, Irvin very soon noticed York's absence from his customary place, and became alarmed. He beckoned the sheriff who stepped forward for a whispered consultation. "Mr. Sheriff, where is York?"

"I don't know, Your Honor."

After a few nervous moments the sheriff was again summoned. "Mr. Sheriff, please step to the door and whistle up the street for York," the judge muttered hoarsely.

The sheriff did as ordered, but he soon tiptoed back, alone.

Judge Irvin was now plainly worried. To continue the case before him was out of the question. York must be in danger!

"Court adjourned!" he exploded, and dashed to the street door. By a prearranged signal the tavern landlord released York at this instant, so that a happy reunion of man and dog took place immediately, while the eager crowd, like children released from school, dashed off to the horse race.

The wags affirmed that if one wanted to win a case he must praise Judge Irvin's horse and dog. It is a historical fact that no prudent lawyer, in this court, ever spoke of Pedro except in terms of adulation or failed to keep on intimate terms of friendship with York, via the bone department.

> Slowly the course of justice on proceeds,
> While ancient Pedro at his manger feeds,
> Till strikes the hour when prairie chickens fly.
> Then "Up and at them!" is the mandate high.
> Come out, swift Pedro, noble York appear!
> Enough of work—let sport our spirits cheer.
> Thus may we long our manly vigor keep,
> While sluggish souls o'er wasted muscles weep.
>
> Told by J. W. Curvin

THE THOUSAND AND ONE

No view of early trickstering would be complete without mention of the Thousand and One, that famous Wisconsin order whose members, among them nearly every one of the state's legal and political personalities of the forties and fifties, made hoaxing the sole raison d'etre of their brotherhood.

Like its secret meetings, the exact origins of the Thousand and One are shrouded in mystery. What little evidence there is suggests that "the joker brigade" of Mineral Point first instituted a chapter in 1846, and that those in whose minds the conception flamed were "the jocund Kelly brothers, Francis Henry and Andrew Hewitt." Not far behind was Janesville, "famous for her wags." Mr. Robert Briggs has been credited with introducing the mystic rites to the legislature in Madison, and the initiated members carried enthusiasm for the order to their various portions of the state. Andrew Elmore, William A. Barstow, and Alexander Randall formed a branch in Waukesha in 1849, and almost simultaneously the "Celestials," as they were known, gained a foothold in Milwaukee, Baraboo, Plover, Fond du Lac, and other communities. The Milwaukee *Sentinel* for August 21, 1851, has a cryptic reference to offshoots in Minnesota, at St. Paul and Willow River.

Only those who had been initiated into the mysteries of the Thousand and One knew that it was dedicated solely to hoaxing and horseplay. The public was led to believe that with such illustrious men as Alexander Botkin, Satterlie Clark, Major Rountree, and E. B. Dean as members, the organization could not but have some nobler purpose. A big public meeting in the old capitol to celebrate the "anniversary" of the order was preceded by a solemn procession, with bands playing and banners flying. The public remained attentive through a long oration on the ancient and honorable lineage of Thousand and One, without once suspecting it was sheer burlesque. Various conjectures were advanced to explain what the title meant. In Baraboo the Reverend Warren Cochran, during a sermon denouncing secret societies, testily remarked that he would interpret the "thousand" to mean the number of rascals in the society, and the "one" the number of decent men. A more complimentary as well as more accurate deduction was that the title referred to the thousand tricks in store for the one poor candidate for initiatory "honors."

The Thousand and One attached so much importance to its initiation ceremonies that it has been said that the initiation was all there was to the order, a fact in some localities. Andrew Elmore is supposed to have devised the ritual for these occasions, published and widely used under the title, *Ethereal Intonations, Pertaining to an Initiation into the Sublime Mysteries of the Oriental Evanic Order 1001*. The hocus-pocus prescribed in this odd pamphlet is a clever parody of secret society procedures.

(The candidate is then led among ruins, or proper representations, three times around the room. He is then addressed by the Sentinel, who, seizing him by the throat, interrogates him:)

"Who is this, possessed of the idle curiosity of puny woman, dare intrude upon the Secret Council of the Order 1001? Speak! or by the shade of the great Confucius, one of earth's mortals shall pay the forfeit of his life!"

Junior Pilot: "'Tis a stranger who seeks admission into our ancient and mysterious Order."

Sentinel: "Has he the password?"

Junior Pilot: "No—but I have it for him."

Sentinel: "Peace, babbler! Brothers, a stranger, prompted by idle curiosity, has dared intrude himself into the august presence of the Grand Council in Secret Session. What shall be done with him?"

(All cry: "Put him out! Put him out!")

Father Abraham: "Listen to the words of one who speaks from age and experience. Hold, brothers! I have but one word to say: Dead men tell no tales."

(The candidate is then thrown down by the Pilot.)

Worthy Senior: "Hold, brethren! Do the tenets of our Order require the shedding of innocent blood? No! 'Tis rather to wipe away the stain of blood and point the erring sons of mortality to a bright and happy future. Rise, brother! and proceed on your journey; and may it be as calm and as peaceful as it has hitherto been stormy and boisterous."

(The brethren then form a procession, and lead the candidate three times around the room singing:)

Air—"Rosin the Bow"

'Twas down by the foot of Mount Aetna,
Close by the rising of sun,
    Our Order sprang into existence,
And was christened 1001.

Then lead on the stranger, good Pilot,
And let him tread carefully on;
    For he's now in the terrible presence
Of the Order 1001.

We are a band of good-hearted brothers,
As ever was under the sun,
    We love ourselves and the Order,
Hurrah for the 1001!

These exercises were preceded by a soul-stirring questionnaire, and some robust physical rites. "Scores of men ... were stripped, branded, bounced, yoked, doused, made a sled of, whirled, tossed into the air, made to drink nauseous concoctions, wear shoemaker's wax for weeks in the hollows of their feet to 'draw out meanness,' carry asafetida in their pockets to 'counteract immoral tendencies,' have their hair greased to prevent foot-rot in sheep ..." In Plover the candidate was required to sit astride a bull, chased around a race track by playful dogs.

Remarking these shenanigans today, we are apt to discount their tonic effects upon the pompous fool and the knave, who were frequent victims of the Thousand and One. A quack doctor, a fake astrologer, or a fawning office-seeker, all were fair game for the "Celestials." Thinking to gain favors by joining the society, these worthies found in the rigors of the initiation their pretenses shredded to pieces, and they themselves the objects of unforgettable ridicule. "Many a neophyte has gone forth with a full diploma," observed James Buck, "and if not a wiser man than when he went in, it certainly must have been for the want of the ability to comprehend its sublime beauties, and not the fault of the institution whose members were in no wise slack in their attention to those seeking after light at their hands." The codified prankstering of this curious, short-lived organization was touched with the spirit of moral comedy.

chapter 10

SUPERSTITIONS AND HOMELY ADVICE

I<small>N WESTERN</small> Wisconsin, around Taylor," says Lucinda Morken, "there are a number of ways in which you may tell that company is coming. It is always a good idea to keep your eye on the chickens, and if you see an old rooster ambling toward the house with the intention of coming up and crowing on the front porch . . . well, company is absolutely on the way."

Also, watch the household cats, and if you notice them washing behind their ears you better expect a visitor, and if you're busy washing the dishes and have a hundred other jobs to do, for pity's sake don't drop the dishrag, or there'll be a knock at the front door right soon. Of course, if you drop the dishcloth somebody is coming who is dirtier than you are. And if the dishcloth is wet it will be a sloppy person. Then, while the family is eating supper, if you take a slice of bread while you already have a slice on your plate, somebody really hungry is going to call on you.

Table conduct is very important as far as visitors to your Wisconsin home are concerned. The dropping of silverware will bring definite results, as follows:

If a knife is dropped a man will come to visit.

If a fork is dropped a woman will come.

If a spoon is dropped a little girl will arrive.

Dropping a butter knife or spreader means that the visitor will be a little boy. And in addition, the direction in which these implements fall will determine the direction from which the company will appear.

Perhaps the worst catastrophe that can befall a busy family is to spill the toothpicks. That means company coming, and the number of toothpicks spilled means the number of visitors that may be expected.

Going back to that rooster that crowed on the doorstep to predict company, the housewives in early-day Wisconsin took this sign so seriously that they generally immediately killed and cooked the rooster and made a pie just to be on the safe side.

When sweeping in the evening it was necessary to sweep the dirt back of the door. If the dirt was swept outdoors, it was the same as sweeping out the company that was coming.

Company on Monday, company all the week, goes an old Wisconsin saying, and if you sneeze before breakfast that's a certain sign, but those of a more scientific turn of mind had a better method of prophecy. The scientists would lay a tea leaf from their teacup on the upper high part of the thumb, and with the other thumb would pound the tea leaf. At the same time they would count the days beginning with the present day. When the leaf stuck to the pounding thumb, that was the day the company would arrive.

If you saw a cat washing herself in a doorway it was a sign that the minister was coming to call. The German grandfather might say: "Preaster kimps." Speaking of doorways, if a mop or broom falls across a doorway you better clean up and prepare!

Superstitions and signs played a big part in the life of the early Wisconsin pioneer. Without scientific knowledge he relied on signs to steer much of the course of his daily living. Many of these superstitions are still with us today, although most of them have been forgotten and are part of our historic past.

Weather was important to the early settler, living much of the time out of doors and close to nature. He came to rely on weather signs to guide his activities, from planting crops to preventing lightning from striking. The advent of rain, and particularly of a storm, was always of interest. Having no radio broadcasts or reliable information he made up his own; it was passed along from neighbor to neighbor and from grandparents to grandchildren.

A storm was surely on its way under the following conditions:

When the wood fire in the old iron stove roared as it burned.

When the water drawn from the well looked cloudy.

When the ground-up feed that was mixed in the swill barrel rose to the top of the liquid instead of staying "mixed."

When there was a circle around the moon.

When the cat slept with her head "turned under and her mouth turned up" instead of in the usual curled-up position.

There were other signs to show changes in the weather and predict just what to expect from the skies:

When the potatoes boiled dry, it was a sign of rain.

When the leaves on the trees curled up or blew wrong side out, it was a sign of rain.

When the chickens ran for shelter in a shower, it wouldn't last long. If they stayed out in it, it would rain for a long time.

When there was a ring around the moon with stars inside the ring, the number of stars indicated the number of days before a storm.

When the sky was flecked with small clouds, called buttermilk clouds, it was a sign of rain very soon.

When your feet burned, it was a sign of rain.

When there was a heavy dew in the evening, the next day would be hot.

When the smoke from the chimney settled to the ground, it was a sign of rain. When the smoke went straight up, it would be colder.

When roosters crew before midnight, it meant a weather change.

When a dog ate grass, it was a sign of rain.

When six weeks had passed after crickets began to sing, you looked for frost.

If streaks could be seen from the earth to the sun, which looked as though the sun was "drawing water," it would rain.

Water beads on outside of a water pail meant rain.

Wind in the south—blows bait in fish's mouth. Wind in the east— fish bite the least. Wind in the west—fishing is best!

When the kitchen range was being used, and sparks clung to bottom of a frying pan or pot, it was supposed to storm.

What the weather was on the last Friday of a month predicted closely what the weather would be like during the following month.

A good time to plant hotbed seeds was on Good Friday.

If rain fell on Easter Sunday, it would be followed by six weeks of rainy Sundays.

If the sun set behind a bank of clouds, there would be rain tomorrow; when the sun set "like a ball of fire," it would be a hot day, or at least a bright sunshiny one.

> Evening red and morning gray,
> Sends the traveler on his way.
> Evening gray and morning red,
> Brings down rain upon his head.

> Rainbow in the morning
> Sailors take warning
> Rainbow at night
> Sailors delight.

And here are some other weather jingles:

> A snow storm in May
> Is worth a load of hay.

> A swarm of bees in May
> Is worth a load of hay.

> A cold April the farmers barn will fill.

> If Candlemas Day be mild and gay
> Go saddle your horses and buy them hay;
> But if Candlemas Day be stormy and black
> It carries the winter away on its back.

If Candlemas Day be fair and clear
There'll be two winters in a year.

A year of snow
A year of plenty.

Much damp and warm
Does the farmer much harm.

When the morn is dry,
The rain is nigh.
When the morn is wet,
No rain you get.

When the grass is dry at morning's light
Look for rain before the night.

The bigger the ring
The nearer the wet.

When the cats played in the evening or the fire popped in a wood stove, the wind was going to blow.

The weather on the last Friday of a month predicted closely what the weather would be like during the following month.

Will the spring be wet or dry? Will the winter be mild or severe? Many residents, especially the older farmers, still observe the direction of the wind on the day the seasons change. The prevailing wind that day has a good chance of being the wind of the season, and so a westerly wind will predict a wet spring, or an easterly wind will bring a dry spring, or many believed it was just the opposite—a west wind dried and an east wind brought rain. A south breeze the first day of winter would forecast a mild winter while a blustery northern forecast a long, cold winter. Thus the state of the weather and the direction of the wind when the sun crossed the line (or the equinox) might forecast the wind and weather for at least the next three months.

One settler said that her grandfather always predicted "thaw weather" in January when the train reverberated loudly down the railroad tracks. And if the moon was on its back it meant dry weather ahead, but if the moon was tipped over on its face there was sure to be wet weather.

Northern lights suddenly showing at night predicted a change in the weather or might be interpreted to precede cold, stormy weather.

Some of nature's weather signs which were noted were: a thick shell on hickory nut husks which denoted a long winter ahead; or heavy silk on corn ears or many layers of husks, which predicted a hard, cold winter. Trappers foresaw a severe winter when pelts on fur-bearing animals were unusually thick.

When butchering it was well to plan to do it in the "gain of the moon" as then the meat would not shrink so much as it would when butchered during the "wane of the moon." If a butchered animal's spleen was seen to be long and thin, it was a sign of a long winter. If short and thick, it meant a short winter.

Superstitions pertaining to lightning and thunder storms were many—if one didn't want to be struck:

Never stand in the path of two windows, or have them both open. Don't stand near an open door or window or near a stove or a chimney. Do no sewing, have no needles, pins, or thimbles in or on the hands. Don't hold any metal objects; these were thought to draw the lightning very fast. Don't sit, or be near an animal of any kind.

No tree which had been hit by lightning would be used for fuel, as the house where it was used would be struck also.

Anyone who worked in the fields on Good Friday might be struck by lightning, and in fact it was very bad to start any important work on a Friday.

One hundred years ago the Wisconsin farmer glanced at his almanac, hung conveniently in the kitchen, and noted this uncomfortable verse:

> Now winter with his icy shroud
>   Wraps nature in one general gloom;
> The piercing winds blow long and loud,
>   And make us fear a snowy tomb.

He then discovered the sage advice printed underneath:

> Be wide awake in industry, alive and alert in that for which you were created, which is to "use the world, as not abusing it," and following the golden rule of doing kind offices to all around, and no gossiping.

Estella Bryhn of Mindoro, Wisconsin has something to say about superstitions and farming in the Coulee Region:

As a little girl I helped my father plant potatoes. We lived in the village of West Salem in the heart of the beautiful Coulee region of western Wisconsin. At that time each family raised its own supply of vegetables for the winter, especially potatoes. To buy store "spuds" was not only extravagant, but also proof of poor gardening.

Father raised good potatoes, but somehow there were never quite so many large potatoes under a hill as our neighbor, a little man of Norweigan descent by the name of Martinus, found in his garden plot, which was the identical size of ours. This particular spring Father cut his potato seed pieces a little larger than usual. This year for sure his potatoes would be better than those Martinus raised!

Father dug one hole. I carefully placed one potato piece in the hole with the "eyes" pointing up, "So they can see to grow," my Father would remind me. Then he dug another hole and threw that spadeful of dirt into the first hole, so as he dug one, he filled the one behind him. When we finished Martinus came to voice his disapproval of our work.

"You won't get many potatoes this year," he gloomily informed us. "You are planting in the wrong time of the moon!"

Father laughed. "You plant yours in the moon if you want to, but I'll bet on mine in the ground!"

Almost before we knew it, the summer was gone, and we were digging our potatoes. By a coincidence Martinus chose the same day to dig his. As we dug we kept watching Martinus pile his potatoes up, up, up. Finally Father reluctantly agreed that Martinus had beat us again!

The next spring Father carefully sorted out the seed potatoes from the big bin in the cellar. Then, instead of cutting and planting as he usually did, he impatiently waited until Martinus finally decided the moon was just right, and then they both planted what turned out to be really bumper crops.

The superstition in the Coulee region in regard to planting is that vegetables that grow in the ground, such as potatoes, carrots, turnips, should be planted in the dark of the moon, and crops that grow above the ground, such as corn, cabbage, lettuce, should be planted when the moon is light.

Even today, the proper time to plant corn is when the buds on the hickory trees are as big as squirrel ears.

We had butchered a hog and a beef, and the meat lay on long tables in the "summer kitchen" to cool. Deep freezers were undreamed of and the year's supply of meat on many farms was preserved either by canning, smoking, or packing in a salt brine strong enough to float an egg. We showed our meat, which we thought was very fine grade, to some guests who solemnly informed us that we should have waited a while until the moon was right.

According to this superstition meat butchered in the light of the moon will not shrink or fry away so much, and will also keep better. Chicken will also bleed better, will can nicer, and the feathers will come off much easier.

The Wisconsin farmer who laughs loudly while planting corn is likely to get ears with uneven rows of kernels on them, and the kernels may be too far apart. It may be better, actually, to plant corn in the dark of the moon; many farmers believe so. Planting corn in the light of the moon will give you tall stalks and a lot of fodder, but precious little ears. Planting in the Coulee region apparently differs from this advice.

Allied to agricultural lore is that fascinating mystery of the water witch—that individual who has the apparent power of locating water beneath the surface of the earth. In earlier days water witching was much more important than it is now, but there are still a few witchers in Wisconsin. Their favorite method is similar to that practiced by witchers everywhere. Peach twigs are considered best, and the witcher will cut a branch of peach which has a fork and will trim it, leaving the fork and an extension at the thick end somewhat like the fork and handle of a lad's slingshot, except that the witcher's twig is larger and longer. Willow may also be used and is indeed preferred by some.

With the twig cut and ready, the witcher will hold the twig by the forked end, one side of the fork in each hand, and will walk slowly over an area where he is anxious to locate water. The long extension of the twig is held out in front of him parallel to the earth.

When the witcher comes just over the water, the twig will suddenly point downward, and here the witcher will drive a stake to mark the spot. Men digging later will, in an amazing number of instances, find good water.

Water witching is so widely known and widely practiced that there is evidence supporting belief that some persons have a natural affinity for water. It certainly isn't just the twig alone, for the twigs will not perform for just anybody. Anyway, many of the older wells in Wisconsin were located by witchers, and they were considered indispensable.

But if Wisconsin farmers believed in witchers, they believed in other things as well. Thomas D. Wage, who moved to Wisconsin from Pennsylvania in 1856, would never have his hair cut during the month of March—to do so would cause him to have a year-long headache. He also said that a good farmer had to watch the direction of the wind on March 21 and 22. If in the south, southeast, or southwest, it would be a good corn year. This appears to have been a common belief among old settlers. Mr. Wage, and many of his neighbors, always carried in an extra load of wood on New Year's Day—that indicated that there would be plenty to carry into the home during the year.

There are many sections in Wisconsin where a fly observed in the house at Christmastime foretells a time of prosperity in that house and the certainty of making a thousand dollars. In fact, good luck omens, death omens, or just omens in general seem to play a big part in the lives of many Wisconsin folk. Mrs. Belle Miller out in the Kickapoo Valley wrote us a word about crowing hens:

You questioned [she wrote] whether a hen ever crows. Once in

a while you'll find one that makes a real attempt to. They stretch
their necks way out the way a rooster does, but the sound is awful—
never musical like a rooster's crow. That didn't happen often in our
small flock of chickens, but when it did, my mother got that worried
look on her face, sure that something desperate was going to happen.

Once or twice during my childhood, before 1900, I remember
finding a small, round egg when gathering the eggs. As we had no
pullets at that time it was very unusual. Mother always said that
somebody was going to die in the relations. It seems to me that once
when I found a small egg, my grandmother died. Mother said, "I told
you so."

And white horses are good for an omen anywhere, and Wisconsin
isn't any exception. There are mystic Wisconsin rites concerning
white horses. The record of the number a girl sees must be kept in
this way: kiss the two first fingers of your right hand; imprint that
kiss on the inner palm part of your left thumb with three good
knocks of the right fist. When sufficient white horses have been
counted and recorded, something wonderful will happen to the
counter, probably not in the distant future but in the immediate
present.

May Augustyn of Fond du Lac told us about some of the omen
signs of her Irish grandmother at Janesville:

"Grandma, why are you rubbing the palm of your left hand on the
chair?" I asked one day when I was very small.

"Because it itches, and the old saying is, 'Scratch it on wood it
will surely come good,' and that means I will get money," she
answered with a smile. "If my right palm itched it would be a sure
sign that I would have a handshake with a friend."

The whole performance was a puzzle to me, but I said no more
then. Many times I tried this magic but never found my palm
crossed with gold.

This was only one of the many quaint Irish superstitions my pretty
little grandmother brought with her when she came to the New
World and went to live at Janesville, Wisconsin, where there was
a large settlement of her own countrymen.

Those were the days when Irishmen in that thriving town had real Irish fights between the Patch and the Gashouse gangs, and St. Patrick's evening was always good for a final roundup of the boys who had been celebrating all day. Many a sturdy son of Erin found his sore and swollen head too heavy to lift off the pillow the next morning. His battered body also found the bed soothing, but those Pats and Mikes considered it worth the price of their aches and pains if their gang had been victorious.

Folklore from the Emerald Isle was a part of Grandmother's life and governed many of her decisions through the long years I loved her.

Friday was the Devil's day, and under no circumstances would she start a new undertaking of any kind. Sewing on a new dress was unheard of, and she never ventured forth on a trip until this day of ill luck was over. Home and ordinary routine was her schedule on Friday. She religiously counted her beads to keep the evil spirits away.

Her ideas of death seemed queer but fascinating, and I still remember my mother telling about them. Her belief in the wailing dirge of the banshees was firm, and many stories she related down through the years became family traditions. One in particular was often repeated by her family, long after she was gone.

My mother then had two small children who were safely tucked into bed the night Grandmother came to the house in a great hurry. "For goodness sake, why are the little ones crying so hard? I heard them way down the street," she exclaimed.

"But Mother, the children are not crying and have been asleep for a long time," my young mother replied.

After satisfying herself that it was true, she murmured, more to herself than to Mother, "Old Mrs. Dawson must be dying, and it was the wail of the banshees I heard. They have come to help her on her journey to the other world. It will be over any time now."

"But I did not hear any crying; why should you?" Mother asked.

"Not everyone can hear the banshees. It is a special gift, and in my young days I heard them often in Ireland," Grandmother went on.

Mother was unconvinced, but old Mrs. Dawson did pass on that night, and Grandmother heard no more cries of mourning from the female fairies.

When a member of her family passed on she would not allow anyone to touch them for three hours, as she firmly believed it would take at least that long for the departed to reach the other shore and make his peace with his Maker. Why three hours was the chosen time I was never able to find out, but it was three hours with her, and that settled it. They had always done it that way in Ireland.

None of her loved ones were ever laid to rest without shoes or soft slippers, as she did not want them to walk the streets of Heaven for all eternity in their bare feet. So firmly had this thought been dwelt upon that even the younger members of her family made the same request. Our family still adheres to this custom. My own mother had been in a coma for days, but one afternoon she frightened me badly by suddenly opening her eyes and saying in a harsh whisper, "Shoes."

"Yes, Mother," I answered quickly, for I knew what she meant, though she never leaned to the mysterious as far as I had known. I kept my promise; she wore shoes.

The day Mrs. Griffin's son, Mikie, was to be taken to his final resting place torrents of rain fell. Mrs. Griffin's tears were almost as profuse as the rain, and to comfort her Grandmother said, "Happy is the bride the sun shines on, and happy is the corpse the rain rains on."

The howling of a dog in the night sent the cold shivers down Grandmother's spine, for to her, a dog howling was an evil omen, a sure sign somebody she knew was going on a long journey, never to return. "God rest their soul," was her favorite reaction to the noisy dog. She took good care that her dog was in the house.

Once when I visited Grandma, I wanted to sew on Sunday, but these were her words, "No sewing on Sunday, for if you do you will have to rip out every stitch with your nose. That is true because my mother taught me that when I was a little girl like you."

"Oh, dear," I sighed.

"You must not sigh like that, child. It is bad for your heart," she cautioned.

Grandmother's life work has been finished many years, but her grandchildren still remember her with love and wish they might live those golden days again and listen to her queer and interesting superstitions brought from the Old Country.

While, from Baraboo, Doris Brecka recalls some omens and superstitions of luck or otherwise as related by her German-born parents:

As a child of German-born immigrants farmers, I came in for my share of superstitions, sayings, and proverbs. Though my older sisters and brothers no doubt absorbed many of the old sayings in the original German idiom, by the time I came along, most of them were being rather freely translated into English. But there is one I have managed to retain—perhaps it appealed to me in some special way. Anyway, it seems like just yesterday that I stood at the kitchen table helping can string beans, quart after quart of the tiresome vegetable. Any expression of distaste for a garden product never failed to bring forth this admonishing proverb: *"Wen tunpole hat a weiss hut, dan schmecht die zure apfel gut!"* * which not quite so rhythmically in English states, "When the fencepost has a white hat, then the sour apples will taste good!"

I feel again that lonely terror in my childhood days upon hearing a hen crow or a bird fly against a window. The former was supposed to herald bad luck, the latter bad news. After a long day of cowering close to my mother's skirts after either of these phenomena, I breathed a sigh of relief when night would fall on no worse a calamity than Nellie, the mare, having a light case of colic, or a bill in the mail from the doctor. If I happened to be bold enough to express disbelief, Mother tersely informed me that certainly those things couldn't be considered good luck or good news. Be that as it may, I resolved that my children would never know of the crowing hen!

On growing up, with the usual adolescent consciousness of any flaw in home or dress, I was frequently assured that at night all cats are gray. My best chum complained that in her home her English-born grandmother expressed the same thought: "You won't see that on a flying horse!"

The advent of the holidays brought their own superstitions. One of the most widely known of the German ones is that of the cattle

---

* This wild mixture of Low German, High German, English, and aberrations of memory is left uncorrected here.

in the stable being possessed of the power of speech on Christmas Eve. I was very curious as to which language they would converse in, but I had no intention of finding out for myself. Imagine the terror of having Bessie, the Holstein, roar out at me, "Okay, Sis, what was the big idea of that kick in my shins the other day?"

New Year's Eve brought with it a dark warning about sweeping the house dirt directly out the door. Bad luck, they said.

Sometimes it seemed like every ordinary occurrence foretold the future. Dare to sing before breakfast, you'd cry before dinner. Your palm itched, you were due to get money. Itching nose, you'd kiss a fool. A broom falling across the door, better straighten up quick, for company was on the way! Likewise with silverware falling. Dishes empty of food meant a good day tomorrow.

It was destined years in advance that I would make a good wife, for "good to the dog, good to your husband"!

Between my own German ancestry and that of my Bohemian-ancestored husband, I guess that life in our family could be just one good or ill omen after another. Actually we prefer the good old American concept of living: Faith in the Future!

Mrs. Martin Williams of Green Bay related a wish omen as it was practiced in the Wisconsin Belgian settlements:

The second Sunday of Lent marked the end of activities, social and others, regardless of what date it fell on. Four or five families would get together to make as big a bonfire as possible. The Christmas trees from the preceding Christmas, the prunings from the orchard, and donations of whatever straw that could be spared—anything burnable that could be salvaged—was gathered for this bonfire. To have the biggest fire was an honor.

There was corn popping, apple roasting, even homemade pork sausage and Belgian tripe, with very much merrymaking. This was the last social event until the next fall. There were to be no more card-playing parties or even quilting bees. This was the hint—that anyone who had any more sewing or quilting had to wait until fall. There was work to be done, and people wanted to stay home to get it finished. Seeds had to be sorted by hand, beans shelled, and seeds taken out of the pods. It meant early to bed for an early rising the next morning during this busy season. The horses were fed early and taken out to be tempered for the hard work ahead.

The superstition was that everybody made a wish before activities started during the evening of the big bonfires. By the end of the evening whoever had seen and counted the most fires would get his wish. You had to see the fire first from your own fire. You were not permitted to get into trees or on the housetop. This lucky person would also take home a prize—a homemade something like a scarf, socks, or even tripe.

In the Belgian dialect there is a saying that rhymes and means, "At the big fire, the social evenings are set afire."

And here is a whole list of signs and portents that the Wisconsin citizen had better be on the watch for:

If you rock an empty chair, it means bad luck.

If you sing before breakfast, you'll weep before night.

If a bird taps on the window with his bill, it means someone will die in that house within a year. (This is also interpreted to mean merely that something unusual will happen.)

If you are weaning babies, calves, little pigs, the signs of the zodiac must be in the feet. If weaned while the signs are in the head, the young will never forget the nursing habit. You must wait until the signs have moved down to the feet or any future weakness will settle in the breast, bowels, or arms.

If meat pops in the skillet when you are frying, it means that the animal was killed in the wrong time of the moon.

If cream is churned for a long while and doesn't make butter, it should be stirred with a twig of mountain ash and the cow should be beat with another twig of mountain ash. This will break the spell.

If you kill a wren, you will break a bone before the year is out.

If you kill a robin, there will be no spring.

If you put on a garment wrong side out, leave it that way or bad luck will be the result.

Olive Hope, Salem, Wisconsin enlarges on this one:

A neighbor of ours in early days firmly believed it was bad luck to remove a piece of clothing and turn it right side out if it had been put on wrong side out. One winter's day when we were playing in the snow, one of the boys had, in his haste, donned his shirt wrong side out. When he was about to take it off to change it, his mother stopped him saying, "Now Ora, you know that something would happen to you if you did that, and I will not let you do it. You leave your shirt on wrong side out until you go to bed tonight."

So Ora came out to coast down the hill with us, the garment still wrong side out. In spite of the precaution, by a queer twist of fate, Ora fell and broke his arm, and was bundled off to a doctor's office looking like a scarecrow and, of course, terribly humiliated in that day—far more than one would be in this modern age.

Sabrina Miller, of West Salem, expands our list with the following bits of advice:

If two friends, when walking along together, come to a pole or other object and one goes on one side and one on the other, they must say "bread and butter" or they will soon quarrel.

If you happen to put some garment on wrong side out, leave it that way or bad luck will be the result. Another says it may be turned right side out if it is first spit upon.

Comb your hair after dark, comb sorrow to your heart.

If your right ear burns, someone is talking good about you. If your left ear burns, someone is talking bad about you.

See a pin and pick it up, all the day you'll have good luck. See a pin and let it lie, all the day you'll sit and cry. If you find a straight pin with the head pointing toward you and pick it up, you will have your luck blunted for the day. If point is towards you, good luck will follow.

One must not rock an empty rocking chair or cradle, or the owner will get sick.

Don't start any work on Friday, thirteenth or otherwise, or you'll have bad luck with it.

If a black cat crosses one's path, turn back or you'll have bad luck.

If you forget something when going out, don't go back to the house or bad luck will follow you.

One must not walk under a ladder, or one will have bad luck.

One's first glimpse of the new moon must be over one's right shoulder in order to have good luck.

A black cat coming to one's place presages bad luck. Or, passing in front of you when you're driving on the road, it's a sign of disaster. Brother John would say, "Sure, if it had a white stripe down its back, it might bring disaster!"

A horseshoe over the door, open ends down, means good luck will pour down on you.

Finding a horseshoe is good luck. The number of nails in it foretells how many years of good luck.

If a bird hits the house with a thud, it's a sign a death is coming in that house.

If an owl lights on a house and hoots, it must be killed or a death will follow.

A mysterious rapping on the bed or any part of the house forecasts a death.

You must never give a blade of steel away, or the friendship of giver and receiver will be severed; you should always charge something for the blade. And don't drive fenceposts in the dark of the moon. They will rot and the wire will come loose.

Sewing a garment that you are wearing on your body can have unfortunate consequences. Pauline Easterson says that her mother in northwestern Wisconsin admonished her:

"Paula, how many times have I told you not to sew anything when it is on your body? You know as many falsehoods will be told about you as you take stitches therein."

"Oh Mother, that is just an old country superstition. How could it possibly make any difference if I take a few stitches to keep my big toe in when my stocking is on my foot, or if I pull it off and hold it over by hand?"

"Ja, all right, you wait and see. Shame to do it so careless."

That is the way my day started off, and I forgot all about it in my haste to get dressed and off to school. Later it came back to me. There was to be a party the coming Saturday. All the girls were invited except Mabel and me. We couldn't understand why we had been left out. Next Monday the rest of the girls were talking about their good time at the party. Mabel couldn't resist asking, "Why weren't Paula and I asked?"

"Oh, Hulda said you two had invitations to go to the Twin Cities for the weekend."

We knew Hulda was jealous of us and didn't want us at the party. Mother's sayings would come to mind.

With these memories comes the memory of Mother, sitting by the stove, knitting or mending.

Hedwig Poehler of Milwaukee says that:

"Whistling girls and crowing hens always come to some sad end."

If one's nose itches he is apt to be kissed, cursed, or vexed, or shake hands with a fool.

> If your nose itches
>> Your mouth is in danger
> Shake hands with a fool
>> Or kiss a stranger.

> Haste makes waste
>> And waste makes want
> And want makes strife
>> Between a good man and his wife.

If the chickens laid a tiny egg we were supposed to stand with our backs to the chicken coop and throw the egg over the roof. This was to ward off evil.

If a young man or woman happens to meet a pile of dirt in the doorway that the housewife is sweeping up, they will not be wed that year.

We could not cut a baby's fingernails before he was a year old or he would get to be a thief. My mother always bit off the baby's nails.

We could not let the baby look in a mirror before he was a year old for fear of his being conceited.

Olive Hope says that:

If you sing before breakfast, you will cry before supper.

If a baby is allowed to see himself in a mirror before he is one year old, he will not live to reach adulthood.

If a dog is heard howling after midnight, there is going to be a death in the family. Though I never knew whether it meant the family of the dog or of the family who owned the dog.

It was unlucky to seat thirteen people at the table. One of them might die within the year.

Kill the first snake you see in the spring and you will overcome the difficulties you meet during the whole year.

It is impossible for a pregnant woman to make jelly or vinegar. The jelly will not set and the vinegar will not ferment.

If it is a habit of a girl to splash water on the front of her apron as she leans over the washboard, she is going to marry a drunkard.

Snow or rain in an open grave meant there would be another death in the family within the year—or someone in the relationship will die very soon.

Neither must a corpse be taken over the same road twice, that is going to the church and later to the graveyard, for that certainly would bring another death to the family very soon.

Seeing the moon over your left shoulder is bad luck.

If a black cat crosses your path, it is bad luck.

If your ears burn, someone is talking about you.

Dream of the dead and you'll see the living. Dreaming about horses or muddy water is a sign of death coming.

Get married in green and you'll live like a queen. Get married in blue, he'll always be true.

A barking dog doesn't bite.

The longest way round is the shortest way home.

A green Christmas means a fat graveyard.

Dreaming of a white or gray horse meant a death in the family.

Never begin a piece of work on Friday, for it will never be finished. Never start on a journey on Friday—you will never get there.

To raise an umbrella inside the house is to invite death to your home.

Mrs. Kenneth Lindsay wrote us in a letter that:

When you move to a different house, never take a cat or an old broom with you or bad luck will follow you.

If you go out of the house and forget something and have to go back after it, sit down and cross your legs and wish so your luck will be good.

If a sick person picks at the bedclothes, it is a sign death is near.

If children grate their teeth in their sleep, it is a sign they have worms.

White spots on your finger nails from thumb to little finger mean: friend, foe, present, beau, journey to go.

Cut your finger nails on Monday for crosses, Tuesday for losses, Wednesday the best day of all, Thursday a letter, Friday something better, Saturday see your true love tomorrow, and on Sunday the devil will follow you all week.

Never count the number a bell tolls—bad luck to you.

If you spill the salt, hurry and put some in the fire or throw some over your right shoulder so you won't have a quarrel with someone.

To see three teams of horses on the road, sign you'll hear of a funeral.

To meet an empty hearse is a sign of a death in your family.

If your shoestring is dangling, it is a sign your lover is thinking of you.

If there are three dots of tea grounds in your teacup, wish and you'll get your wish.

If the Wisconsin moon shines on you as you sleep, there may be a death in the family, and if you dream of something white it may be a sign of death. Rain falling in an open grave means a death within a year. Three knocks at the door and nobody there means a death in the family. Dream of the dead, hear of the living. If a death occurs at the end of a week, so that the corpse is held over Sunday, some relative is going to die within three months. If two persons living in the same block die in the same week, a third in that city block will die very soon. To set two lighted lamps on the same table means certain death to someone close to you.

It is the custom in some parts to announce to the bees a death in the family, especially the death of the father or the head of the family. The bees will then bring consolation to the family members. If a swarm of bees settle on the dead branch of a live tree in the yard, a death will occur in the family within a year.

It is unlucky to plant a bed of lilies-of-the-valley, as the person who does so will surely die within the next twelve months. Cows forecast the future. If they moo after midnight, it is warning of an approaching death.

See a black cat cross the road in front of you and . . .

But Mrs. John Carlson of Ogema doesn't believe that one.

It was County Fair time in Phillips, Wisconsin, she says, a time when farmers laid down their hoes, school children were given a holiday to attend the fair, and the whole county looked forward to a day of festivity:

The 1914 model Ford that we owned at the time gave poor promise of a twenty-two-mile-long ride to the fair in the fall of 1926.

"I'm not going and that's that," said our lord and master. "Fairs are all the same, and you and the children have been to others."

Well, that should have been an end to that, but it was such a lovely day. Looking at the tearful faces of our five children, my husband finally relented. He said that we could try and see how far we would get with the bad tires and all. So we all dressed hurriedly and climbed into our tin Lizzie. My husband couldn't quite join in the festivity as he felt the car would break down at any time.

We hadn't traveled a mile from home when it happened. The biggest black cat that we had ever seen crossed our path. Being so terribly superstitious, I felt that almost anything could happen that day. And it did. With difficulty I repressed my fears and we finally reached the County Fair without having encountered anything more disastrous than two flat tires.

We had a wonderful day at the fair, seeing the sights and visiting with old friends, many of whom we saw only on such rare occasions. About four o'clock in the afternoon, my husband remarked that we had better start for home. The children wanted no part of it, as they still had a few coins burning holes in their pockets. But my husband insisted, so we started for the car. On the way we met a friend, who was much surprised that we were on our way home.

"Aren't you going to stay for the drawing?" he asked.

"We have no tickets," I said. "I know they are giving away a new Ford so I wish that we did have some." My oldest daughter spoke up. "Mama, the man at the gate threw some tickets in the back seat when we came in." We went to the car, found the tickets and signed them and then deposited them in the big barrel. And just in the nick of time, as officials were already on the platform preparing for the drawing.

A little girl was called upon to draw the tickets. She was to draw four, and the fifth ticket was to be the winner. The announcer started to call out each number slowly. On the fifth ticket every number he called out corresponded with those on my ticket stub. I had won the Ford.

"It's our car! It's our car!" I screamed at my husband. He thought that I had gone completely out of my mind and refused to even go up on the platform. Half dragging him, I finally reached the platform with him. Disappointed holders of tickets were throwing them right in his face.

We were a happy and proud family riding out of the County Fair grounds in our brand-new Ford. Crowds surged around the car and here and there cheers would go up. We beamed, waved, and felt much like royalty riding in a Coronation Parade. The old tin Lizzie was later brought home by a friend.

Black cats? They don't scare me.

Granddaddy Longlegs will give the location of the cows in the pasture when asked, and witch hazel will cast spells on its encounterers. Moonstones are good-luck charms, but an opal is an unlucky stone portending injury and mental or physical trouble. An agate insures its wearer health, long life, and prosperity. A diamond may disperse storms, and a topaz prevents bad dreams. Rubies are said to discover poison and correct evil, but the finding of purple hyacinths can only denote sorrow. Broken straws or sticks foretell a broken agreement, and in summer, if you are not careful, snakes may milk your cows dry in the pasture. If your nose itches you will hear some good news. If you drop your comb while combing your hair you are in for a scolding that day; also a scolding if you button your dress the wrong way. If the teakettle sings there is sure to be trouble, or an argument—the only remedy is to keep putting cold water in the kettle! If it rains on your wedding day you will shed many tears during your wedded life; but if you eat raw cabbage on New Year's Day you will have plenty of money in your pocket all the year.

One thing you better watch out for, though, is sneezing because, as Mrs. Clarice Moon of Rock County writes:

> Sneeze on Monday, sneeze for danger.
> Sneeze on Tuesday, kiss a stranger.
> Sneeze on Wednesday, get a letter.
> Sneeze on Thursday, something better.
> Sneeze on Friday, sneeze for sorrow.
> Sneeze on Saturday, lover's tomorrow.
> Sneeze on Sunday, your safety seek,
> For hard luck you will have all the week.

chapter 11

PROVERBS AND PLAIN TALK

Though possibly many of the old tales and legends are dying out from sheer lack of the telling, one traditional folklorist's category is flourishing: that of the popular saying, or proverb.

The popularity of the proverb may be accounted for in several ways. It has a universal appeal, is custom-made and saves thinking; it belongs where it is found and recognizes no birthplace; it often has rhyme and rhythm; it always has some grains of wisdom succinctly expressed; it has achieved a kind of authority from long acceptance.

Also, the proverb can very effectually close down an argument unless the opposition comes back with an equally authoritative old saw as refutation.

Where did the proverbs come from? The answer is, "Anywhere and everywhere." A partial answer might be, "The Bible and Ben Franklin." But Shakespeare wouldn't like that; neither would a million and one nameless ones who have contributed to the treasury of popular sayings, or have had a hand in twisting them into almost unrecognizable versions of the original proverbial expression. For example, that statement of truth in Lear, "How sharper than a serpent's tooth to have a thankless child ..." has become in the crude

315

hand of a punster, "How sharper than a serpent's thanks to have a toothless child..."

The popular saying recognizes no native land, necessarily, but belongs to him who quotes it; even so, in the Wisconsin scene we now and then run across one that gives a clue to its origin. The exhortation not to be "penny wise and pound foolish" bears proof that it has crossed the ocean in spite of the fact that the beer barons of Milwaukee express the same thought in a warning that it is "foolish to save at the spigot and waste at the bunghole."

A contributor prefaces her sheaf of homely proverbs with the remark that she heard them from her Danish grandmother. Some of these same proverbs are to be seen in a book of New York State folklore, are current throughout Wisconsin, and are doubtless the common property of every one of our states and of many foreign countries.

It is easily understandable that they are widely spread, also that they have, for the most part, lost their identity.

Our ancestors recognized the truth of the saying, "Wrong possessions do not last," whether they first heard it in German, "*Unrecht gut gedeihet nicht*," or translated in Wisconsin or New York into "What comes over the devil's back goes under his belly." Also they thought it worthwhile to bring with them from the East such custom-made warnings and advice as "Listeners never hear any good of themselves," or "A dog that will fetch a bone will carry a bone," or "What is spoken vanishes, what is written remains," so "Don't write and fear no man."

Pioneer times demanded perseverance and patience, but so does life everywhere. "Leg over leg the dog goes to Dover" may have originated in England, but it went by boat, Conestoga wagon, and oxcart to Wisconsin, where it must have been repeated to buoy waning spirits with the hope that leg over leg the dog would get to the frontier that was to be Wisconsin. New York maidens, too, appear to be equally convinced with their sisters in Milwaukee, Madison, and Mineral Point that "A ring on the finger is worth two on the phone."

Albertine Schuttler of Milwaukee has something to say about Old World sayings brought to Wisconsin:

These sayings show that the Germans brought more than food and band music to the New World.

"In der Not frisst der Teufel Fliegen." In great need the Devil devours flies. In time of famine or extreme hunger men will eat anything.

"Ein Faulpelz kommt auf keinen grünen Zweig." A lazy fellow doesn't ever reach the green branch. This comes from the folk custom of builders placing green branches on gables of newly finished houses for having completed them in record time; thus, the branches showed that they were industrious.

"Selber essen macht fett." What you eat makes you fat, i.e., strong. Meaning: The do-it-yourself job is best.

"Milch und Brot macht die Wangen rot." Milk and bread puts rosy color in your cheeks. Old-fashioned way of adding calories.

"En gut swin et all." Low German proverb, meaning "A good pig eats everything." However it did not mean eating in a piggish way, but finishing what is served to you; eating the plate clean. Also, the Low Germans were the original plate luncheon people, serving the whole meal on one plate. They were the opposites of the Yankees, who used separate dishes.

"Komm' ich nicht heute, komm' ich morgen." Procrastination: If I don't come today, I'll come tomorrow."

"Komm' ich über den Hund, komm' ich über den Schwanz." If I jump over the dog, I'll get over the tail, i.e., to stretch a budget or a sum of money to include a luxury or something extra.

"Hand immer in der Tasche." Has his hand always in his pocket; a spendthrift. *"Hat die Faust in der Tasche."* Has his fist in his pocket; a stingy person.

"Mit dem Hut in der Hand kommt man durch das ganze Land." With the hat in your hand, you'll journey throughout the land. Polite manners get you everywhere.

"Eine Hand wäscht die andere." One hand washes the other. Exchange of favors.

"Oben hui! unten pfui!" A careless person dressed up but wearing soiled underwear.

Whenever we received unfair criticism my grandmother would

say: *"Die Wespen stechen nicht die schlechte Ftrucht."* The wasps don't feed on the bad fruit.

Helen C. Smith of Evansville is the busiest collector of Wisconsin proverbs. She has sent us over three hundred, and presently we will present selections from her list. What Mrs. Smith and the other proverb hunters are really demonstrating is that Wisconsin folks still live their daily lives by the proverbs, just as their ancestors did. In general, Wisconsin people are very thrifty, and the proverbs of thrift are heard in every part of the state. The advice, "Always remember that a pin a day is a groat a year," has resulted in many savings accounts or well-filled piggy banks; and the well-known characteristic of neighborliness among Wisconsin farm people has been stated in proverbial form: "Life has taught us that love does not consist in gazing at each other, but in looking outward in the same direction."

This spirit of being good neighbors is just as real now as it ever was in Wisconsin. Our friend Charlie Drewry, supervisor of Wisconsin District and County Fairs, told us how one night his big barn burned to the foundations. In a few days, all his neighbors from around Plymouth came early to Charlie's farm and by nightfall they had made a new barn, larger even than the first. This kind of tale is repeated many times and in many places in the Badger State.

Nevertheless, good neighborliness is always tempered with caution and good sense. The proverbs say: "Love your own house better than your neighbor's," and "Never borrow from neighbors. It is better to buy what you need. Never fail to return what you borrow promptly, and with thanks... and in as good or better condition or quantity, if possible."

There is sound warning too, for those neighbors who might not follow such advice. Many a borrowing neighbor, returning an implement in poor condition, has taken comfort from this one: "If you do not use your head, then you must use your feet."

Wisconsin mothers advise their daughters: "Never sew cotton lace on a silken garment." Or, "Do not always use an unsound apple." If you do, you may never get to use a good one. Or, "Remember, after the laughing comes the weeping." Or, somewhat more obscurely:

> Yes, yes, so it goes in the world,
> One has the purse, the other the gold.

As advice to a daughter who was, perhaps too young to marry the Wisconsin mother would say: "Don't marry until you're dry behind the ears." Or,

> Give him the mitten
> Before you're too smitten.

The mother might also say: "Beware! He'll have you as deep in the mud as he is in the mire."

On the other side of the fence, Wisconsin fathers have some worthwhile wisdom for their sons:

> A woman, a dog, and a walnut tree,
> The more you beat 'em the better they be.

This may not have so much point in Wisconsin as it does in Michigan, but it is still heard in the Badger State, too. Or he may say: "Now remember, son, 'A woman who paddles your canoe may cast you up a rocky shore.'"

Most male advice, however, isn't given in regard to women. More likely it is given in the nature of living a respected life: "The fault of others is easily perceived, but that of oneself is difficult to perceive. A man winnows his neighbor's faults like chaff, but his own fault he hides, as a cheat hides an unlucky cast of the die."

Mrs. Bert Winterling of Jefferson said that her grandfather, who was of Swedish descent, came to live with her family after grandmother died. Grandfather was a wonderful addition to the house, and the children were fond of him. Gramp didn't have many superstitions, but he was strong on proverbs.

"Lost time is never found again." Gramp would call up to the children at 5 A.M., and they always obeyed his order, jumping out of bed and dressing as quickly as they could. In Richland County, winters were quite cold, but Gramp had a big fire going in the fire-place to welcome them.

Mrs. Winterling, when she was a child, liked to whistle. "Whistling girls and crowing hens always come to some bad end," Gramp told her, and she didn't whistle as much as she wanted to. Gramp taught the children to feed the birds and said, "Never destroy even a scrap of bread."

He would always make a weather prediction at evening and in the morning, "Red sky in the morning, sailor take warning. Red sky at night, sailor's delight." When an older sister broke several dishes while carrying to the cupboard, Gramp called to her: "You took a lazy man's load."

When she was seven, Mrs. Winterling planted a garden. She had some beets, carrots, and radishes, and her father told her he'd buy the vegetables from her when they were ready. Gramp heard her planning what she was going to do with the money. "Catch your chicken before you grease your pan, child," he said. And when the little girl lost her purse one day Gramp said, "Don't put your eggs in one basket."

Helen Smith's list contains many of the proverbs that are used today throughout Wisconsin. She says that her list only really scratches the skin of those that are in common use.

Here are the ones she selected for us:

A narrow mind begets obstinacy.

A word to the wise is sufficient.

All men are equal; there is naught in birth; 'tis Virtue only makes the difference.

A new broom sweeps clean.

America is the schoolhouse of the world.

A fault which humbles a man is of more use to him than a good action which puffs him up with pride.

A rolling stone gathers no moss.

As won, so flown. Light come, light go.

A pleasant word on a rainy day is a ray of golden sunshine.

As snug as a bug in a rug.

A red sunset turns water crimson.

As like as two peas.

Arguing in anger wins no victory.

A penny for your thoughts.

A hearty laugh is sunshine in a house.

A man at bay seldom hesitates.

A person's manners indicate his morals.

A loving heart's worth gold.

An earnest man finds a way.

A wise man seeks to shine in himself. A fool seeks to outshine others.

A penny saved is a penny earned.

Ambition is one of those passions that is never satisfied.

A good book is the best teacher.

A good cause makes a stout heart and a strong arm.

A college education cannot make brains.

At the workingman's house, hunger looks in but dares not enter.

Always call a spade a spade.

All men are equal while they sleep.

All but the determined fail in the race of life.

A burden well borne becomes light.

A friend is a second self.

A boy's mother is his best friend.

A good name is worth more than a girdle of gold.

Above the clouds is the sun, still shining.

A swallow of water may save a life.

After an unselfish deed the heart is light.

A bird in the hand is worth two in the bush.

By doing nothing we learn to do ill.

Big head and little wit.

Boast not of the morrow.

Before you sign it, read it and think; look at the water before you drink.

Breakfast with the fork (i.e., a meat breakfast).

Before men made us citizens, great Nature made us men.

Belly to the ground (at great speed).

Borrowing makes sorrowing.

Cast the log out of your own eye.
Character is what we are.
Children and fools speak the truth.
Conduct and courage lead to honor.
Cleverness is serviceable for everything, sufficient for nothing.
Capital is not what a man has, but what a man is.
Certain winds will make men's temper bad.
Childhood shows the man as morning shows the day.
Clowns are best in their own company, but gentlemen are best everywhere.

Don't ride a free horse to death.
Do not squander time; for that is the stuff life is made of.
Don't be a small potato!
Dispatch is the soul of business.
Despair has raven wings.
Don't be penny wise and pound foolish!
Drink deep or taste not the Pierian spring.

Everybody's business is nobody's business.
Experience bought with pain teaches.
Even a fly has its spleen.
Every difficulty yields to the enterprising.
Everyone complains of his memory, no one complains of his judgment.
Every good gift cometh from above.
Each man is the servant of all men, and all men of each.
Enough and to spare.

Friendship is not given to you—you must earn it.
From the older ox the younger learns to plow.
Forbidden fruits are the sweetest.
Flies thick of a night means rain before it's light.
"First sweep your own doorstep."
Full many a flower is born to blush unseen.
Friendship is a gift, but it is also an acquirement.

Give a rogue rope enough and he will hang himself.
Genius is an immense capacity for taking trouble.
Gather the rosebuds while you may.
Great sins make great sufferers.
Gossip sets every tongue in motion.

He that plods will reach the goal.
Honesty is more valuable than brillancy.
He only is exempt from failure who makes no effort.
He is not worthy of the honeycomb who shuns the hive because the bees have stings.
Home is home, be it ever so homely.
He that would thrive must rise at five.
He who faints is lost.
Health and plenty cheer the industrious man.
He who runs may read.
He is a wise man who talks little.
He who loves praise loves temptation.
He whose house is made of glass must not throw stones at another.
He gives twice who gives promptly.
He is a fool of twenty-four carats. He is a goose of the first water.
He comes "like fresh fish in Lent."
He who praises everybody praises nobody.
He did not invent gunpowder. He will never set the Thames on fire.
He who loves truly loves always.
He lives happily who lives for others.
He who quells an angry thought is greater than a king.
Heaven still guards the right.
Hunger makes coarse meats delicate.

If you make your bed poorly, you may have to sleep in it.
It is not good to wake a sleeping hound.
Incessant scribbling is death to thought.
It's a good sign when a new lamb comes with a new moon.
It's a bad sign when the cream whips stiff instead of churning.
It is an ill wind that blows no good.
It is not all of life to live.

If a man empty his purse into his head, no one can take it from him.

If you love life, then do not squander time.

It is easy to struggle, but the hardest thing in the world to surrender.

I weep more deeply, because I weep in vain.

Idle gossip runs on wheels, and every hand oils the wheels as they run.

Ill fares the land where men decay.

It is wisdom to dislike folly.

Idleness is the mother of all the vices.

If you fear difficulties you will fail.

Justice is the end of the law, and love is the work of the ruler.

"Just wait until you put your feet under your own table."

Keep your tongue from evil and lips from guile.

Knowledge wanes, but wisdom lingers.

Listen—with erect ears.

Loves makes all things beautiful.

Look before you leap.

Little minds are subdued by misfortune, but great minds rise above it.

Loss of sincerity is loss of vital power.

Let the buyer beware.

Labor that you may have.

Love is mighty, but money is almighty.

Lost time is never found again.

Let not the cobbler venture above his last. (Let one criticize only what he understands.)

Laziness travels so slowly that poverty soon overtakes him.

Let the world run by while you think.

Let it pass for what it is worth.

Little by little all tasks are done.

Laws are not masters, but servants, and we rule them if we obey them.

Little gain, little pain.

Like natures like the same things.
Living is not breathing; it is acting.
Lying, you have neither friends nor gold.
Like produces like.
Love yourself last, and others will love.

Make hay while the sun shines.
Merit wins the soil.
Men are but children of a larger growth.
Man can be great when great occasions call.
Make haste slowly; speed with heed.
Misfortunes never come singly.
Money makes money.
Man is a wonderful piece of work.
Men know what we are by what we do.

Never make a defense or apology before you be accused.
No one is useless in this world who lightens the burden of it for another.
No capital earns such interest as personal culture.
No fountain is so small that heaven may not be imaged on its bosom.
Never put off until tomorrow what you can do today.
No evil thing can harm the dead, but the living are in constant danger.
Naked words—plain language.
No one else can earn a man's success for him.
Nothing that is dishonest is profitable.

Out of the head (i.e., from memory).
On earth are no fairies. (The Irish won't believe that!)
Our sweetest songs are those that tell of saddest thoughts.
Only men of industry succeed.
Old accounts breed new disputes.
Our good deeds live after us.
Our todays and yesterdays are the blocks with which we build.
One ought to wash one's soiled linen in private.
One swallow does not make a summer.

Patience is the best remedy for all trouble.
Pure salt (i.e., true good sense, or wit).
Pot calling kettle black.
Pleasant words are all remembered.
Perseverance is the road to success.
Politeness costs nothing and wins everything.
Punctuality is the politeness of kings.
Poverty wants few things, avarice wants everything.

Raindrops and rills have their work to do.
Reputation is what we seem.
Reading in haste gives small knowledge.

Simplicity is always right.
Seldom is a person at the same time wise in his own eyes, wise in the eyes of the world, and wise in the sight of the Creator.
Shoemaker, mind your shoe.
Some temptations come to the industrious, but all temptations attach the idle.
Small pitchers have wide ears.
Stand where you are!
Silence gives consent.
Seconds are the gold dust of time.
Short horse, soon curried.
Spring hangs infant blossoms on the trees.
Summer clothes herself in green and decks herself with flowers.
Soon ripe, soon rotten.
Something else is coming; expect it!

There is a time for all things.
Those who make the worst use of their time complain most of its shortness.
To look poor among rich women is humiliating.
To choose time is to save time.
Two souls and one thought, two hearts and one beat.
Trouble teaches how much there is in manhood.

The world globes itself in a drop of dew.
The mold of a man's fortune is in his own hands.
The water runs smooth where the brook is deep.
The path of industry is the path to success.
The sublime and the ridiculous are often nearly related.
The only jewel you can carry beyond the grave is wisdom.
They have rights who dare maintain them.
The first step towards greatness is honesty.
There is no such word as fail.
The freeman is he whom the truth makes free.
Though the mills of Gods grind slowly, yet they grind exceeding small.
Talking is the disease of age.
There is always a song somewhere.
There is no sauce like appetite.
The more haste, the less speed.
The stone you throw the farthest, you will pick up first.
The more the better. The more the merrier.
The wheel that does the squeaking is the wheel that gets the grease.
The best way to get out of trouble is to stay out.
Time goes by, by little minutes.
Things that injure teach; we burn and learn.
The bright stars playing in the sky are the children of the sun.
Time and the clock go as they please.
To succeed is every man's desire.
To hesitate is to be lost.
The sun has drunk the dew that lay upon the morning grass.
There's no wound deeper than a pen can give.
To look for pears on the elm.
There's no slipping up a hill.
To leave no stone unturned.
Those who bring sunshine to the lives of others cannot keep it from themselves.
The mountains are in labor; there will be born a ridiculous mouse.
The truest self-respect is not to think of self.

Tempest in a glass of water.

Truth needs not the foil of rhetoric.

The good is always the road to what is true.

To go for wool and come back shorn.

The absent are always in the wrong.

Time wasted is existence, used is life.

Things fit to give weight to smoke.

Trifles show character.

Thought takes man out of servitude, into freedom.

The rain comes when the wind calls.

The down of the dandelion tells our fortune.

There must be work done by hands or none of us could live.

Truth is the highest thing that man may keep.

The love of money causes untold suffering. It is the root of all evil.

To the intelligent and virtuous, old age presents a scene of tranquil enjoyment.

They that would have more and more can never have enough.

The joy of success does not equal that which attends the patient working.

The noblest mind the best contentment has.

Truth is fearless, yet it is meek and modest.

The service of a friend is to make us do what we can (are capable of).

To think a score of times of helping your neighbor is good, but to help him once is far better.

The path of life is full of thorns.

They conquer who believe they can.

The buds are the children of the flowers.

Talkers are not good doers.

There's some ill planet reigns. (Said when in bad luck.)

The trolley makes the farmer a city dweller.

To live long it is necessary to live slowly.

To profess regard and to act differently marks a base mind.

Virtue is an effectual anchor.

Virtue is an angel, but she is a blind one.

With oars and sails (i.e., with all one's power).

We do not have to eat the whole pie (or apple) to know if it is good (or bad).

When he had five sons, we had five farms.

Whatever you hold closest, that it is that burns you first.

Whatever is good is beautiful.

Wisdom is better than wealth.

Where the honey is, there are the bees.

What cannot be cured must be endured.

Winds whispering from the west will bring rain.

With a grain of salt.

Word for word and letter for letter.

Winter lingering chills the days of May.

Wise men know the place to stop.

When the cat's away, the mice will play.

What I do not know does not make me glow. Nothing out of sight wakes appetite.

Wear the old coat and buy the new book.

Who grasps much, holds little.

Wings are for angels, but feet for men.

Working men have few wants.

We live in deeds, not years, in thoughts, not breaths.

Wisdom is better than rifles.

What is worth doing at all is worth doing well.

Walls have ears.

When a fool makes up his mind, the market has gone by.

Who never tries will never win.

Who keeps one end in view makes all things serve.

Who steals my purse steals trash.

Worth makes the man.

Wealth may seek us, but wisdom must be sought.

Where the heart is well guarded, temptation cannot enter.

When a lady walks the streets she leaves her frowns at home.

Whoever labors deserves reward.

With running pen....

Wise men teach their sons wisdom.

What is done wisely, is done well.
Whispering tongues can poison truth.

You are of more value than many sparrows.
You can't teach an old dog new tricks.
Youth is the springtime of life.
You may drive out nature with a pitchfork, yet she will come back.
You give me chalk for cheese.
You will lose your loaf of bread right out of your basket if you aren't supposed to have it.
You have touched the thing will a needle; you have hit the nail on the head.

Mrs. Paul Meier of Rudolph wrote us that an old French neighbor of hers, now dead, used to speak of a tall, thin, sickly-looking person as a "coffin dodger." In describing a very odd-looking person he said, "Why, she's homely as a pan full of warts!" Which brings up the subject of the salty proverbial expression. Mrs. Clarice Moon of Delavan has supplied us with some gems of this sort of earthy Wisconsin speech.

As busy as a man on the town.
Able to set up an' eat a few porridges (convalescent).
A boarding house reach.
A hen's time ain't much.
All deacons are good but there's odds in deacons.

By the living laws.
Black as zip.
Bug bite and moonshine (disgust).
Bay yer head, or pull in yer horns.
Burn his candle at both ends.
Blacker'n a stack of black cats.

Came up amongst the missing (to be lost or die).
Can't spin a thread (can't do a thing).
Cold as a north side of a January gravestone by starlight.

Dunnowz I know (ignorance of a matter).
Dark as a pocket.
Darker'n a wolf's mouth.
Dust your back (throw a man).
Dead clear up to yer navel (lifeless).
Devil and Tom Walker.
Don't know enough to pound sand in a rathole.

Enjoyin' dretful poor health.
Essence pedler (a skunk).

Fixin' for a spell of sickness.
Fogs so thick you could cut 'em up in chunks with your jackknife.
Faster than a cat lappin' chain lightning.
Fell bluer'n a whetstone.
Fresh—little salt in cooking.
Fog's so darn thick this morning you can hardly spit.
Fatter'n a settled minister.
Fits like a shirt on a bean pole (a bad fit).

Great keezers ghosts.
Got up so early that he often met himself going to bed.
Go at it 240.
Get thy spindle and distaff ready and God will send the flax.
Gettin' too big fer yer boot or britches.

Him and work had a fallin' out (lazy man).
Her house was a regular hurrah's nest.
Homely as hell is wicked.
He has no more use for it than for water in his boats.
Huffle-brained (stupid).
Homely enough to stop a clock.
Hot as the Devil's kitchen.
Hungry as a graven image.
He don't need it anymore than a pig needs a wallet.
He's the whole team and the little dog under the wagon.
Handy as a pocket in a shirt.

Hired man looking for salt pork and sundown.
He pries up the sun with a crowbar.
He could sell a fiddle to a one-arm deef and dumber.
He's as straight as a yard of pump water.
Hell-bent and crooked.
He don't need it any more than a dog needs two tails.
Heavy branded—a lot of salt in cooking.
Homely as a hedge fence (or mud fence).
Hook-a-hendum, a whatyouacallit, a thingamajig (any small gripping tool).
Hotter'n Dutch love at midnight.
Her head looks like it had worn out two bodies.
Hotter'n love in hay time.
Homely as a mud post.
Homely enough to stop a down train.

It was cold enough to freeze two dry rags together.
In one's naked bed (down sick).
I've trotted around all day in a bushel.
It's a poor back that can't press its own shirt.
I take my tea barfoot.
In your own dish.
Independent as a hog on ice.

Just feelin' peaked.
Jumped like a cat out of the woodbox.

Know enough to lap salt.
Kicked to death by cripples.

Last of pea time (hard up).
Like haulin' a hog out on a scalding tub (different).
Like the mill-tail a-thunder.
Lollygags (love-making).
Longer'n (taller'n) the mortal law.
Laugher'n a bailed owl.

Madder'n tunket.
Mean enough to steal acorns from a blind hog.
Make long arms (reach at the table).
Mad as hops—madder'n snakes in hayins; madder'n a wet hen.
Mean enough to steal the coins from a dead man's eyes.

Nine months of winter and three months late in the fall.
No great kill or cure.
No bigger'n a pint of cider or a goolthrite (very small).

Oh, be joyful, or Ah, be rich and happy (hard liquor).
Oh just staggerin' around (inquire as to health).
On the mending hand (convalescent).

Prayer-handles (knees).
Pale as dishwater (very pale).
Pell-mell fer a cat race or pell-mell fer Kittry (very fast).
Peg out (be ill or die).
Premlico order.
Pop'lar as a hen with one chick.
Poor's poodue also poor's poverty in a gale of wind, or Poorer'n
skimmed whey (extremely poor).

Rub the time close (allow little time).
Ride out (untidy).

Stands out like a blackberry in a pan of milk.
So thievish they hev to take in their stone walls nights.
Slower'n molasses in January.
Stone's got a pretty heavy mortgage on that land.
Starved fit to eat the Lord's Supper or the Lamb of God.
Salter'n the briny ocean (very salt).
Stingy enough to skim his milk at both ends.
Slower than a hoptoad in hot tar.
Slick's a ram, cat, greased pig, or a schoolmarm's leg.
Spoon victuals (invalid diet).
So homely 'twould gag ye.

Slow as a hog on ice with his tail froze in.
Safe as in God's pocket.
Slacker'n dishwater (untidy).
Sick abed in the woodbox (in good health).
Sight by su'thin' to see if he's moving (lazy).
Slower'n a jill poke. Slower'n stock still.
Sick abed.

Thick as fiddlers in hill (plentiful).
Ther's no more heat in the sun than a yeller dog.
Twenty tailors around a buttonhole.
Twice around a toothpick and halfway back.
The last one in the back row when the faces was handed out.
Taller'n a stack-pole.
The cussed critter was so tough then you c'd hardly stick a fork in his gravy.
'Twould break a snake's back to faller the last furrow.
Tight's ye can jump fer luck (fast as you can go!)
To go it ball-headed.
To make a Virginia fence (walk drunken).
Thinner'n a hayrake.
Thin's vanity.

Upon your shoetops (feeling fine).
Upon one's bean water (feeling lively).

Wee wau (shaky loose).
Wrappin' round yer finger (slight value).
We have two seasons—winter and the fourth of July.
White hen's chickens (better).

Yr Uncle Dud (the narrator).

Robert E. Gard is widely recognized for his interest in preserving the lore and legends of American regions. Since 1945 he has been a professor at the University of Wisconsin-Madison where he has directed various programs in cultural arts and native literature. He is the founder of the Wisconsin Idea Theater, an internationally known movement to spread the idea of a native American Drama. He is the author of some thirty-five books.

L. G. Sorden is one of the best-known personalities in Wisconsin. He was on the faculty of the University of Wisconsin-Madison for forty years and has long had a major interest in Wisconsin stories and people. He is joint author with Robert E. Gard of *The Romance of Wisconsin Place Names*. He is also the author of *I Am the Mississippi* with E. Louise Miller and *Lumberjack Lingo*.
